THE BEST OF The MAILBOX® Magazine

SCIENCE Made Simple
BOOK 2
GRADES 4–6

Explore the wonder and beauty of science with *The Best Of* The Mailbox® *Science Made Simple • Book 2*! This compilation of teaching units—selected from 1994 to 1998 issues of *The Mailbox®* magazine for intermediate teachers—will energize your science lessons and strengthen students' skills. Inside this invaluable classroom resource, you'll find:

- Skill-based science units
- Whole-group, small-group, and independent activities
- Literature links
- Reproducibles
- Patterns

Editor
Cindy Mondello

Art Coordinator
Cathy Spangler Bruce

Cover Artist
Jennifer Tipton Bennett

Manufactured in the United States
10 9 8 7 6 5 4 3 2 1

Table Of Contents

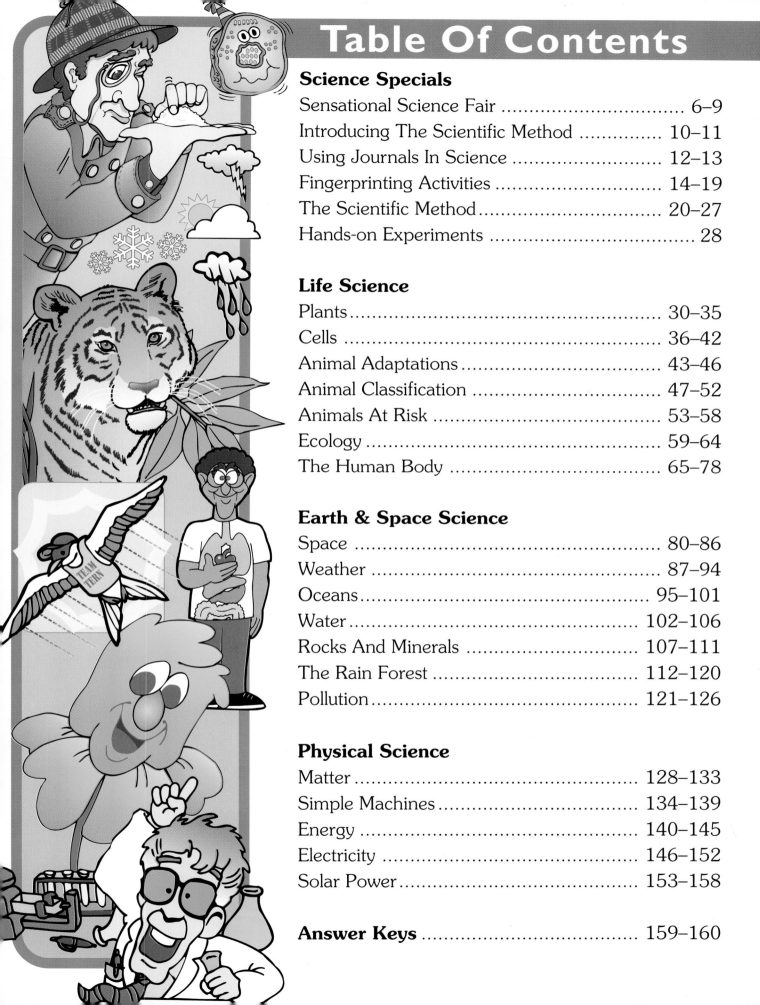

Science Specials

A Sensational Science Fair

It'll be here before you know it. No, not the holidays—this year's science fair! And preparing for it doesn't have to be a hassle, thanks to our science-savvy subscribers. Use the following tips and ideas to guarantee a science fair that's nothing short of sensational!

Getting Started

Good-Bye To Competition!

Encourage increased participation in your school's science fair by eliminating unnecessary competition among students. Instead of judging projects to see which ones are best, award a special certificate to every student who participates in the event. To further avoid creating a competitive environment, refer to the event as an expo instead of a fair.

Andrea Bayroff—Gr. 5, Washington School, Westfield, NJ

Calling All Volunteers!

Enlisting the help of volunteers makes putting on a science fair a lot easier! Prior to your scheduled science fair, contact a local university or high school. Ask for student volunteers to act as official judges for your fair. Draft additional volunteers by sending home a request to parents. Give parents several options such as conducting a science demonstration, helping students develop their projects and presentations, setting up the fair, or helping manage the fair. With the extra help, you'll quickly prove one hypothesis—volunteers are a key ingredient in a successful science fair!

Terry Healy—Gifted K–6, Eugene Field Elementary Manhattan, KS

Pre-Fair Checklist

Organize your students for the science fair by providing them with a special pre-fair checklist. Include important reminders such as those listed below:

- On the morning of the science fair, bring all necessary materials to school including your presentation board, display-table items, and bibliography.
- Review the information on your presentation board.
- Dress appropriately for the occasion.
- Make eye contact with the person(s) to whom you are speaking.
- Speak clearly as you give your presentation.
- Smile and relax!

Provide each student with a copy of the checklist on the day before the science fair.

Andrea Bayroff—Gr. 5

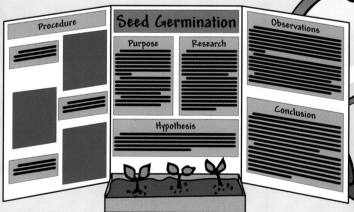

It's All In The Presentation

Help your students create eye-catching science displays with the help of some inexpensive presentation boards. Ask your school principal or P.T.A. to purchase a supply of trifold cardboard presentation boards. Loan these boards to students to use in displaying their science fair projects. To avoid unnecessary wear and tear, have each student use staples or pins to attach his project to the board for easy removal. Then store the boards and reuse them the following year.

Mary T. Spina—Gr. 4, Bee Meadow School, Whippany, NJ

Science Project Log

Developing a science fair project is not something that can be done overnight. Help your students stay on track during the development process with the help of a project log. Give each student a small notebook; or staple several small sheets of lined paper together to make a project log. Direct each student to write detailed notes about progress on her project and any questions she has in her log. Collect each student's log on Monday morning; then make comments and answer the questions. Count each student's project log as a portion of her final project grade. Keeping your students on task and excited about their science fair projects has never been easier!

Andrea Bayroff—Gr. 5, Washington School, Westfield, NJ

What Can I Do For A Project?

Use the following practical suggestion to help each of your students come up with a topic for her science fair project. Post the following science areas on the right side of a bulletin board: geology, chemistry, electricity, space, weather, plants, animals, physics, and nutrition. On the left side, display the question words *who, what, when, where,* and *why*. Spend five to ten minutes each day coming up with questions for one of the posted areas, such as "Why do leaves change color in the fall?" and "What is the best type of soil to use for growing beans?" Record each question on a sentence strip and post it beside the related topic. Continue holding daily sessions until questions for each area have been posted. Encourage each student to select one of these questions to focus on in her science fair project. Then stock your classroom library with periodicals and books for students to use in researching their topics.

Terry Healy—Gr. K–6, Eugene Field Elementary Manhattan, KS

Why?	How?
Why do leaves change color in the fall?	How do some plants survive living in the desert?
Why do plants need roots?	

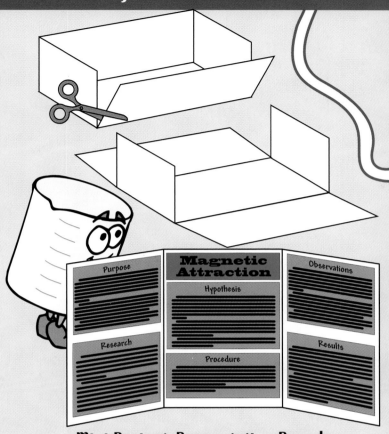

Mini Project-Presentation Boards

Need an easy way to teach your students how to organize and present their science projects? Have each student bring in a shoebox. Then conduct a simple whole-class experiment to test a scientific concept such as magnetic attraction. As you conduct the experiment, review the scientific process with your students:

Purpose—Why is the experiment being conducted?
Research—What kind of data is necessary to support the experiment?
Hypothesis—What might happen?
Procedure—What materials are needed? What steps need to be taken to prove the hypothesis?
Observations—What happens during the experiment?
Results—Do the results of the experiment prove the hypothesis?

Next have each student cut along the four corners of his box as shown. Have him cut away the box's end flaps, leaving a trifold cardboard form. Direct the student to cover the trifold form with construction paper; then have him glue a label naming each part of the scientific process to the box. Instruct the student to attach information gathered during the class experiment below each label. Have him save his completed display to use as a model for his science fair entry.

Barbara Chojnacki—Gr. 6, Cold Water Elementary Florissant, MO

Stress-Free Science Fair

Ease your students' anxiety about preparing for your science fair with this practical idea. Several weeks before the fair, have each student pose a simple science-related question he would like to answer. Direct the student to bring in the materials to conduct an experiment that answers the question. Also have him record the purpose, research, hypothesis, and procedure of his experiment on a sheet of paper. On a designated day, arrange students' desks in a circle; then have each child conduct his experiment for the rest of the class. Ask parent volunteers to help photograph each student with his experiment and film the event. Then have each student make observations and draw conclusions about his experiment; next have him record his information on a poster or presentation board. Attach the photo of the student with his experiment to the poster. When the day of the science fair arrives, display each student's poster along with the videotape of your class conducting its experiments.

Jo Anne Risley—Gr. 4, Waldron Mercy Academy
Merion Station, PA

Other Helpful Ideas

Color-Coded Organization

Make organizing your science fair a snap with this easy-to-do idea! Purchase a different color of duplicating paper for each grade level taking part in your science fair. Have each participant record his name, grade, project title, and project description on an entry form (see page 9) duplicated on the color assigned to his grade level. Then direct the student to attach his form to his science fair entry. As students bring their entries to the display area, organize the projects by grouping those with the same-colored forms together. Locating projects at each grade level will be much easier with this simple system!

Mary T. Spina—Gr. 4, Bee Meadow School
Whippany, NJ

Don't Forget tonight's P.T.A meeting! 7:30 P.M. SPECIAL FEATURE This year's super Science Fair!

A Good Turnout

Ensure that your next P.T.A. meeting is well-attended by scheduling it on the same night as your science fair. Have each student bring her project to school on the morning of the date scheduled for the P.T.A. meeting. Direct each teacher to display her class's entries in a central classroom location. Throughout the day, have parent judges visit each room and meet briefly with the owner of each project for a demonstration and explanation. After all judges have viewed the projects, tally the scores and list the top three projects from each class. Keep the award winners secret until the evening's meeting. Allow attendees to view the science fair projects prior to the start of the P.T.A. meeting. Then announce the winners at the meeting's conclusion.

Amy Westendorp—Grs. 5–6, Barry County Christian School
Hastings, MI

Come One, Come All!

Don't forget to attend Foster Heights Elementary's Science Fair on Wednesday, February 25. Science projects from students in grades K–5 will be on display in the school gymnasium that evening.

Also...

Flaget Memorial Hospital will set up an information booth and offer free cholesterol screening for anyone who is interested.

We hope to see you there!

Healthy, Wealthy, And Science-Wise

Give the attendees at your next science fair a dose of health awareness with this practical suggestion. Ask a local hospital to set up a health screening or information booth during your science fair. When you send out reminders about the science fair, be sure to include an announcement about the health services being offered.

Patricia E. Dancho—Gr. 6, Apollo-Ridge Middle School Spring Church, PA

Well-Read Scientists

Looking for a way to publicize your school's science fair throughout your community? Establish a cooperative partnership with your local library. Ask the librarians to display posters promoting your upcoming science fair alongside some of the library's science books. Then encourage your students to go to the library to conduct research for their science fair projects. The positive exposure generated for your science fair and the library is just one of many benefits of the partnership.

Patricia E. Dancho—Gr. 6

You're Invited To A Science Fair!

Who: Students in grades K–5
What: Interesting science projects on a variety of topics
When: Thursday, May 21
Where: Lynnhaven Elementary School,
210 Dillon Drive, Virginia Beach, VA
Why: To learn more about science and have fun

We hope you can attend!

SCIENCE FAIR ENTRY FORM

Name(s) _____

Grade level _____

Project title _____

Project description _____

_____

_____

Note To The Teacher: Use with "Color-Coded Organization" on page 8.

SCIENCE SUMMITS

Scale the summits of scientific reasoning by introducing your students to the scientific method. Use the science lab form on page 11 as you conduct the following experiments.

by Christine A. Thuman

Activity 1: Air Pressure

Purpose: What happens when the air pressure inside an object is not equal to the pressure outside the object?

Materials (per group or individual): small plastic tumbler, index card (large enough to cover the opening of the cup), water, tray to catch spills

Procedure:

1. Hold the index card over the mouth of the cup. Turn the cup over. **Predict** what will happen if you let go of the index card. Let go of the index card. **Observe and record** what happens.
2. Fill the cup 1/2 full of water. Hold the index card over the cup opening by placing your palm over the card. While holding the card in place, quickly turn the cup over.
3. **Predict** what will happen if you let go of the index card. Gently pull your hand away from the card.
4. **Observe and record** what happens.

Conclusion: Compare your predictions to what actually happened. Tell why you think this happened. What did you learn from this experiment?

This is why:

This experiment demonstrates *air pressure.* Since the air pressure inside and outside the empty cup is the same, gravity pulls the paper off the cup. In the case of the water-filled cup, the air pressure inside and outside the cup starts out the same. When the cup is turned, a few drops of water spill out, and the water level in the cup drops. Therefore the *volume,* or space, above the water increases; however, the amount of air in that space remains the same. Since the volume occupied by that air is greater, the air pressure decreases. This creates a situation in which the outside air pressure is greater than the inside air pressure. At this point the paper is pushed in and the escape of water is stopped. Since air pressure pushes the paper in (rather than it being sucked in), the paper holds the water in the cup.

Activity 2: Force

Purpose: How can you keep a facial tissue from tearing?

Materials (per group or individual): empty cardboard tube, rubber band, sheet of double-ply facial tissue, salt, broomstick, empty trash can

Procedure:

1. Wrap the tissue around the end of the cardboard tube. Secure it with a rubber band. Pour four inches of salt into the tube.
2. Place the rounded end of a broomstick into the tube. Stand with one hand holding the broomstick and the other holding the tube firmly without crushing it. Hold the tube over the empty trash can.
3. **Predict** what you think will happen if you try to push the broomstick through the tissue. Using constant, firm pressure, try to push the broomstick through the tube to break the tissue. (Don't jab.)
4. **Observe and record** what happens.

Conclusion: Compare your predictions to what actually happened. Tell why you think this happened. What did you learn from this experiment?

This is why:

This experiment demonstrates how force works against an object. Salt is composed of many tiny *crystals.* When an object, such as a broom handle, is pressed against the thick layer of salt, the crystals send the force in many directions. By the time the pressure reaches the tissue, it has become too weak to tear it. Have your students try this experiment using a pencil instead of a broom handle. Be sure to hold the tube over a trash can. What happens this time? *(The pencil goes through the salt and tears a hole in the tissue.)* Have your students discuss the difference in results.

Name _____

1. **PURPOSE:** What do you want to find out? _____
_____

2. **PREDICT:** What do you think will happen?
_____
_____
_____
_____
_____

3. **MATERIALS:** What items do you need in order to do this experiment? _____
_____
_____
_____
_____

4. **PROCEDURE:** What steps will you follow? _____
_____
_____
_____
_____
_____
_____
_____
_____
_____
_____
_____

5. **OBSERVATIONS:** What happened during this experiment? _____
_____
_____
_____
_____
_____
_____
_____
_____
_____
_____
_____

6. **CONCLUSION:** What did you learn from this experiment? _____
_____
_____
_____
_____
_____
_____

Using Journals In Science

Leonardo da Vinci was one of the most gifted inventors and artists the world has ever known. Today we know about his ideas because he recorded much of what he saw and thought in his notebooks. His notebooks ranged from ones as large as wall posters to some that were small enough to carry on his belt. Some of Leonardo's notebooks have survived to this day. They're filled with lines and lines of neat print—written from right to left—along with numerous drawings and diagrams.

Journaling in science helps students reflect on skills they've learned, and creates orderly notes for later study. Use the suggestions below and the reproducible on page 13 to get your budding scientists into journaling.

by Irving P. Crump

Getting Started

Reproduce one copy of the journal cover (the top half of page 13) for each student. Have students color and decorate their covers; then have them cut lined paper the same size as the cover to make pages for their journals. Instruct each student to punch a hole in the top left corner of the cover and each journal page, then bind all of the pages behind the cover with a brad or ring. Make a journal for each major topic of study throughout the year.

Suggestions For Using Science Journals

Science Experiences:

Provide each student with a copy of the form on the bottom half of page 13 to complete after a science experiment or laboratory activity, a nature walk, or a field trip. Have the student follow the directions on the page, then add the completed page to his journal.

Free Writing:

Have students write about any aspect of a science or health topic of their choice. Let them express their opinions about a person, an event, or a thing. Anything goes!

Current Events:

Have students bring in magazine and newspaper articles dealing with science subjects. Share an article; then have students react to it in their journals.

Question Of The Day:

On the board write a question that relates to a topic you're studying, a news item, or a science-related subject. Examples: "Would you like to be a paleontologist? How would your family adjust if there were a gasoline shortage? What's the greatest environmental problem facing our community?" Have students respond to the question in their journals.

Vocabulary Words:

Have students write science words and their definitions in their journals.

Lists:

Have students list important facts, causes and effects of events, or statements comparing and contrasting the characteristics of objects or events. Examples: "List the characteristics of mammals. Compare and contrast tornadoes with hurricanes. List some of Leonardo da Vinci's ideas that have become realities in the past 300 years."

Observation Skills:

Have students observe an object or event over a period of time and record their observations. Examples: "Observe and record weather patterns for one month. Observe the growth of two plants: one that is fertilized and one that is not."

Writing From Another Perspective:

Have students write about an event from a different perspective. Examples: "Write about an oil spill from the perspective of a seal. How does a deer family feel about suburbs encroaching on its woodland home? How does a furniture manufacturer feel about a ban on the import of mahogany?"

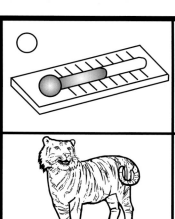

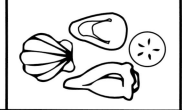
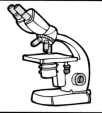

My Science Journal

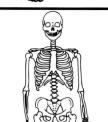

_____
name

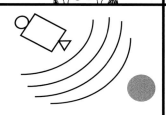

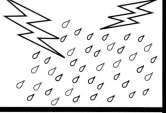

○ name _____ date _____

_____
science experience

① Briefly describe the experience: _____
_____
_____

② What special materials, if any, were used? _____
_____
_____

③ Write a sentence describing something new you learned. _____
_____

④ In the space below, draw a diagram or picture that would help you describe this science experience to a friend.

Let Your Fingers Do The Walking

Investigating Science Through Fingerprinting Activities

Looking for a fun way to introduce your students to the skills of scientific investigation? The answer is right at your fingertips! Use the following fingerprinting activities to point your students in the direction of some fingers-on science fun!

by Gregory Grambo

Background For The Teacher

What do emperors of ancient China and modern-day computers have in common? Both have used fingerprints as a means of identifying people. What makes fingerprints so reliable? No two people have the same set of fingerprints, not even identical twins! In the late 1800s, two British police officers developed an official system for classifying fingerprints. Since then people have used fingerprints to identify criminals, prevent un-authorized admission into restricted buildings, and identify victims of war and other tragedies.

No Two Alike

Hold up a penny and a dime. Ask students, "If a person cannot see, how can he tell the difference between a penny and a dime?" Students will point out that a dime has ridges around its edge and is slightly smaller than a penny. Next divide your class into groups of four. Give each group two pennies that have the same date. Instruct each group to examine its pennies. Then ask, "How can you tell the difference between these two pennies?" Students will point out that while the pennies have many similarities, they can be distinguished because they have different scratches or marks on them. No two pennies are exactly alike. Point out that the same is true of fingerprints. That's why they are such a reliable means of identification.

A Lasting Impression

It only costs a few pennies to teach your students the fundamentals of fingerprint-making. Provide each group with a black stamp pad, a pad of paper, and a penny that has been glued—head side up—onto the end of a tongue depressor as shown. Have each member press the penny onto the pad and then onto the top sheet of paper. Ask students, "Does the print of the penny look just like the face of the penny?" Students will note that only the top edges of the penny left any impression on the paper. What conclusions can students draw from this experiment? *(In printmaking only the hills or ridges touch the paper and leave an inked impression.)*

Your Not-So-Secret Identity

Divide your class into groups of two or four. Provide each group with a stamp pad and white paper. Using the conclusions drawn from "A Lasting Impression" on page 14, have students predict what will happen if they press the tips of their index fingers into the ink and then onto the paper. Then have them explain *why* their fingers will leave prints. Students should predict that they will leave a lined print on the paper because the tips of their fingers have high spots (hills, ridges) and low spots (furrows, valleys) just like the penny (see the diagram). Allow students to experiment with making more fingerprints.

It's best to roll the finger from one side to the other while a partner presses gently on the finger. Demonstrate the technique (see the diagram on page 16). Then have each student work with a partner to practice making fingerprints with this method. Follow up by duplicating page 16 for each student to complete with a partner. Save page 16 to use again in "Is There A Pattern?" below.

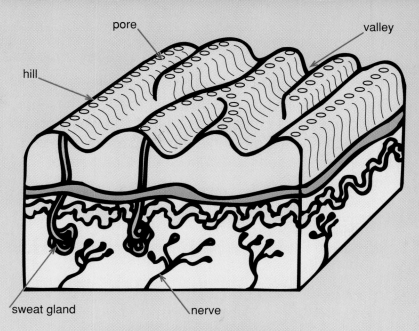

Cross Section Of A Fingertip

Is There A Pattern?

Do fingerprint patterns run in a family? Conduct the following investigation to find out. Duplicate page 18 for each student. Have each student use the page to collect a complete set of fingerprints from three members of her family. Instruct each student to label each print with the initials of the person. After everyone has collected their prints, have each student take out her copy of page 16. Instruct the student to cut out and glue the Common Fingerprint Patterns in a column on a 12" x 18" sheet of paper. Next have her cut apart the prints she collected from family members, arrange them in rows next to their matching patterns, and glue them in place to form a bar graph. Have the student use her graph to determine which (if any) patterns are most common in her family.

Do You Have A Clue?

For this super sleuthing activity, duplicate five copies of page 17. Number four of the sheets identically 1 to 30; leave the last sheet unnumbered. Spread the five sheets on a table. In turn help each student make one thumbprint in the same box on each sheet, including the unnumbered one. When you have collected the thumbprint of each student, write the letters *A* through *Z* randomly in the boxes on the unnumbered sheet. (Add *AA, BB, CC,* and *DD* if you have more than 26 students.) Make a key matching each number to its corresponding letter. Cut apart the lettered sheet; then shuffle the thumbprints and divide them into four sets.

Group your class into four teams. Give each team a numbered sheet and one set of thumbprints. Challenge each group to correctly match each separate print with its partner on the numbered sheet. After a short time, have each group rotate its set of prints to the next group. Continue until each group has seen every set of prints. Read the correct answers and reward the group that correctly matches the most prints.

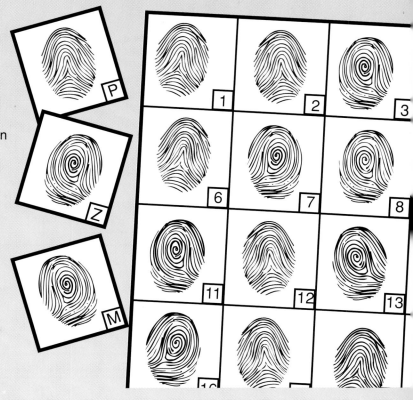

Who Are You?

Have you ever had your fingerprints taken? Chances are, if you were born in a hospital, they took your fingerprints or footprints so that you would not be confused with the other infants. Grab an ink pad and follow the directions below to create a new set of fingerprints.

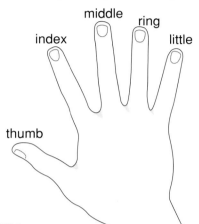

Roll your finger to the right.

Directions:
1. Work with a partner.
2. Place this paper so that the bottom edge meets the edge of your desk.
3. Roll your right thumb across an inked pad. Be sure to ink the sides of the thumb.
4. Lift your thumb from the pad; then have your partner help you roll your inked thumb inside the box labeled "Right Thumb" (see the illustration). Repeat this process with your index, middle, ring, and little fingers.
5. Wash your hands with soap and water.
6. Compare your five fingerprints with the eight common fingerprint patterns pictured below. Next to each pattern, record which of your fingers has a similar pattern. (You may not have all the patterns.)

Common Fingerprint Patterns

plain whorl

plain arch

radial loop

double loop whorl

accidental whorl

tented arch

ulnar loop

central pocket loop

Bonus Box: On the back of this page, record the fingerprints of your left hand. Label each print. Compare each print to the Common Fingerprint Patterns. What patterns do you see in the prints of your two hands?

Right Thumb (RT)	Right Index (RI)	Right Middle (RM)	Right Ring (RR)	Right Little (RL)

Note To The Teacher: Use this page with "Do You Have A Clue?" on page 15.

Person #1				
right thumb	right index	right middle	right ring	right little
left thumb	left index	left middle	left ring	left little

Person #2				
right thumb	right index	right middle	right ring	right little
left thumb	left index	left middle	left ring	left little

Person #3				
right thumb	right index	right middle	right ring	right little
left thumb	left index	left middle	left ring	left little

Note To The Teacher: Use this page with "Is There A Pattern?" on page 15.

The Scene Of The Crime!

Private Eye Pete and his assistant, Kitty, are investigating the scene of a crime. Pete and Kitty have already determined that there were two intruders. One thief stuck his hand on a painted wall and left some *visible* fingerprints. But the other thief was more careful. He missed the paint, but left some *latent* (not visible) prints. Pete and Kitty know how to lift latent prints. Grab a partner and follow the directions below to discover their techniques.

Materials for each pair of students: a clean glass surface; vegetable oil; dark-colored powdered tempera paint; cornstarch; a soft, fluffy paintbrush; paper towels; one-inch-wide, clear transparent tape; a two-inch square of black paper

Lifting A Dark-Colored Fingerprint
Directions for the student:
1. Place a small amount of oil on a paper towel.
2. Rub your finger in the oil and remove the excess oil by blotting it gently.
3. Press your finger on the surface of the glass.
4. Dip the brush into the tempera paint and tap it lightly to sprinkle the printed area with powder.
5. With the very tip of the brush, gently sweep away the extra powder. Be careful—if you brush too hard, you'll remove the print, too.
6. Carefully place a strip of tape over the print. Peel up the tape slowly.
7. Place the captured print on Box A.

Lifting A Light-Colored Fingerprint
Directions for the student:
1. Glue the black paper square on top of Box B.
2. Follow Steps 1–6 above to create and lift a print. This time, however, substitute cornstarch for the powdered tempera paint.
3. Place the captured print on Box B.

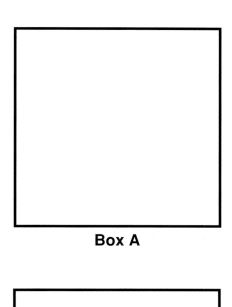

Box A

Box B

Bonus Box: Make a *visible* print by gently rubbing the pointed end of your pencil over the tip of your finger. Place a piece of transparent tape over your fingertip. Carefully lift the tape off your finger and place it on the space under Box B. How clear is this print compared with the prints you lifted above? What other substances around school could be used to create a visible print?

The Great Powder Puzzle

Introducing The Scientific Method To Intermediate Scientists

Puzzled about how to introduce the steps of the scientific method to your students? Then take a closer look at this "powder-packed" unit that combines chemistry, observation, and fun to produce an exciting back-to-school reaction!

ideas by Gregory Grambo

Background For The Teacher

Chemistry is the study of substances: what they are made of, how they act, and how they change. The most basic of chemical substances are *chemical elements*. When two or more elements combine and create a change, a *chemical reaction* occurs. Since early times, people have made many discoveries by observing elements and the changes they go through. Scientists today seek to understand these substances through *the scientific method* of observation and logic.

The following unit is designed to help your students use the scientific method to experiment with five different powders. During the fun hands-on activities, students will discover what these powders are made of, how they act, and how they change.

Safety First!

Safety should be the first order of business when conducting any science experiment in the classroom. The following tips will help you and your students conduct safe experiments:

- Follow all directions and handle all equipment properly.
- Do not taste any of the chemicals in the experiments.
- Do not touch your eyes, mouth, face, or body when working with chemicals.
- Wash your hands thoroughly after completing the activities.
- Be especially careful with matches and open flames; tie back long hair and roll up loose sleeves.
- Remember fire-drill and other emergency procedures.

Scientific Method

Identify a purpose (Why is the experiment being conducted?)
Gather research (What kind of data is necessary to support the experiment?)
Form a hypothesis (What might happen?)
Perform an experiment (What materials are needed and what steps need to be taken in order to prove the hypothesis?)
Make observations (What happens during the experiment?)
Draw conclusions (Do the results of the experiment prove the hypothesis?)

Materials List

Each group will need the following items:

- five same-sized metal spoons
- pot holder
- one 6-inch candle
- matches
- pie tin
- five clear plastic cups, labeled A–E
- container of water
- five paper plates, labeled A–E
- eyedropper
- iodine (Lugol's solution is recommended and is available at science supply centers and some drugstores.)
- vinegar
- silver nitrate (available at science supply centers and some drugstores)
- about 1/3 cup each of flour or cornstarch, baking soda, sugar, salt, and plaster; each powder in a different container labeled A–E*
- one additional container per group (to hold the sample of the "mystery mixture")

Make a key for yourself identifying which powder is in each container.

Ready, Set, Experiment!

Give each group of four students a copy of each experiment on pages 22–27 and the materials needed. Discuss the background and safety information on page 20. You may wish to share the names of the five powders being used, but not tell which containers they are in. Continue to stress student safety as some of the experiments involve potentially harmful materials and procedures. After each experiment, have group members wash their hands. Also have them wash any equipment that will be used in succeeding experiments (spoons, plastic cups, eyedroppers).

The Heat Is On! page 22

In this experiment students will use heat to identify one of the mystery powders. Four of the powders (flour, baking soda, salt, and plaster) should turn brown or have no reaction. The sugar will melt, turn brown, then turn black. Sugar is a carbohydrate made of carbon, hydrogen, and oxygen. When heated, the hydrogen and oxygen will evaporate, leaving the carbon behind. Students may also notice a smell like that of marshmallows or caramel emanating from the cooking sugar. Stress that students must be very careful about working with an open flame, and that they must not taste any substance or put it directly under their noses.

Water Wonders page 23

In this experiment students will use water to identify one of the mystery powders. Four of the powders (flour, baking soda, sugar, and salt) will dissolve in water, some more slowly than others. The plaster will not dissolve. After sitting overnight, the plaster will undergo a chemical reaction—it will harden.

Black And Blue All Over page 24

Iodine is used to test for the presence of a starch (like in cakes and cookies). When iodine is put on a starch, a bluish black color will appear. In this experiment, students will use iodine to identify one of the mystery powders. Four of the powders (baking soda, sugar, salt, and plaster) should turn yellowish brown. The flour or cornstarch should turn bluish black. *Remember that iodine is a poison.* Warn students not to touch their eyes, mouths, faces, or bodies when working with the iodine. Also remind them to wash their hands thoroughly after completing the experiment.

Sizzling Stuff page 25

When added to some substances, vinegar (an acid) causes them to react. In this experiment, students will use vinegar to identify one of the mystery powders. Four of the powders (flour, sugar, salt, and plaster) should not react to the vinegar. The baking soda will produce a reaction because it contains carbon dioxide. The vinegar causes the carbon dioxide to bubble and fizz as the CO_2 is released as a gas. (Students may see some fizzing with the plaster since it contains a calcium carbonate, but not as much as the baking soda.)

High Ho, Silver! page 26

Silver nitrate is a chemical that, when added to a sodium chloride, will produce a chemical reaction. In this experiment, students will add water and then silver nitrate to each powder. Four of the powders (flour, baking soda, sugar, and plaster) should not react. But when the silver nitrate is added to the salt solution, it creates a mixture that will not dissolve in water. The silver nitrate will form a mass and sink to the bottom of the cup. (The nitrate may react with the baking soda solution by bubbling and changing color.) *Remember that silver nitrate is a poison.* Warn students not to touch their eyes, mouths, faces, or bodies when working with the silver nitrate. Remind them to wash their hands thoroughly after completing the experiment.

The Great Powder Puzzle page 27

After each group has discovered the identity of each powder, give students a new mystery mixture to test. Prepare the mixture by combining two or more of the five powders. Give each group a sample of the mixture, a copy of page 27, and the materials determined by the group's members. Instruct students to use the information they learned in the previous experiments to determine which powders are in the mixture. For example, if the new mixture bubbles up when vinegar is added and smells like marshmallows when heated, students can conclude that it contains baking soda and sugar. Evaluate each group's knowledge of the scientific method by observing how its members perform each step of the experiment and by the data they record.

The Heat Is On!

Some substances *melt,* or break down when heated. One of the mystery powders below is a carbohydrate made of the chemical elements *carbon* (like coal) and *hydrogen* and *oxygen* (elements found in water). When heated, the hydrogen and oxygen will evaporate, leaving the carbon behind. Use your powers of observation, knowledge of the scientific method, and heat to discover information about the five different mystery powders.

Purpose: Find the identity of one of the mystery powders by using heat. (**Remember:** Do not taste any substance!)

Hypothesis: What effects do you think heat will have on each powder? What do you think the mystery powder is? _____

_____

_____

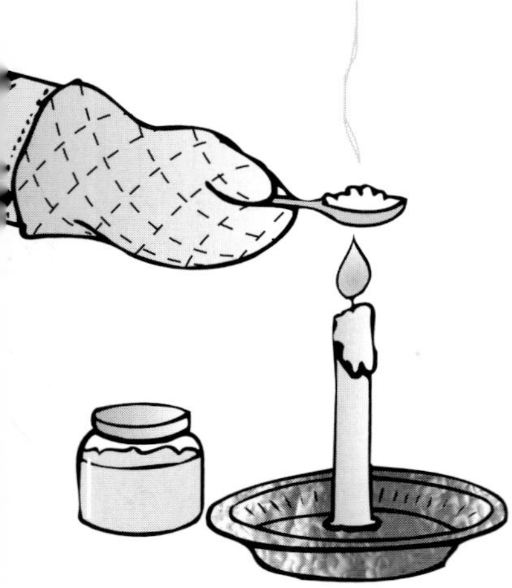

Materials:
five same-sized metal spoons (one for each powder)
candle
matches

pot holder
pie tin
five different powders in
    containers labeled A–E

Procedure:
1. Take a spoonful of a powder out of its container. Observe the appearance of the powder.
2. Place the pie tin under the candle to collect the dripping wax. With your teacher's assistance, light the candle and use a pot holder to hold the spoon over it. Observe what happens to the powder once it has been thoroughly heated and after it cools. Record your observations on the chart below.
3. Follow the same procedure for each of the other powders. Be sure to use a different spoon for each powder.

Observations:

Mystery Powders	What changes do you see in its appearance during heating?	What do you smell?	What happens after it cools?
A			
B			
C			
D			
E			

Conclusions: How can heat be used to help identify a substance? Can you identify one of the powders?

_____

_____

_____

Water Wonders

Some substances *dissolve,* or mix evenly with water. Some substances do not; they undergo chemical reactions when mixed with water. Use your powers of observation, knowledge of the scientific method, and water to discover information about the five different mystery powders.

Purpose: Find the identity of one of the mystery powders by using water. (**Remember:** Do not taste any substance!)

Hypothesis: What effects do you think water will have on each powder? What do you think the mystery powder is? _____

_____

Materials:
container of water
five clear plastic cups (labeled A–E)
five same-sized metal spoons (one for each powder)
five different powders in containers labeled A–E

Procedure:
1. Place a spoonful of each powder into its labeled cup. Observe the appearance of each powder.
2. Add water and stir until the powder dissolves or the cup is filled.
3. Observe what happens to each powder; then record your observations on the chart below.
4. Let each powder sit in its cup for the rest of the day. Tomorrow observe each powder; then record your observations on the chart below.

Observations:

Mystery Powders	About how much water is needed to dissolve the powder?	What changes do you see in the powder's appearance?	What happens to the mixture after it sits overnight?
A			
B			
C			
D			
E			

Conclusions: How can water be used to help identify a substance? Can you identify one of the powders?

_____

_____

Note To The Teacher: See "Water Wonders" on page 21 for more information on using this sheet.

Black And Blue All Over

Iodine is a substance that can be used to test for starch. Starch is found in breads, cookies, and cakes. When iodine is put on a starch, a bluish black color appears. Use your powers of observation, knowledge of the scientific method, and iodine to discover information about the five different mystery powders.

Purpose: Find the identity of one of the mystery powders by using iodine. **(Remember:** Do not taste any substance!)

Hypothesis: What effects do you think iodine will have on each powder? What do you think the mystery powder is?

_____

Materials:

five paper plates, labeled A–E
eyedropper
iodine
five different powders in containers labeled A–E

Procedure:

1. Place a spoonful of each powder on its labeled plate. Observe the appearance of each powder.

2. Use the eyedropper to place three drops of iodine on each powder. **(Remember:** Iodine is a poison! Do not touch any part of your face with the iodine, and wash your hands thoroughly after the experiment.)

3. Observe what happens to each powder after iodine has been added to it. Record your observations on the chart.

Observations:

Mystery Powders	What changes do you see in its appearance?
A	
B	
C	
D	
E	

Conclusions: How can iodine be used to help identify a substance? Can you identify one of the powders?

_____

_____

©The Education Center, Inc. • *The Best Of THE MAILBOX® Science • Intermediate* • TEC1475

Note To The Teacher: See "Black And Blue All Over" on page 21 for more information on using this sheet.

Sizzling Stuff

When an acid is added to some substances, they begin to change. When they change, they give off a carbon-dioxide gas. The chemicals will bubble as they give off this gas. Sodium bicarbonate is a substance that reacts to an acid. It is used in cooking and in medicines. Use your powers of observation, knowledge of the scientific method, and an acid (vinegar) to discover information about the five different mystery powders.

Purpose: Find the identity of one of the mystery powders by using vinegar. (**Remember:** Do not taste any substance!)

Hypothesis: What effects do you think the vinegar will have on each powder? What do you think the mystery powder is? _____

_____

Materials:
vinegar
five clear plastic cups, labeled A–E
five same-sized metal spoons (one for each powder)
five different powders in containers labeled A–E

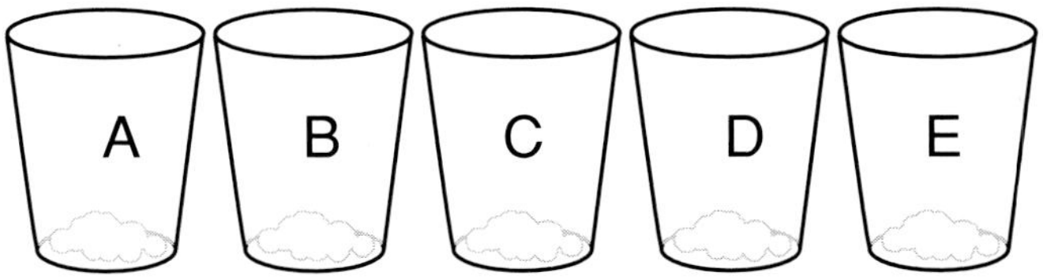

A B C D E

Procedure:
1. Place a spoonful of each powder in its labeled cup. Observe the appearance of each powder.
2. Pour a spoonful of vinegar into each cup.
3. Observe what happens to each powder once the vinegar has been added to it. Record your observations on the chart below.

Observations:

Mystery Powders	What do you see occurring after the vinegar is added?	What changes do you see in its appearance?
A		
B		
C		
D		
E		

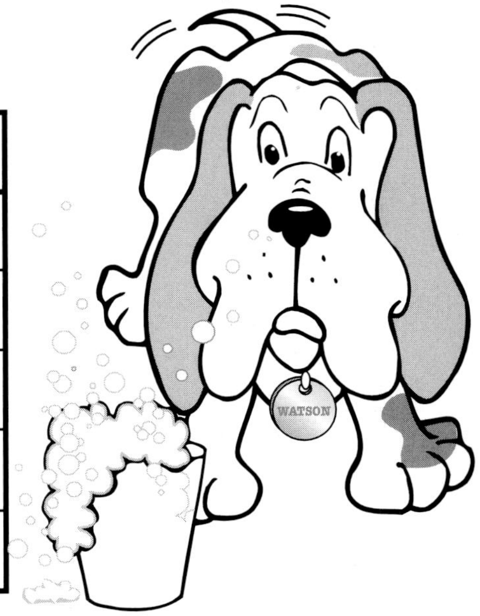

Conclusions: How can vinegar be used to help identify a substance? Can you identify one of the powders? _____

_____

_____

High Ho, Silver!

Silver nitrate is a chemical that when added to a sodium chloride will produce a chemical reaction. Sodium is an element used to flavor certain foods. Use your powers of observation, knowledge of the scientific method, and silver nitrate to discover information about the five different mystery powders.

Purpose: Find the identity of one of the mystery powders by using silver nitrate. (**Remember:** Do not taste any substance!)

Hypothesis: What effects do you think the silver nitrate will have on each powder? What do you think the mystery powder is? _____

_____

_____

Materials: five same-sized metal spoons (one for each powder); five clear plastic cups, labeled A–E and filled halfway with water; silver nitrate; five different powders in containers labeled A–E

Procedure:
1. Place a spoonful of each powder into its half-cup of water. Observe the appearance of each powder.
2. Mix the solutions with separate spoons.
3. Add a small amount of silver nitrate to each cup. (**Remember:** Silver nitrate is a poison! Do not touch any part of your face with it, and wash your hands thoroughly after the experiment.)
4. Observe what happens to each solution once the silver nitrate has been added to it. Record your observations on the chart.

Observations:

Mystery Powders	What changes do you see occurring in the mixture?
A	
B	
C	
D	
E	

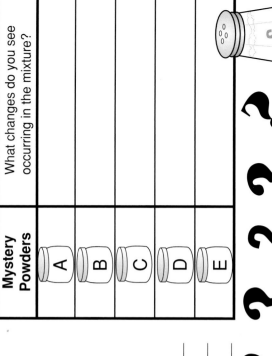

Conclusions: How can silver nitrate be used to help identify a substance? Can you identify one of the powders? _____

_____

©The Education Center, Inc. • *The Best Of* THE MAILBOX® *Science • Intermediate* • TEC1475

Note To The Teacher: See "High Ho, Silver!" on page 21 for more information on using this sheet.

Name(s) ____________________ Group chemistry experiment

The Great Powder Puzzle

Now that you have tested each of the five powders and discovered its identity, can you now identify a new mystery mixture? This mixture contains two or more of the five mystery powders. Your job is to identify which powders are in the mixture. Fill out each step below as you perform the experiment. Remember to follow the scientific method!

Purpose: Find the identity of the powders contained in the mystery mixture. (**Remember:** Do not taste any substance!)

Hypothesis: Which powders do you think are in the mystery mixture? ____________________

____

____

Materials:
List the materials you need to complete the experiment.

one container of the mystery mixture

Observations:

? ? ? ?	Describe what happens to the mixture after performing each experiment.
applying heat	
adding water	
adding iodine	
adding an acid (vinegar)	
adding silver nitrate	

Procedure: List the steps you will follow in conducting your experiment.

1. ____________________

2. ____________________

3. ____________________

4. ____________________

5. ____________________

Conclusions: Can you identify which powders are in the mixture? Explain your choices.

____

____

____

Note To The Teacher: See "The Great Powder Puzzle" on page 21 for more information on using this sheet.

Simply Science

Help students see science more clearly with the following hands-on experiments.

The Long, Long Journey

That chocolate-chip cookie that enters your mouth is just beginning a long journey through your digestive system. Illustrate this point by conducting the following demonstration. Gather these materials: a ball of string, a yardstick, masking tape, and a permanent marker. Beginning at one end of the string, measure each distance listed below. Wrap a piece of tape around the end of each measurement; then label the tape with the name of the corresponding body part.

Distance traveled by food	Body part
three inches =	mouth
ten inches =	esophagus
eight inches =	stomach
22 feet =	small intestine
five feet =	large intestine

Cut the string after the last measurement; then watch the astonished expressions of your students as you stretch it around your classroom.

Jan Drehmel—Gr. 4
Korger-Chestnut School
Chippewa Falls, WI

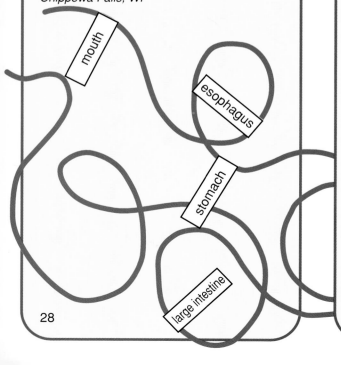

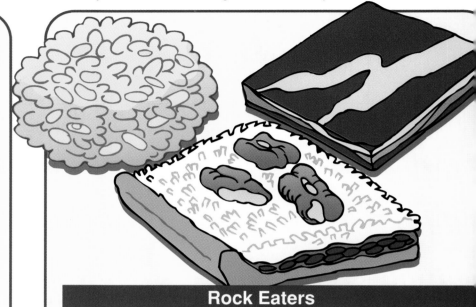

Rock Eaters

Create the following tasty treats with the recipes below to review the three main types of rocks. Divide your class into groups of three and give each group a paper plate containing a sampling of each treat. Instruct each group to observe the treats and—without eating them—record which type of rock each represents. Have each group share its findings with the rest of the class. Finally, invite the students to eat the rocks as a treat.

Cereal Balls: (*Igneous* rock: Air is trapped in the cereal much like air gets trapped in pumice when that molten rock cools quickly.) Melt 1/3 cup margarine with a 10-ounce package of marshmallows. Stir in 6 1/2 cups of crispy rice cereal. Form this mixture into balls and cool on waxed paper.

Layer Bars: (*Sedimentary* rock: Each ingredient represents a different layer of sediment.) Preheat the oven to 350°F. In a 13" x 9" pan, melt 1/2 cup margarine. Sprinkle 1 1/2 cups graham-cracker crumbs over the margarine. Pour one can sweetened condensed milk evenly over the crumbs. Top with 1 cup chocolate chips, 1 1/3 cups coconut, and 1 cup chopped nuts. Press down firmly. Bake for 25 to 30 minutes. Cut the cooled treat into bars.

Almond Bark: (*Metamorphic* rock: The swirling white and dark chocolate resembles marble, a metamorphic rock.) Place 12 ounces of white almond bark and 12 ounces of chocolate chips in separate bowls. Melt each in a microwave for about two to three minutes, stopping midway to stir. Pour the melted almond bark into the melted chocolate. Stir lightly to swirl, not mix. Pour the swirled mixture into a pan lined with waxed paper; then refrigerate till hardened. Break the treat into pieces to share with the class.

Therese Durhman—Gr. 5, Mountain View School, Hickory, NC

Life Science

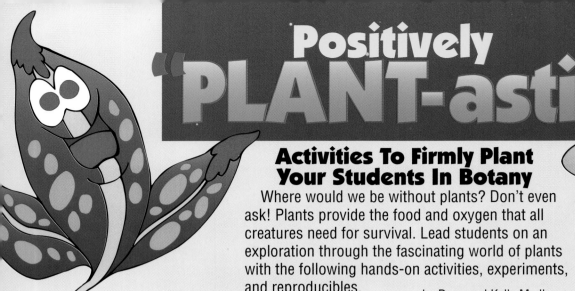

Positively "PLANT-astic"!

Activities To Firmly Plant Your Students In Botany

Where would we be without plants? Don't even ask! Plants provide the food and oxygen that all creatures need for survival. Lead students on an exploration through the fascinating world of plants with the following hands-on activities, experiments, and reproducibles.

by Dean and Kelly Medley

Something New Under The Sun!

Scientists have recently discovered several new plant species in the remote jungles of Asia. Ask your students, "How do you think scientists recognize new plants?" Then have each student create a new plant species that he has just "discovered"! Follow these steps:

1. Gather a supply of craft materials such as colored paper, fabrics, pipe cleaners, straws, buttons, scissors, glue, and other scrap materials.
2. Instruct each student to draw a large diagram of his newly discovered plant on a 12" x 18" sheet of white construction paper. Remind students to include all important parts of the plant.
3. Have students select craft supplies and construct their plants, gluing the pieces on top of their diagrams.
4. Afterwards, have each student write a short article describing the environment in which his plant lives as well as any special adaptations or conditions necessary for its survival. Have each student present his plant and article to the class. Post these botanical discoveries around the room during your study of plants.

Examine students' projects to determine their knowledge of plant characteristics. Did your young botanists create embryophytes—plants with roots, stems, and leaves? Or did they portray thallophytes—plants that lack these structures (such as algae and fungi)? Use your kids' creations as a springboard for discussing the different classifications of plants.

Sticky Situation

Why be concerned about plant and animal extinction? The following game demonstrates the sticky situation that's created when even one element is removed from a delicately balanced food web.

Materials (per small group): 9" x 12" sheet of white construction paper, scissors, pencils, crayons, markers, 1 clean potato chip canister, 6 or more pipe cleaners, masking tape, 6 or more 1-inch squares of tagboard, paper cup

Directions:

1. Wrap the paper around the canister. Trim off any excess paper; then flatten the paper.
2. Research a food web that contains at least six components. Draw a diagram of the web on the paper. Label and number each component on the web. Wrap and tape the diagram around the outside of the canister.
3. Cut a 1/2-inch strip of masking tape for each food-web component. Label and number each tape strip with one component. Wrap each label around the end of a different pipe cleaner. Place the labeled pipe cleaners inside the canister.
4. Count out as many 1-inch squares of tagboard as you have components. Write a different number on each square. Place all the squares in the paper cup.

To Play The Game: Sit in a circle on the floor. Shake the canister and dump the pipe cleaners into a pile in the center of your circle. In turn, select a number from the cup. Then pick that pipe cleaner from the pile without moving or disturbing any of the other pipe cleaners. The student who successfully removes the most pipe cleaners before the teacher calls time wins.

After each student has had several tries, call time-out. Discuss any difficulties students had during the game. Lead students to realize that just as the pipe cleaners are difficult to separate, so are the relationships between animals and plants in a food web. When a species is removed through extinction, other members of the web are affected. Follow up by having students research specific endangered plant species and how their extinction will affect others.

STEP 1 STEP 2

Climbing Colors

You don't have to have a green thumb to understand the importance of chlorophyll to plant photosynthesis! Without this pigment a plant cannot produce its own food. Have students conduct the following experiment to determine the presence or absence of chlorophyll in leaves:

Materials (per pair of students): 1 fresh green leaf, 1 yellow or brown (dead) leaf, penny, two 3 1/2" x 1" strips of coffee-filter paper, 1 oz. nail polish remover, 6-oz. baby food jar, tape, paper towel
Directions:

1. Center a leaf approximately 1/2 inch from one end of the filter strip. Using the edge of the penny, rub a straight line across the leaf so that a mark is made on the filter strip parallel to and approximately 1/2 inch from the edge of the strip (see the diagram).
2. Pour the nail polish remover in the jar. Tape the strip to the inside of the jar so that the edge with the leaf mark just touches the liquid. Place the lid on the jar.
3. Observe as the liquid "climbs" up the filter strip. Record your observations.
4. When the liquid stops climbing, remove the strip and place it on the paper towel to dry. Recap the jar.
5. Repeat the experiment with the other leaf.
6. Return the liquid and jar to the teacher.
7. Compare your observations from each experiment. *(The dead leaves do not produce colors on the filter paper. This indicates that these leaves are no longer producing food for the plant.)*

Sorting It All Out

Plants containing roots, stems, and leaves are easy to locate and make great critical-thinking materials. Invite your budding botanists to examine these plant structures to discover for themselves the varied functions that make plants unique. Begin by gathering a large supply of plant parts. Vary the size, shape, and texture of the parts. For instance, include the fibrous, spreading roots of grass and the solid roots of carrots. Find examples of different types of stems such as potatoes, daffodils, or tree saplings. Include lettuce leaves as well as leaves from trees, flowering plants, and bushes. Set up three tables before students arrive. Place all the roots on one table, the stems on another, and the leaves on the third.

Divide your class into three teams. Provide each team with a 12" x 18" sheet of white construction paper. Have each team begin at a different table and determine how it would categorize the plant parts on its table. Each team's recorder records its findings on the construction paper. After about ten minutes, have each team rotate to a different table and repeat the process with a new sheet of paper. After visiting every table, have the teams report their findings. Discuss the similarities and differences between each team's observations. Then have students use their observations to infer why each plant has that particular type of root, leaf, or stem.

Getting To The Root Of The Matter

Let's hear it for roots! They anchor plants in place and transport the minerals and water necessary for plants' survival. Plus they help hold soil in place—preventing the erosion of precious topsoil and protecting such ecosystems as dunes and maritime forests. Conduct the following experiment over a period of three weeks to demonstrate the holding power of roots:

Materials (for each group of three or four students): eight 8-oz. Styrofoam® cups, tray, tablespoon, waterproof marker, paper, potting soil, water, 2 each of 4 different types of seeds that have been soaked in water overnight (Grass, bean, tomato, and radish seeds are good choices.)
Directions:

1. Poke three holes in the bottom of each cup; then fill each cup to 1/2 inch from the top with potting soil. Place all the cups in a tray to prevent leaking water from damaging tabletops.
2. Following the directions for planting depth on the seed packets, plant one seed in each cup. Use the marker to label each cup with the name of the plant.
3. Predict which roots will best hold soil. Record each group member's predictions on paper.
4. Gently water the seeds. Maintain the soil moisture by adding one tablespoon of water to each cup every day.
5. After three weeks, gently pull each plant out of its soil. Note the difficulty each plant presents as you try to pull it from the cup. Observe the amount of soil clinging to each plant's roots.
6. Compare the size and shape of each plant's root system.
7. Compare the results with your predictions. Note which roots held more soil. What does that tell you about the types of plants that would best prevent erosion? *(Roots with many branches hold soil best. As students pull up each plant, they will see that the grass roots hold more soil than the radish roots.)*

RADISH GRASS GRASS

Pam Crane

31

Survival Of The Fittest

Plants grow almost everywhere. But what happens if the place in which they're growing doesn't receive enough sunlight, minerals, water, or clean air? Conduct the following simulation to predict the growth of four "plants" under different conditions:

Materials (per group of four students): 1 empty cereal box; scissors, 1 copy each of pages 34 and 35; 4 yellow, 4 purple, 4 green, and 4 orange Skittles® candies; glue stick; plastic cup

Directions:
1. Cut the front panel from the empty cereal box.
2. Glue the top flaps back together so that the box has four sides.
3. Glue page 34 faceup on the inside "bottom" panel of the box. Each circle represents the area in which a plant's roots have spread.
4. Cut apart the four graph pieces on page 35 and distribute one to each group member. Have each group member note the plant number indicated on his graph.
5. Place the candy pieces in the cup.
6. With the box sitting still on a desk, have one group member hold the cup three inches above the X and dump the candy pieces into the box.
7. Have each group member find column 1 on her graph and record the number of each colored piece that fell within her plant's circle.
8. Pick up all the candy pieces and repeat the process of dumping and recording nine more times.
9. Complete the group questions at the bottom of page 35. *(Rooted plants cannot move and are subject to the conditions of their locations. Many plants die for want of water, minerals, sunlight, or clean air. However, plants grow even where conditions are not always favorable. Plants adapt to survive in diverse environments.)*

Where Is The Water?

Students may already be aware that plants expel oxygen durin*photosynthesis.* However, do they know that plants also release water through a process called *transpiration?* Most water is released through small openings in the leaves called *stomates.* Scientists use an instrument called a *potometer* to measure the amount of water expelled by a plant during transpiration. Challenge your students to prove the process of transpiration by usin a student-made potometer and a *control.*

Materials (per small group): 2 identical 16-oz. foam cups with plastic lids, water, 1 small seedling (see page 33 for directions on growing seed lings), fine-point permanent marker, modeling clay

Directions:
1. Peel back the plastic from the straw hole in the lid; then carefully thread the seedling through the hole. Seal any openings around the hole with clay. Be careful not to injure the seedling.
2. Lay the lid on the cup to determine the location of the roots in the cup. Remove the lid and fill the cup with enough water to cover the roots.
3. Place the lid securely on the cup.
4. Mark the waterline on the outside of the cup with a marker. Write the date next to the line.
5. Create a control by filling the other cup to the same level with wate
6. Seal the straw hole with clay and place the lid on the control cup.
7. Expose both cups to light for two weeks.
8. Observe both cups each day. Record any changes in the water leve by drawing a new line on each cup to mark the new level. Write the date next to the line.
9. Compare all data recorded on both cups. *(The students should no the decreased water level in the plant cup. This phenomenon occu because the plant has released water during transpiration.)*

A Bibliography For Budding Botanists

Eyewitness Books: Tree
Written by David Burnie; Published by Alfred A. Knopf

Growing With Gardening: A Twelve-Month Guide For Therapy, Recreation, And Education
Written by Bibby Moore; Published by The University Of North Carolina Press, Chapel Hill

Grow Lab: A Complete Guide To Gardening In The Classroom and *GrowLab™: Activities For Growing Minds*
Both titles written and published by the National Gardening Association, 180 Flynn Avenue, Burlington, VT 05401

Let's Grow!: 72 Gardening Adventures With Children
Written by Linda Tilgner; Published by Storey Communications, Inc.

Plants And Flowers
Written by Brian Holley; Published by Hayes Publishing Ltd.

The Clover & The Bee: A Book Of Pollination
Written by Anne Ophelia Dowden; Published by HarperCollins

Flowers For You: Blooms For Every Month
Written by Anita Holmes; Published by Bradbury

Starting Seedlings In Your Classroom

Many hands-on activities require a seedling. Grow plants for your experiments right in your classroom with these helpful tips and instructions.

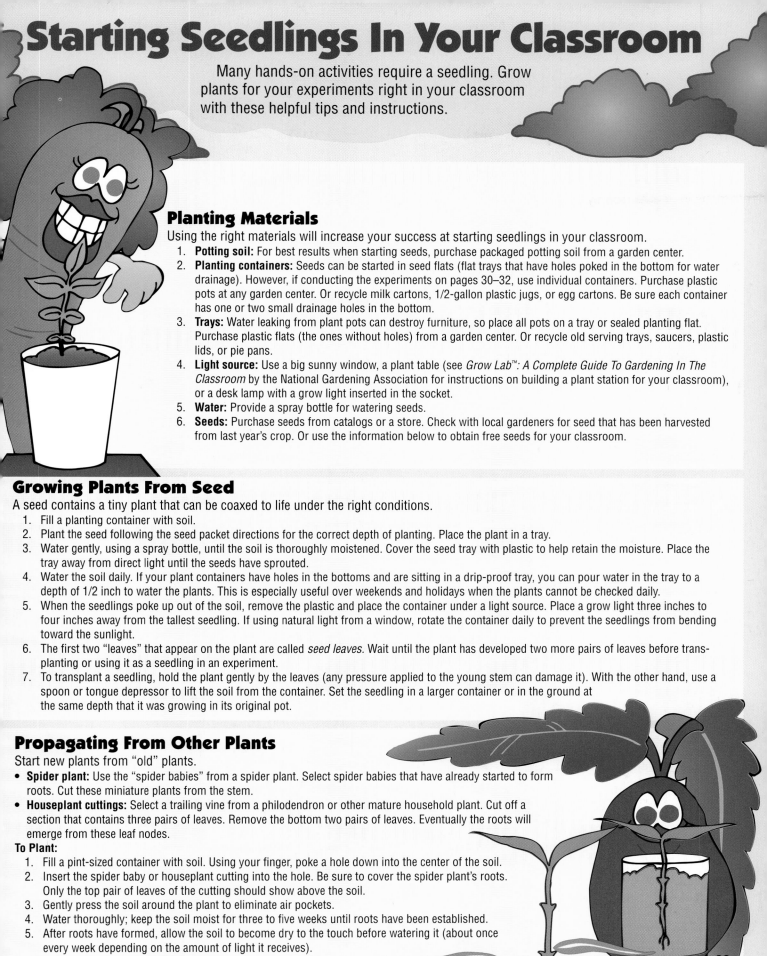

Planting Materials

Using the right materials will increase your success at starting seedlings in your classroom.

1. **Potting soil:** For best results when starting seeds, purchase packaged potting soil from a garden center.
2. **Planting containers:** Seeds can be started in seed flats (flat trays that have holes poked in the bottom for water drainage). However, if conducting the experiments on pages 30–32, use individual containers. Purchase plastic pots at any garden center. Or recycle milk cartons, 1/2-gallon plastic jugs, or egg cartons. Be sure each container has one or two small drainage holes in the bottom.
3. **Trays:** Water leaking from plant pots can destroy furniture, so place all pots on a tray or sealed planting flat. Purchase plastic flats (the ones without holes) from a garden center. Or recycle old serving trays, saucers, plastic lids, or pie pans.
4. **Light source:** Use a big sunny window, a plant table (see *Grow Lab™: A Complete Guide To Gardening In The Classroom* by the National Gardening Association for instructions on building a plant station for your classroom), or a desk lamp with a grow light inserted in the socket.
5. **Water:** Provide a spray bottle for watering seeds.
6. **Seeds:** Purchase seeds from catalogs or a store. Check with local gardeners for seed that has been harvested from last year's crop. Or use the information below to obtain free seeds for your classroom.

Growing Plants From Seed

A seed contains a tiny plant that can be coaxed to life under the right conditions.

1. Fill a planting container with soil.
2. Plant the seed following the seed packet directions for the correct depth of planting. Place the plant in a tray.
3. Water gently, using a spray bottle, until the soil is thoroughly moistened. Cover the seed tray with plastic to help retain the moisture. Place the tray away from direct light until the seeds have sprouted.
4. Water the soil daily. If your plant containers have holes in the bottoms and are sitting in a drip-proof tray, you can pour water in the tray to a depth of 1/2 inch to water the plants. This is especially useful over weekends and holidays when the plants cannot be checked daily.
5. When the seedlings poke up out of the soil, remove the plastic and place the container under a light source. Place a grow light three inches to four inches away from the tallest seedling. If using natural light from a window, rotate the container daily to prevent the seedlings from bending toward the sunlight.
6. The first two "leaves" that appear on the plant are called *seed leaves.* Wait until the plant has developed two more pairs of leaves before transplanting or using it as a seedling in an experiment.
7. To transplant a seedling, hold the plant gently by the leaves (any pressure applied to the young stem can damage it). With the other hand, use a spoon or tongue depressor to lift the soil from the container. Set the seedling in a larger container or in the ground at the same depth that it was growing in its original pot.

Propagating From Other Plants

Start new plants from "old" plants.

- **Spider plant:** Use the "spider babies" from a spider plant. Select spider babies that have already started to form roots. Cut these miniature plants from the stem.
- **Houseplant cuttings:** Select a trailing vine from a philodendron or other mature household plant. Cut off a section that contains three pairs of leaves. Remove the bottom two pairs of leaves. Eventually the roots will emerge from these leaf nodes.

To Plant:

1. Fill a pint-sized container with soil. Using your finger, poke a hole down into the center of the soil.
2. Insert the spider baby or houseplant cutting into the hole. Be sure to cover the spider plant's roots. Only the top pair of leaves of the cutting should show above the soil.
3. Gently press the soil around the plant to eliminate air pockets.
4. Water thoroughly; keep the soil moist for three to five weeks until roots have been established.
5. After roots have formed, allow the soil to become dry to the touch before watering it (about once every week depending on the amount of light it receives).

"Survival Of The Fittest" Activity Board

Use with the "Survival Of The Fittest" activity on page 32.

Plant #1	1	2	3	4	5	6	7	8	9	10	Plant #2	1	2	3	4	5	6	7	8	9	10
sunlight (yellow)											sunlight (yellow)										
minerals (purple)											minerals (purple)										
water (green)											water (green)										
clean air (orange)											clean air (orange)										
Plant #3	1	2	3	4	5	6	7	8	9	10	Plant #4	1	2	3	4	5	6	7	8	9	10
sunlight (yellow)											sunlight (yellow)										
minerals (purple)											minerals (purple)										
water (green)											water (green)										
clean air (orange)											clean air (orange)										

Names of group members: _____

Answer the following questions using the information on your graphs:

1. Which plant received the largest amounts of sunlight, minerals, water, and clean air combined? _____

2. How do you think this plant would have survived compared to the other three plants? _____
   _____

3. Which of the plants received the least amount of water? _____

4. Could a plant survive if it did not receive much water? Explain your answer. _____
   _____
   _____

5. Could a plant receive too much water? Explain your answer. _____
   _____

6. Could a plant survive if it did not receive sunshine or minerals? Explain your answer. _____
   _____

7. How would a lack of clean air affect a plant? _____
   _____

8. Have each group member research a different plant that manages to survive in adverse conditions (conditions in which the plant would not receive large amounts of sunlight, minerals, water, or clean air). On separate paper, write your findings on how each plant has adapted to survive in these conditions.

Note To The Teacher: Use this page with the "Survival Of The Fittest" activity on page 32 and the reproducible activity board on page 34. Examples of plants students can research in Step 8 include plants of the tropical rain forest or the high mountains, desert vegetation, or aquatic plants.

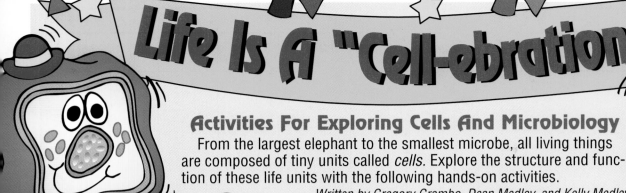

Life Is A "Cell-ebration"!

Activities For Exploring Cells And Microbiology

From the largest elephant to the smallest microbe, all living things are composed of tiny units called *cells.* Explore the structure and function of these life units with the following hands-on activities.

Written by Gregory Grambo, Dean Medley, and Kelly Medley

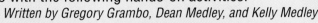

Plant And Animal Cell Models

Create these three-dimensional cell models and lead your students toward a greater appreciation of the varied functions of a single cell.

Materials:
1 shoebox, without lid
2 one-gallon zippered plastic bags
2 bunches green grapes
8 cups clear gelatin
30 jelly beans
2 Ping-Pong® balls
2 tangerines
4 tablespoons candy sprinkles
2 plastic straws
glue
2 paper plates
scissors

Cell Structures Represented And Their Functions

cell wall: nonliving structure surrounding plant cell; provides shape and support
cell membrane: encloses the cell, controlling the inward and outward flow of materials
chloroplasts: contain chlorophyll, used by plants to make food
cytoplasm: jellylike material where chemical processes take place
mitochondria: rodlike structures that control the release of energy in cell processes
vacuoles: fluid-filled sacs that store different substances in liquid form
nucleus: contains DNA; stores information used to control cell activities
ribosomes: particles in cytoplasm that build the proteins needed by a cell
endoplasmic reticulum (ER): membranes that run throughout the cytoplasm; form tubes through which materials move to all cell parts

Before class: Construct the endoplasmic reticulum by putting glue in one paper plate and the sprinkles in another. Roll both straws in the glue and then in the sprinkles. After the straws dry, cut them into one-inch pieces.

Building the plant cell model:

1. Remind students that a plant cell has both a *cell wall* and a *cell membrane* (unlike the animal cell, which has only the cell membrane). These structures contain all the other parts of the cell. Line a shoebox with a plastic bag. Explain that the shoebox represents the rigid cell wall, while the plastic bag represents the cell membrane. Explain the function of each additional part (steps 2–7) as you add it to the model.
2. Add four cups of the gelatin *(cytoplasm)* to the bag.
3. Scatter 15 of the jelly beans *(mitochondria)* throughout the gelatin.
4. Place a Ping-Pong® ball *(vacuole)* to one side in the gelatin.
5. Put a tangerine *(nucleus)* in the center of the bag.
6. Scatter half of the sprinkle-covered straw sections *(endoplasmic reticulum and ribosomes)* throughout the gelatin.
7. Position the grapes *(chloroplasts)* throughout the gelatin.

Building the animal cell model:

Use the same materials and steps as in the plant cell model with the following exceptions:
- Animal cells have no cell wall. Eliminate the shoebox.
- Animals do not produce their own food through photosynthesis. Do not include the chloroplasts (grapes).

After building the models: Have students compare the two models. Help them notice that the models are basically the same, except for the cell wall and chloroplasts.

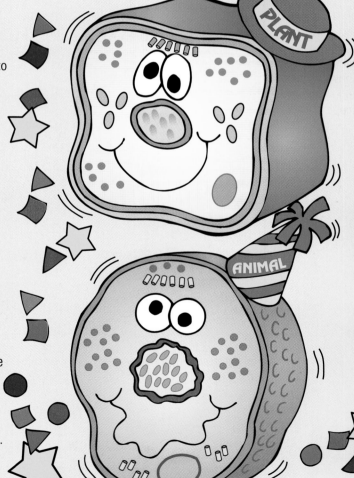

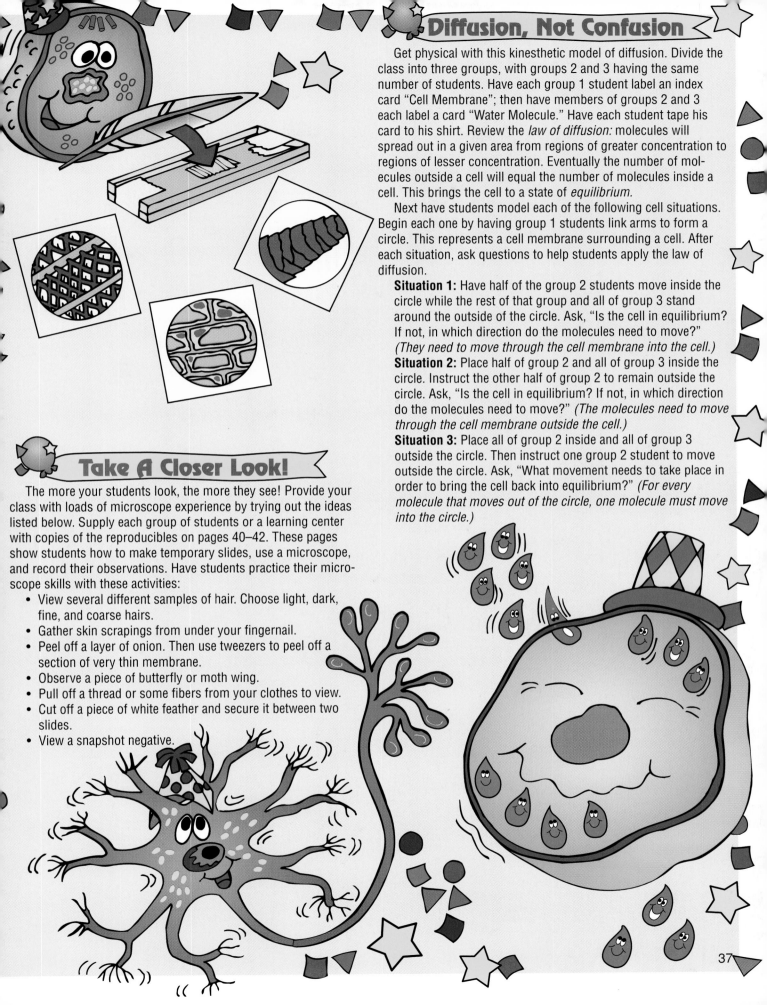

Diffusion, Not Confusion

Get physical with this kinesthetic model of diffusion. Divide the class into three groups, with groups 2 and 3 having the same number of students. Have each group 1 student label an index card "Cell Membrane"; then have members of groups 2 and 3 each label a card "Water Molecule." Have each student tape his card to his shirt. Review the *law of diffusion:* molecules will spread out in a given area from regions of greater concentration to regions of lesser concentration. Eventually the number of molecules outside a cell will equal the number of molecules inside a cell. This brings the cell to a state of *equilibrium.*

Next have students model each of the following cell situations. Begin each one by having group 1 students link arms to form a circle. This represents a cell membrane surrounding a cell. After each situation, ask questions to help students apply the law of diffusion.

Situation 1: Have half of the group 2 students move inside the circle while the rest of that group and all of group 3 stand around the outside of the circle. Ask, "Is the cell in equilibrium? If not, in which direction do the molecules need to move?" *(They need to move through the cell membrane into the cell.)*

Situation 2: Place half of group 2 and all of group 3 inside the circle. Instruct the other half of group 2 to remain outside the circle. Ask, "Is the cell in equilibrium? If not, in which direction do the molecules need to move?" *(The molecules need to move through the cell membrane outside the cell.)*

Situation 3: Place all of group 2 inside and all of group 3 outside the circle. Then instruct one group 2 student to move outside the circle. Ask, "What movement needs to take place in order to bring the cell back into equilibrium?" *(For every molecule that moves out of the circle, one molecule must move into the circle.)*

Take A Closer Look!

The more your students look, the more they see! Provide your class with loads of microscope experience by trying out the ideas listed below. Supply each group of students or a learning center with copies of the reproducibles on pages 40–42. These pages show students how to make temporary slides, use a microscope, and record their observations. Have students practice their microscope skills with these activities:

- View several different samples of hair. Choose light, dark, fine, and coarse hairs.
- Gather skin scrapings from under your fingernail.
- Peel off a layer of onion. Then use tweezers to peel off a section of very thin membrane.
- Observe a piece of butterfly or moth wing.
- Pull off a thread or some fibers from your clothes to view.
- Cut off a piece of white feather and secure it between two slides.
- View a snapshot negative.

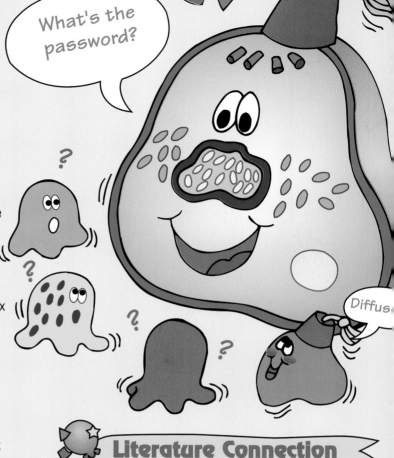

Demonstrating Diffusion

Amaze your students with this demonstration of a cell membrane's ability to allow only certain molecules to enter the cell.

Materials:

test tube
water
index card
iodine
dialysis tubing (available from a science supply store)

eyedropper
empty jar
rubber band
scissors
soluble potato starch (1 g starch/100 ml water) —available from a science supply store

Directions:

1. Fill the jar with water.
2. Add a few drops of iodine to the water until the water is yellow in color.
3. Using the scissors, cut a small *x* in the center of the index card.

4. Fill the test tube with the starch solution.
5. Cover the opening of the test tube with the dialysis tubing; then secure the tubing with a rubber band.
6. Place the test tube through the opening in the index card as shown.

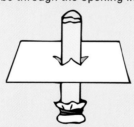

7. Place the test tube in the jar as shown.

8. Set the jar aside until the next day. Observe and discuss changes with students.

Diffusion is the spreading out of molecules in a given area from a region of greater concentration to a region of lesser concentration. Dialysis tubing is semipermeable like the cell membrane. Large particles, like starch, cannot pass through the tubing. However, small particles—like iodine—can. The iodine that passes through the dialysis tubing mixes with the starch in the tube, turning the liquid black. As more iodine enters the tube, the water in the jar will become clear.

Literature Connection

These books on cells and microbiology are worth a closer loo

The World Of The Microscope by Chris Oxlade and Corinne Stockley (Scholastic Inc.)
Atoms And Cells by Lionel Bender (Scholastic Inc.)
Cells Are Us and *Cell Wars* by Dr. Fran Balkwill (Carolrhoda Books Inc.)
Mysterious Microbes by Steve Parker (Raintree Steck-Vaughn Publishers)
From the **DISCOVER HIDDEN WORLDS** series (Western Publishing Company, Inc.):
The Home by Heather Amery and Jane Songi
Nature by Heather Amery

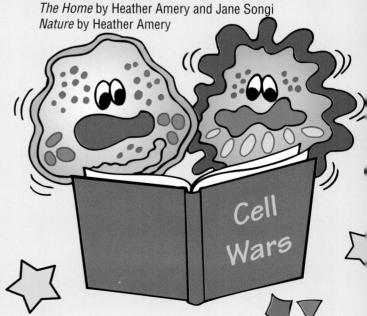

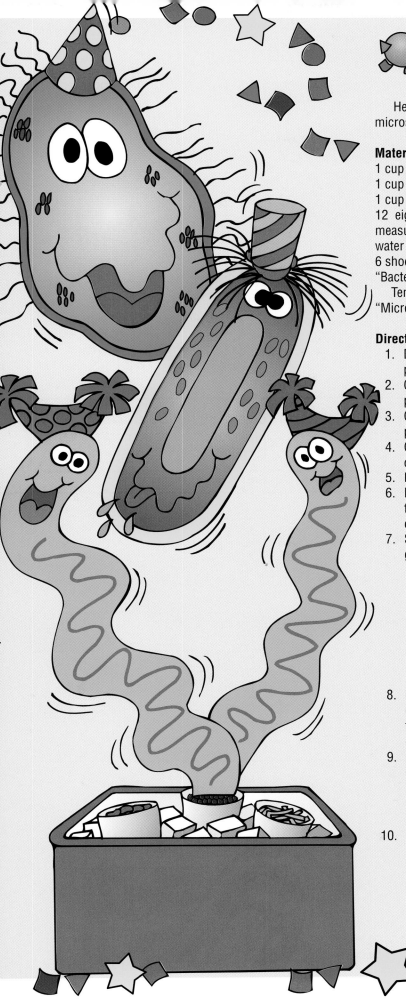

Bacteria: To Grow Or Not To Grow!

Help students grow their own bacteria to observe under microscopes with this exciting experiment!

Materials:
1 cup peppercorns
1 cup straw, cut into 2-inch sections
1 cup dried pinto beans
12 eight-oz. paper cups
measuring cup
water
6 shoeboxes
"Bacteria Growth Chart" and "Making
   Temporary Slides" (page 40) for each group
"Microscope Observation Sheet" (page 42)

3 permanent markers
2 small ice buckets or
   coolers filled with ice
closet (optional)
warm spot, such as a
   radiator or sunny
   windowsill

Directions:
1. Divide the class into three groups. Give each group four paper cups.
2. Give group 1 the peppercorns to sort equally into its four paper cups.
3. Give group 2 the straw to distribute equally into its four paper cups.
4. Give group 3 the beans to sort equally into its four paper cups.
5. Have each group add 3/4 cup of water to each cup.
6. Have each group use markers to label its four cups with these captions (one per cup): warm/light, warm/dark, cool/light, cool/dark.
7. Set up the following stations in your room; then have each group bring its cup to the appropriate station:
   Warm/Light (a sunny windowsill or near a radiator)
   Warm/Dark (near a heat source; cover each cup with a shoebox)
   Cool/Light (nestled in ice in a cooler without a lid; add ice daily to the cooler)
   Cool/Dark (nestled in ice in a cooler; cover each cup with a shoebox or store the cooler in a closet; add ice daily to the cooler)
8. Have each group check its cups daily for five to ten days to observe any bacterial growth. Growth will be evident when the water turns cloudy. Have each group track its bacteria growth on a copy of the chart on page 40.
9. Based on a comparison of each group's chart data, have the class determine which conditions are most conducive to bacterial growth. Ask students if they can come up with other real-life situations where bacteria will easily grow (on shower curtains; inside damp, hot sneakers; etc.).
10. Following the directions for preparing microscope slides on page 41, have groups prepare slides of their bacteria to observe under the microscope. Use the open microscope observation sheet on page 42 to record observations.

Making Temporary Slides

Many specimens can be examined using temporary slides. These slides are considered temporary because after a while, the water used evaporates and the material decays.

Materials: slides and coverslips, tweezers, eyedropper, water, specimens

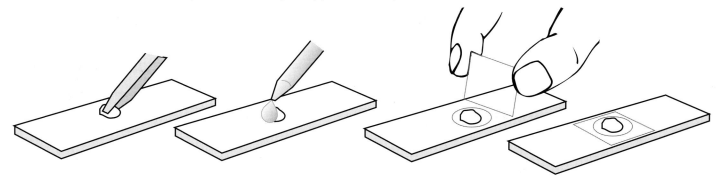

1. Place the specimen in the center of the slide.

2. Cover it with a drop of water.

3. Holding a coverslip by its side edges, place the bottom edge on the slide near the water drop.

4. Carefully lower the coverslip onto the specimen.

Clean slides and coverslips in warm water that contains a little dish detergent. Handle each slide by its sides. To dry a slide, stand it up at an angle on a dry paper towel. Let its upper end rest against a clean jar. Then soak the slide in rubbing alcohol to sterilize it. Allow the slide to dry completely before storing it.

Name(s) _____ Observation chart

Bacteria Growth Chart

Circle the specimen your group is observing: peppercorns   straw   pinto beans
Chart the growth of bacteria by noting whether the water is clear, cloudy, or colored. Also note any odors and/or other characteristics of the water.

	Day 1	Day 2	Day 3	Day 4	Day 5	Day 6	Day 7	Day 8	Day 9	Day 10
Warm/ Light										
Warm/ Dark										
Cool/ Light										
Cool/ Dark										

Based on your observations, which condition was best for growing bacteria? _____

Name _____

How To Use A Simple Compound Microscope

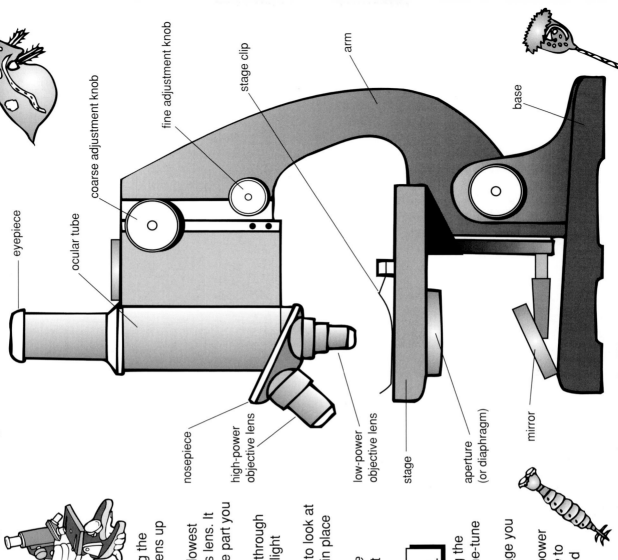

eyepiece

ocular tube

coarse adjustment knob

fine adjustment knob

stage clip

arm

base

nosepiece

high-power objective lens

low-power objective lens

stage

aperture (or diaphragm)

mirror

1. Handle with care! When carrying the microscope, grasp the *arm* with one hand while supporting the *base* with the other.

2. Position the microscope on a steady table near a good source of light. If possible, tilt the *ocular tube* so that you can get a clear view through the microscope without leaning over the *eyepiece*.

3. While looking at the microscope from the side, practice turning the *coarse* and *fine adjustment knobs* to see how they move the lens up and down. Raise the lens as far as possible.

4. Turn the *objective lenses* so that the microscope is set at the lowest power (probably 10X). Always start your observations with this lens. It allows you to see more of the object so that you can locate the part you want to observe more closely.

5. If the microscope has an *aperture*, open it fully. While looking through the eyepiece, tilt the *mirror* to reflect the maximum amount of light through the lens. You should see a white circle.

6. Place a prepared slide on the *stage* so that the part you want to look at is positioned over the hole and under the lens. Hold the slide in place with the *stage clips*.

7. While looking at the microscope from the side, turn the *coarse adjustment knob* to bring the lens down very close to—but not touching—the slide.

** Never lower the lens while looking through the eyepiece. You could hit the slide, breaking it or breaking the lens itself.

8. Looking through the eyepiece, slowly raise the lens by turning the coarse adjustment knob. After the object comes into focus, fine-tune the picture by slowly turning the *fine adjustment knob*.

9. Slowly move the slide around until you find the part of the image you wish to observe.

10. To look at the image in more detail, change to a higher-power objective lens. First raise the lenses. Turn the *nosepiece* to select the higher-power lens. Lower the lens as explained in step 7, and refocus as in step 8.

Note To The Teacher: Use this page with "Take A Closer Look!" on page 37.

Microscope Observation Sheet

Draw the images you see through your microscope in the circles below. Don't forget to label each drawing with the name of the object, the date, and the lens power used.

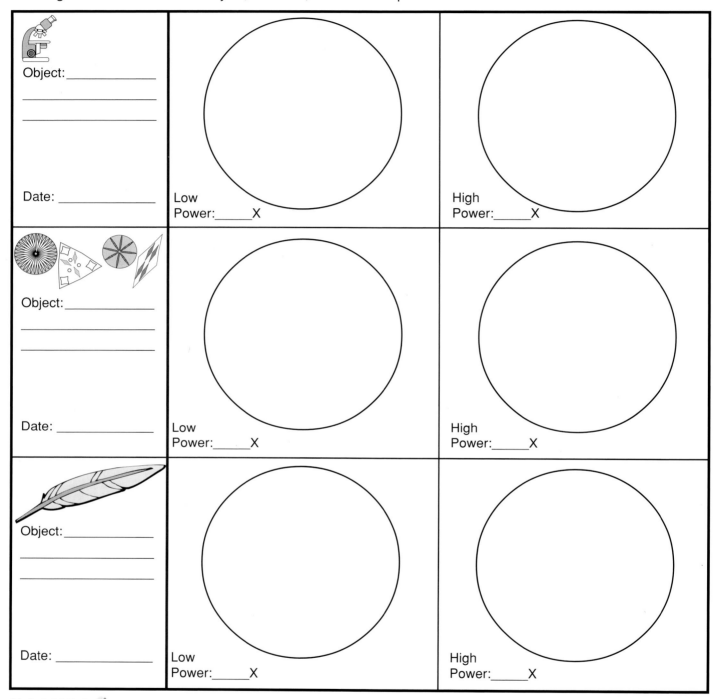

Object:_____

_____

_____

Date: _____   Low Power:_____X   High Power:_____X

Object:_____

_____

_____

Date: _____   Low Power:_____X   High Power:_____X

Object:_____

_____

_____

Date: _____   Low Power:_____X   High Power:_____X

Helpful Hints:
• Look down the microscope with one eye and at your paper with the other.
• Use a sharp pencil when drawing. Give your drawing a title.
• Some objects are not transparent enough to be seen with bottom lighting (lighting reflected from the mirror under the stage). These objects need to be lit from above to see them in detail. To get the best top lighting, aim a lamp at the object on the stage. Move the lamp around to get the best lighting. Move the mirror so that no light comes up through the stage.

Note To The Teacher: Use this sheet with "Take A Closer Look!" on page 37, with "Bacteria: To Grow Or Not To Grow!" on page 39, or in other microscope experiences.

THE ANIMAL OLYMPICS

Getting your students in tip-top physical and mental shape has never been easier! Combine the study of animal adaptations and math with the six challenging events in this exciting, one-of-a-kind Olympic activity.

by Daniel Kriesberg and Stephanie Willett-Smith

PREPARING FOR THE ANIMAL OLYMPICS

Choose an outside location in which to hold the events. Then assemble these materials: a yardstick for every two students, a tape measure, a stopwatch, masking tape, paper cut into four different-sized squares (8" x 8", 4" x 4", 2" x 2", 1" x 1"). To make the booklets for recording data, provide each student with a copy of pages 44, 45, and the top half of page 46. On these pages students will find facts about animal adaptations that are related to the events. Direct the student to cut the pages apart along the dotted lines, place the pages in order, and staple them between the front and back covers. Be sure students bring their booklets and pencils with them to the events.

HOLDING THE EVENTS

Event 1: Sprints—Have each student stand on a starting line. Next have each student estimate the distance of 100 yards by walking from the starting line to that point. Check students' estimations by measuring the actual distance with  the yardstick or tape measure. Have your students stand single file at the starting line. Use the stopwatch to time each student as he runs the 100-yard distance. Have the student record his running time on page 3 of his booklet.

Event 2: Long Jump—Have your students return to the starting line. One at a time, allow each student to get a running start and jump. Then use the tape measure to measure his jump. Direct the student to record his jump distance on page 4 of his booklet.

Event 3: Wing Rotation—Divide your students into pairs. Have one partner rotate his arms in a circular pattern as many times as possible in one minute while his partner counts the number of rotations. Have the student record the number of rotations on page 5 of his booklet.

Event 4: Accuracy Jump—Place the 8" x 8" piece of paper on the ground. Have each student jump onto the  paper, trying not to fall off. Continue the process, using a smaller piece of paper each round. Direct a student to record the dimensions of the last paper onto which he jumped without falling on page 6 of his booklet.

Event 5: High Jump—Head back indoors for this event. Have students work in the same pairs as they did for the Wing Rotation event. Give each student a small piece of masking tape. Then direct the student to jump up as high as she can and stick the tape to the wall. Have the student use the yardstick to measure the distance she jumped from the ground to the tape. Then have her record the distance on page 7 of her booklet.

Event 6: Long-Distance Marathon—Direct each student to complete this last event for homework. If a student does not have access to a car, provide your own car's mileage and age data for the student to record on page 8 of his booklet.

At the conclusion of the six events, have each student complete the math problems at the bottoms of her booklet pages. Direct the student to use the back of each sheet for her computation. (See page 159 for an answer key.) After each student has completed her booklet, present her with a copy of the award on the bottom of page 46.

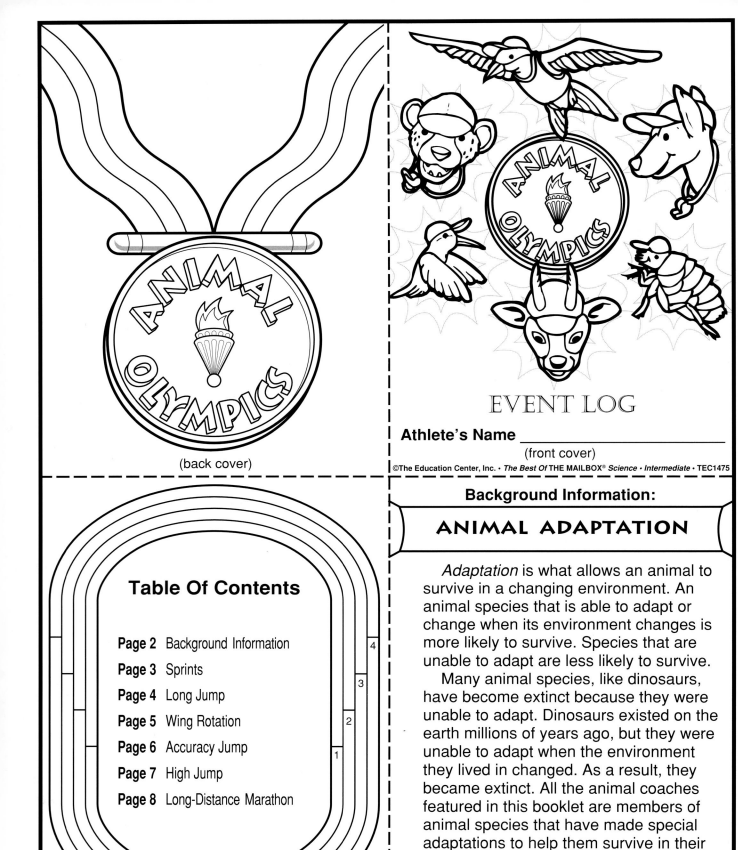

(back cover)

EVENT LOG

Athlete's Name _____

(front cover)

Table Of Contents

Background Information:

ANIMAL ADAPTATION

Adaptation is what allows an animal to survive in a changing environment. An animal species that is able to adapt or change when its environment changes is more likely to survive. Species that are unable to adapt are less likely to survive.

Many animal species, like dinosaurs, have become extinct because they were unable to adapt. Dinosaurs existed on the earth millions of years ago, but they were unable to adapt when the environment they lived in changed. As a result, they became extinct. All the animal coaches featured in this booklet are members of animal species that have made special adaptations to help them survive in their environments.

1

2

Sprints

TEAM COACH: Cheetah
FACTS: The fastest land animal is the cheetah. The cheetah can reach speeds of up to 60 miles per hour. That is equal to about one mile per minute!
SPECIAL ADAPTATIONS: The cheetah has long legs for running. Its spine is flexible, allowing it to extend its legs even farther. A small head and thin body make the cheetah's body streamlined.

1. How fast did you run 100 yards?
   _____
2. There are three feet in one yard and 5,280 feet in a mile. How many yards are in one mile? _____
3. How long would it take you to run a mile if you continued at the same pace as you ran 100 yards? Clue: (Answer #2 ÷ 100) x Answer #1
   = _____

3

Long Jump

TEAM COACH: Kangaroo
FACTS: The kangaroo can jump up to 40 feet in a single bound.
SPECIAL ADAPTATIONS: The kangaroo has small front legs and powerful, large hind legs. A kangaroo moves only its hind legs when it hops, and its long tail is used for balance.

1. How far did you jump in the long jump event?
   _____
2. How many more feet can a kangaroo jump than you?
   _____
3. How many jumps would it take a kangaroo to cover a distance of one mile?
   _____

4

Wing Rotation

TEAM COACH: Hummingbird
FACTS: A hummingbird can flap its wings up to 4,200 times in one minute.
SPECIAL ADAPTATIONS: The hummingbird has wings that can move in a circular pattern. This adaptation allows the hummingbird to hover in one spot. The hummingbird is also able to move both forward and backwards, enabling it to back out of flowers it has entered to obtain the nectar it feeds upon.

1. How many times can you rotate your arms in a circular pattern in one minute?
   _____
2. How many times can a hummingbird rotate its wings in one hour? _____
3. How many times can you rotate your arms in one hour? _____

5

Accuracy Jump

TEAM COACH: Klipspringer Antelope
FACTS: The klipspringer is a small antelope that lives on the rocky slopes of the African mountains.
SPECIAL ADAPTATIONS: The klipspringer is an excellent climber thanks to its rubbery hooves. These hooves allow the klipspringer to grip rocks when jumping from one to the other.

1. What was the size of the smallest paper you were able to jump on without falling? _____
2. Using the area formula *length x width,* compute the total area of that piece of paper.
   _____
3. What is the total area of the largest piece of paper you jumped on? _____

6

High Jump

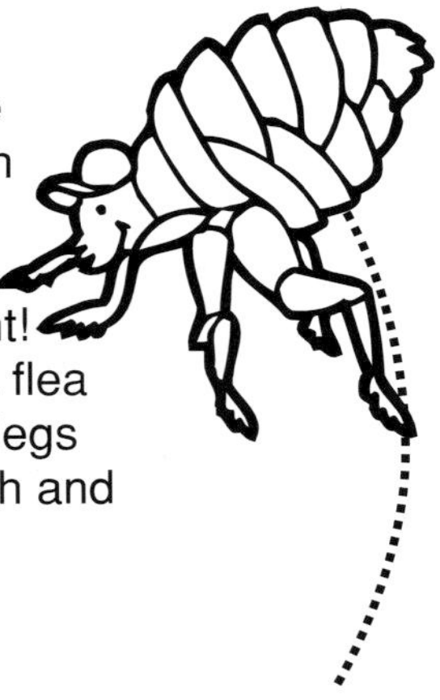

TEAM COACH: Flea
FACTS: The flea is a parasite that measures about 1/16 inch in height. It can jump up to eight inches in the air or about 130 times its own height!
SPECIAL ADAPTATIONS: A flea has very long, powerful back legs that enable it to jump very high and reach the hosts it feeds upon.

1. How high did you jump from the ground? _____
2. What is your height in inches? _____
3. How high would you jump if you could jump 130 times your height? _____
4. What is the difference between how high you actually jumped and the number you came up with in problem 3? _____

7

Long-Distance Marathon
(To be completed at home)

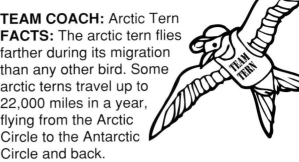

TEAM COACH: Arctic Tern
FACTS: The arctic tern flies farther during its migration than any other bird. Some arctic terns travel up to 22,000 miles in a year, flying from the Arctic Circle to the Antarctic Circle and back.
SPECIAL ADAPTATIONS: The arctic tern has pointed wings enabling it to fly great distances and for long periods of time.

1. How far has your family car traveled in all? (Check the odometer.) _____
2. How many years old is the car? _____
3. What is the average number of miles traveled per year by the car? _____
4. On average, does the car or the arctic tern travel farther per year? _____

BONUS: How far would the arctic tern travel in a decade? _____

8

CONGRATULATIONS!

_____

has successfully completed the
six challenging events of the
Animal Olympics

this _____ day of _____,

_____.

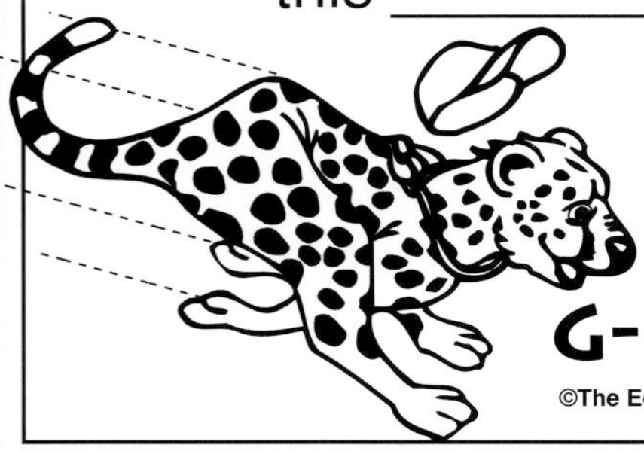

G-R-R-R-REAT JOB!

©The Education Center, Inc. • *The Best Of* THE MAILBOX® *Science* •
Intermediate • TEC1475

Note To The Teacher: Use with the activity on page 43. Make one copy of the award above and program the specific date on it. Then duplicate a copy for each student who successfully completes the Animal Olympics.

TOP SECRET

Classified Information

Activities To Introduce Budding Zoologists To Animal Classification

So many animals, so little time! How *do* scientists keep them all straight? It's no secret that they *classify,* or group, animals according to their common characteristics. Use the following activities to help your students uncover the hows and whys of animal classification.

by Gregory Grambo, Dean Medley, Kelly Medley, and Christine Thuman

Carl The Crocodile
(Crocodylus porosus)

Alias: Crocodilly Willy

Info: 20 feet long. Last seen in salty waters.

Case Number: 103-28A

Agent: Polly Pye–Private Eye

Sharky
(Carcharodan carcharis)

Alias: Great White Shark, Jaws

ECRET

Info: If he smiles, run!
Case Number: 56-224-5D

...lly Pye–Private Eye

Manty
(Mantella aurantiaca)

Alias: Mantella

Info: Poisonous! Watch out for arrows.

Case Number: 4770-3C

Agent: Polly P...

Twenty Questions

Play the familiar game Twenty Questions to demonstrate the thinking processes that take place during classification. Prior to class place a telephone book in a paper bag and hide it in a desk. When class begins, have students try to identify the book you are hiding by asking you 20 yes/no questions. Take note of the questions that your students ask. Do they inquire about color, size, number of pages, genre, or illustrations? All of these are categories by which we classify books. Afterward, point out how the types of questions students asked helped them to narrow down the possibilities. Tell students that this process is similar to what scientists go through when they are trying to *classify,* or group, a new species of animal.

The Flip Of A Coin

Scientists use observation to classify animals. How closely do your students observe the world around them? Test their observation acumen with the following demonstration. Quiz students about an object they probably see every day—a penny. Instruct students to write down the answers to the following questions on notebook paper. Warn them not to peek at a penny while answering these questions.

- We know that Lincoln's image is on the front, or *head,* of a penny. Who is pictured on the back of a penny? *(Lincoln. He can be seen sitting inside the Lincoln Memorial.)*
- What building appears on the back of a penny? *(the Lincoln Memorial in Washington, D.C.)*
- How many times does the phrase "one cent" appear on the coin? *(once, on the back)*
- Is the edge of a penny smooth or ridged? *(smooth)*
- What word appears to the left of Lincoln's head on the front of a penny? *("Liberty")*

Check to see how many students answered every question correctly. Point out that in order to distinguish between the thousands of species of animals, scientists must use careful, not casual, observation.

Observe And Draw

A picture is worth a thousand words. However, drawing pictures of animals is challenging when the animals move about. Scientists have learned to capture animal images in fast, simple drawings. They add the details later, after many repeated observations. The key to making animal drawings is to observe and draw as rapidly as possible.

If you don't have plans to visit the zoo, you can bring a live animal into the classroom for observation. The animal should be one that's used to being around large numbers of children. Set up a table where four to five students can sit around the animal. Place the animal in a large, see-through cage. Have small groups of students take turns drawing the animal using pencil and paper. Encourage students to use simple lines to capture the shape and movement of the animal's spine before adding the arms, legs, head, and tail. Help students focus their attention by posing the following questions: "What lines make up the animal's form?", "Which way does it bend or twist?", and "How can you capture that twist in a few strokes?" Afterward, place several how-to-draw-animals books in a center for students who wish to practice.

WANTED

Link The Skink
(Dasia smaragdina)

Last seen hiding among the leaves.

Spinning A Web Of Classification

Brainstorm a list of items that can be classified in our world such as stores, foods, furniture, transportation, school supplies, or musical instruments. Using *books* as an example, show students how to break down a category into its smaller classifications by modeling the webbing technique. Begin by writing *books* in an oval on the chalkboard. Explain to students that books can be divided into two main categories: fiction and nonfiction. Connect two other ovals to the center. Write *fiction* in one oval and *nonfiction* in the other. Have students help you name categories that would fit in each of these two divisions. Continue expanding the web by adding additional categories. See the diagram for ideas.

Next, divide the class into teams of three to four students. Supply each team with markers and a three-foot length of light-colored bulletin-board paper. Have each team select one of the topics you brainstormed at the beginning of the lesson; then have the team make a web that divides that category into more specific groups. Afterward, have each team share its web with two other teams.

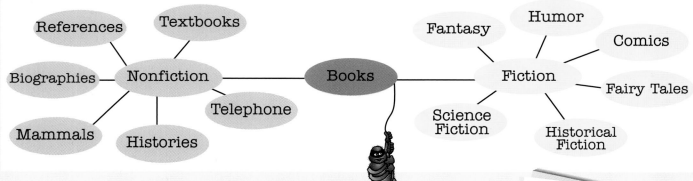

Toying With Taxonomy

Observing and classifying is child's play when your students examine their favorite toys. Instruct each student to bring in one toy or stuffed animal. Divide the class into teams of four to five students each. Instruct each group to sit in a circle with its toys placed in the center. Direct each team member to carefully examine each toy. Then have the team categorize its toys by grouping them according to similar characteristics. Give the group a copy of "Toying With Taxonomy" (page 50). Inform students that when they group some of their toys into one category, the remaining toys must then be grouped into an opposite category. For instance, if some of the toys are grouped under the heading "contain plastic parts," the remaining toys must fit into the category "contain no plastic parts." Encourage students to devise as many specific categories as they can for their toys.

After giving them about ten minutes with the first group of toys, have teams exchange toys with another team. Instruct teams to devise different categories for grouping this new set of toys. Have teams record their findings on the "Toying With Taxonomy" sheet.

The Hood
(Pitohui
dichrous)

Alias:
Hooded
Pitohui

Info: Warning: skin, feathers, and internal organs are poisonous.

Case Number: 4770–3C

Agent: Polly Pye–Private Eye

TOP SECRET

I.D. Me!

No two people are exactly alike. Prove this statement to your students by creating a *dichotomous key* of your class. Explain that a dichotomous key allows you to make decisions between two choices until a specific organism is identified. Begin the key with the heading *Our Class* as shown in the diagram. Divide the class physically into two groups—*boys* and *girls.* Fill in the next two spaces on the key with these headings. Next divide each of these two groups further using the categories *brown eyes* and *blue/green eyes.* Record these categories on the key; then divide the students physically into these groups. Continue subdividing the class using one or more of the following categories: left-/right-handed; light/dark hair; can curl/can't curl tongue; attached/detached earlobes; can wink/can't wink one eye; can raise/can't raise one eyebrow; can touch/can't touch nose with tongue. The key is complete when each student is in an individual group by himself. Select one student and demonstrate how you can follow a pathway on the key to identify that student.

Next have students practice making their own dichotomous keys. Divide your class into groups of eight. Provide each group with a copy of "If The Shoe Fits!" on page 51. Instruct groups to complete the reproducible according to the directions.

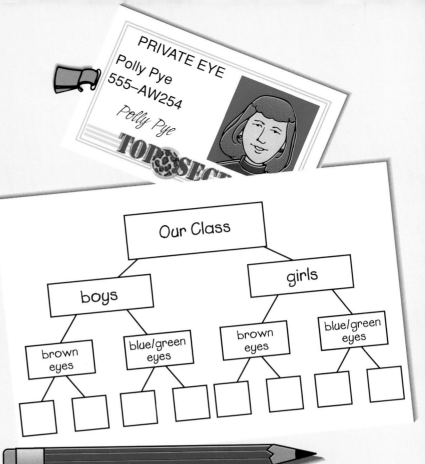

Arthropod Animation

While most students have a clear understanding of the backboned animals known as *vertebrates*—fish, birds, mammals, reptiles, and amphibians—they may not have extensive knowledge of the phylum of invertebrates (animals without backbones) known as *Arthropoda.* Use art to familiarize your students with a few of the millions of species in this phylum. Divide students into seven teams and give each team a copy of the "Arthropod Breakdown" on page 52. Assign each team a different class of arthropods to research. Instruct each team to research the body characteristics of its particular class of arthropod. Then have each team use craft materials to construct a three-dimensional model of an arthropod in that class. Provide craft materials such as paint, pipe cleaners, Styrofoam® balls, cardboard tubes, and glue. Have each team share its completed animal and describe the animal's body characteristics.

Literature/Software Connection

Big Bugs; written by Jerry Booth; Harcourt Brace & Company, 1994

Do You Know The Difference?; written by Andrea and Michael Bischhoff-Miersch; North-South Books Inc., 1995

Everything You Never Learned About Birds; written by Rebecca Rupp; Storey Communications, Inc.; 1995

Invertebrates; written by Bradford Burnham; Thomson Learning, 1995

The Kingfisher First Encyclopedia Of Animals; written by David Burnie and Linda Gamlin; Kingfisher, 1994

Tongues And Tails; written by Theresa Greenaway; Raintree Steck-Vaughn Publishers, 1995

A Wasp Is Not A Bee; written by Marilyn Singer; Henry Holt and Company, Inc.; 1995

How We Classify Animals: CD-ROM for Windows™ and Macintosh®; teaching module written by Helen Hansen; AIMS Media, 1995

Name(s) ____

Toying With Taxonomy

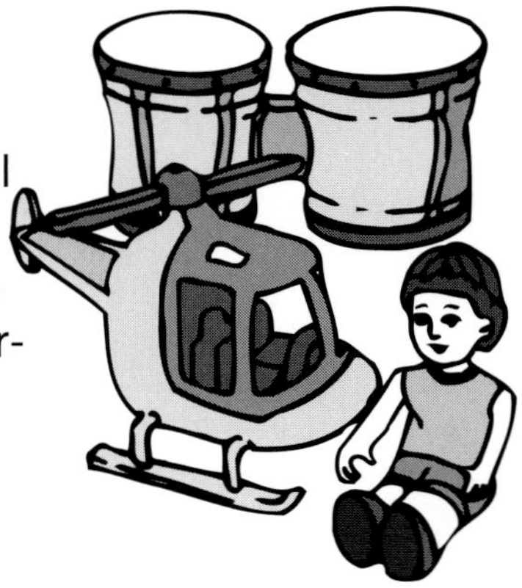

Here's your chance to play around in the name of science! In Part I, list the toys in your group. Then carefully examine each toy for details that will help you *classify,* or group, the toys. Divide the toys into two different groups. On the first set of lines under "B. Classifications," write the names of the two groups and the number of toys in each one. Try to list four different pairs of groups on the remaining lines. Repeat these steps in Part II using another team's set of toys.

Part I: Your Team's Toys

A. Write the name of each toy: ____________ ____________

____________ ____________ ____________

B. Classifications

Group A	# of toys	Group B	# of toys
____________	____	____________	____
____________	____	____________	____
____________	____	____________	____
____________	____	____________	____
____________	____	____________	____

Part II: Another Team's Toys

A. Write the name of each toy: ____________ ____________

____________ ____________ ____________

B. Classifications

Group A	# of toys	Group B	# of toys
____________	____	____________	____
____________	____	____________	____
____________	____	____________	____
____________	____	____________	____
____________	____	____________	____

 Note To The Teacher: Use this reproducible with "Toying With Taxonomy" on page 48.

Name(s) _____

Animal classification: dichotomous key

If The Shoe Fits!

What makes your shoes unique? Find out by creating your own dichotomous key.

Directions for a group of six to eight students:

1. Have each member of your group remove one of his shoes and place it in the center of the table.
2. Carefully examine each shoe, noting its characteristics.
3. Have a group recorder write "Group Shoes" in the top box of the dichotomous key below.
4. Brainstorm to come up with two categories into which each shoe either fits or doesn't fit. No shoe should fit into *both* categories.
5. Physically divide the shoes into your two categories. Then write the names of these two categories in the next two boxes of the key.
6. Examine the two piles of shoes. For each pile, decide on another pair of categories into which each shoe either fits or doesn't fit. Write the names of these categories in the key.
7. Divide the shoes into additional categories, recording the names of the categories on the key, until each shoe stands alone.

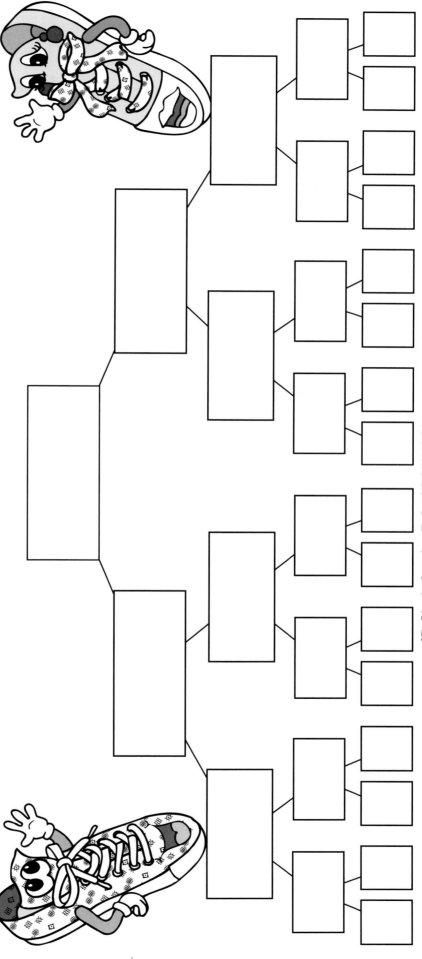

©The Education Center, Inc. • *The Best Of THE MAILBOX® Science • Intermediate* • TEC1475

Note To The Teacher: Use this page after completing "I. D. Me!" on page 49. Some possible categories for shoes are: left/right, fasten/slip-on, leather/not leather, or sneaker/not sneaker.

51

Arthropod Breakdown

There are a lot of arthropods out there!
In fact, this phylum contains the largest variety of creatures
in the animal kingdom. But as varied as they are, all arthropods do
have some common characteristics including a tough exoskeleton,
jointed limbs, and a nerve cord running the length of the body. Look over
the chart below to learn about some of the classes contained in the phylum
Arthropoda and its subphylum, Crustacea.

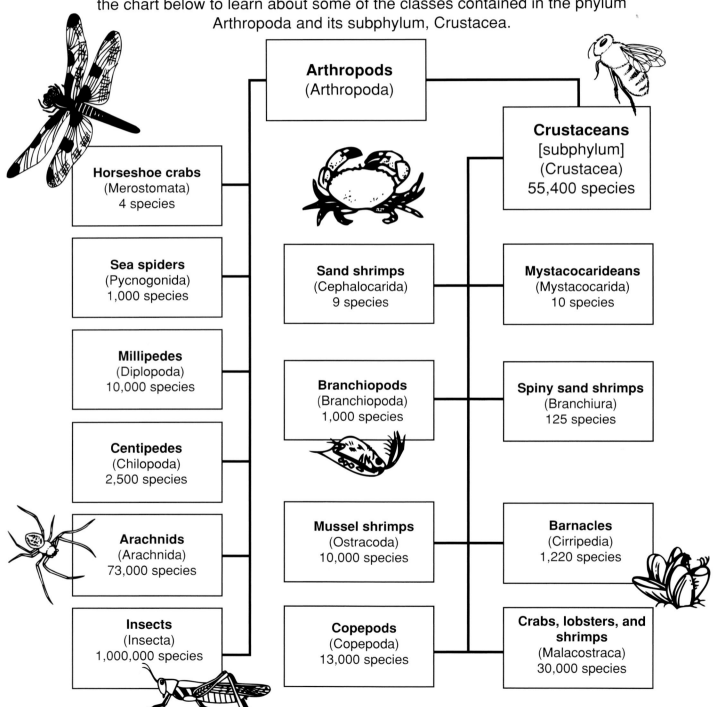

Arthropods
(Arthropoda)

Crustaceans
[subphylum]
(Crustacea)
55,400 species

Horseshoe crabs
(Merostomata)
4 species

Sea spiders
(Pycnogonida)
1,000 species

Sand shrimps
(Cephalocarida)
9 species

Mystacocarideans
(Mystacocarida)
10 species

Millipedes
(Diplopoda)
10,000 species

Branchiopods
(Branchiopoda)
1,000 species

Spiny sand shrimps
(Branchiura)
125 species

Centipedes
(Chilopoda)
2,500 species

Arachnids
(Arachnida)
73,000 species

Mussel shrimps
(Ostracoda)
10,000 species

Barnacles
(Cirripedia)
1,220 species

Insects
(Insecta)
1,000,000 species

Copepods
(Copepoda)
13,000 species

**Crabs, lobsters, and
shrimps**
(Malacostraca)
30,000 species

Animals At Risk

Creative Activities For Studying Endangered Animals

Heighten your students' awareness of endangered animals and the laws protecting them with this collection of thought-provoking activities.
by Judith Cummings and Jim Martino

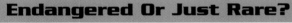

Endangered Or Just Rare?

Endangered, threatened, rare, extinct—what do these words really mean? Begin your unit by asking students what they think these words mean; then clarify the definitions of these key terms using the descriptions that follow:

Extinct is used to describe animals that have died out completely, such as dinosaurs, dodo birds, and passenger pigeons.

Endangered animals are those animals that are in immediate danger of becoming extinct. The American crocodile, the black-footed ferret, and the mountain lion are all endangered animals.

Threatened animals are those animals whose numbers are low or declining. These animals are not in immediate danger of extinction, but will likely become endangered if they are not protected. Loggerhead sea turtles and African elephants are both threatened animals.

Rare animals have small populations. They live in protected areas and are not necessarily decreasing in number. The kakapo is a rare *and* endangered species of parrot.

Searching For Answers

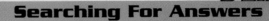

Who's to blame for so many animals at risk? Animals used to become endangered or extinct due to natural causes. Today animals become endangered primarily because of humans. To illustrate why people cause some animals to become endangered, read the picture book *Jaguarundi* by Virginia Hamilton (Scholastic Inc., 1995). This fantasy takes its readers inside the rain forest to meet some animals who are concerned about losing their homes. After reading the book, have students determine why Rundi and the other rain-forest animals feel as though their lives are being threatened. Then introduce the four main reasons why animals become endangered—*destruction of habitat, wildlife trade, overhunting,* and *competition with domestic and nonnative animals.*

Next assign each student or pair of students one of the endangered animals listed on page 56. Provide each student with a copy of page 57 and access to a variety of reference materials. Have each student use the materials to research his animal, complete the reproducible, and share his findings with the class. Assemble the completed research pages into a book titled "Animals At Risk: Searching For Answers."

Six-Sided Search

For a variation of the "Searching For Answers" research activity on page 53, try this 3-D project. Assign each student an endangered animal from the list on page 56. Duplicate a class set of the cube pattern on page 58 and distribute one copy to each student. Provide the class with access to a variety of research materials; then have each child fill in all six sides of the cube pattern with information about her animal. Finally have each student follow the steps on page 58 to assemble her cube.

To share the projects, have each student read aloud the information on her cube without revealing the animal's name. After all sides have been read, invite her classmates to guess the name of the endangered animal.

It's The Law!

The *Endangered Species Act Of 1973* was passed to protect both plants and animals that are officially listed by the U.S. Fish and Wildlife Service as *threatened* or *endangered.* This law protects at-risk wildlife from being hunted, collected, or threatened. It also restricts the construction of dams and other federal projects that would destroy the habitat of an endangered animal.

Sometimes human needs conflict with the very protection offered by this law. In the late 1970s, the completion of the Tellico Dam on the Little Tennessee River threatened to destroy a species of fish called the *snail darter.* The completed dam would destroy this fish, but would save water, provide electricity, and prevent flooding for the people living in that area. Explain the conflict over the Tellico Dam to your class; then take a class vote to see which side students would support—the protection of the snail darter or the building of the dam. After having each student list the pros and cons of building the dam, divide the class into two groups: one to support the protection of the snail darter and the other to side with the building of the dam. Direct each student to write a persuasive paragraph to convince others of his group's point of view. Have each student share his paragraph with the class; then take another class vote to see if students voted for the same side again. As a follow-up activity, challenge your students to find out if the dam was ever completed and whether or not the snail darter was affected.

Success Stories

Use this activity to communicate to your students the positive steps humans are taking to protect some endangered animals. Divide your class into groups. Assign each group one book in the Save Our Species series by Jill Bailey (Raintree Steck-Vaughn Publishers). Titles in that series include: *Mission Rhino, Save The Tiger, Project Panda, Save The Snow Leopard, Gorilla Rescue,* and *Polar Bear Rescue.* Instruct each group to read its book to find out what is being done to protect the animal. Then have each group prepare and give a brief presentation to inform the class about efforts to protect its animal. Are there any success stories?

Endangered Animal Collages

Introduce students to an alphabet full of endangered animals with this literature/art activity. Read *V For Vanishing: An Alphabet Of Endangered Animals* by Patricia Mullins (HarperCollins Children's Books, 1994), a simple picture book that names an endangered animal for each letter of the alphabet. The illustrator uses a unique collage technique to illustrate each featured animal. Share this technique with your class; then let each student try her hand at it!

Materials for each student: one 8 1/2" x 11" sheet of construction paper, several sheets of tissue paper in various colors, scissors, a glue stick, crayons, reference materials, a copy of the reproducible on page 56

Directions:

1. Choose an endangered animal from the list on page 56; then find a picture of your animal in one of the reference books.
2. Draw an outline of the animal's body on a sheet of construction paper.
3. Cut or tear pieces of colored tissue paper; then use a glue stick to paste the pieces onto the animal collage-style to fill in the body.
4. Use crayons to add other details to the animal.

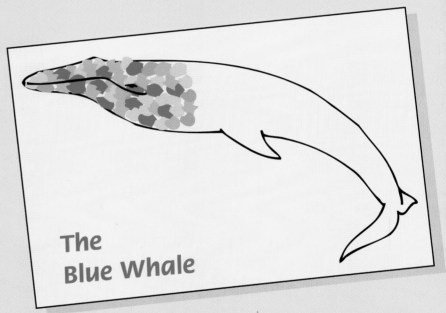

The
Blue Whale

A Welcome Change

Some animals can adapt to an environmental change and stay off the endangered list. At one time all the peppered moths in the industrial areas of Britain were white with black spots (except for a few mutant, black moths). Because the peppered moths blended in so well on the white trees, they could not be easily spotted by birds. In the early 1800s, the white trees turned black because of the soot from newly built factories. Over time the peppered moth adapted to its environment and now most of the population is dark colored. Ask your students how they think this change in the moths occurred. Explain that the moths were able to survive because they adapted to their environment. The white-colored moths—more easily spotted and eaten by birds—declined in number, but the dark-colored moths were able to survive in their habitat and produce offspring that were also dark colored.

Discuss with students how some animals are able to make changes to survive in their environment; then instruct each child to examine the characteristics of the animal he researched in "Searching For Answers" on page 53 or "Six-Sided Search" on page 54. Have each student decide on one adaptation that would save his animal from being endangered and illustrate it on a sheet of drawing paper. Have each student share his illustration with the class and explain why this change would help the animal. Display students' illustrations on a bulletin board titled "Welcome Changes."

Literature Suggestions

- *Any Bear Can Wear Glasses: The Spectacled Bear & Other Curious Creatures* by Matthew & Thomas Long; Chronicle Books, 1995
- *The Great Kapok Tree: A Tale Of The Amazon Rain Forest* by Lynne Cherry; Harcourt Brace & Company, 1990
- *Just A Dream* by Chris Van Allsburg; Houghton Mifflin Company, 1990
- *Will We Miss Them?* by Alexandra Wright; Charlesbridge Publishing, Inc.; 1991
- *Wolves* by Brian J. Heinz; Dial Books For Young Readers, 1996
- *The Bald Eagle: Free Again!* by Carol A. Amato; Barron's Educational Series, Inc.; 1996
- *The Modern Ark: Saving Endangered Species* by Daniel Cohen; G. P. Putnam's Sons, 1995

Animals At Risk

The following lists name animals that are considered *endangered*—in immediate danger of becoming extinct*.

North American Animals

American Crocodile	Key Deer	Red Wolf
West Indian Manatee	Jaguarundi	Gray Wolf
Bald Eagle	Jaguar	New Mexican Ridge-
Mountain Lion	Ocelot	Nosed Rattlesnake
Black-Footed Ferret	Whooping Crane	Gray Bat
California Condor	Florida Panther	Eastern Cougar
Steller Sea Lion		Woodland Caribou

Animals Around The World

Asiatic Lion	Snow Leopard	Bobcat
Black Rhinoceros	Tiger	Lemur
Blue Whale	Chimpanzee	Brown Hyena
Cheetah	Giant Armadillo	Spider Monkey
Giant Panda	Gorilla	Chinchilla
Asian Elephant	Indigo Macaw	Leopard
Orangutan	Brown Bear	Mountain Zebra

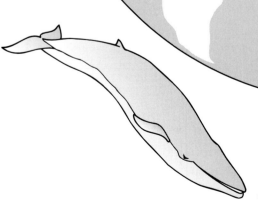

current as of December 1996

Note To The Teacher: Use with "Searching For Answers" on page 53, "Six-Sided Search" on page 54, and "Endangered Animal Collages" on page 55. Duplicate one copy for each student or post a copy in the classroom.

Name_____

 # Searching For Answers

Name of animal: _____

Habitat: _____

_____

_____

Range (where it lives): _____

_____

_____

Draw a picture of your animal in this box.

1. Animals with very specific food requirements can easily become endangered. What does this animal eat? _____

   Do you think this contributes to the animal's endangerment? If so, how? _____

   _____

2. Does this animal have any predators? If so, what are they? _____

   _____

   Do you think they contribute to the animal's endangerment? If so, how?_____

   _____

3. Is this animal considered rare? _____

4. Animals that only produce a small number of offspring are at risk of becoming endangered. How many offspring does your animal produce and how often? _____

   _____

5. Are humans doing anything to endanger this animal? If so, what? _____

   _____

6. Why should humans be concerned about saving this animal?_____

   _____

   _____

7. What is currently being done to save this animal? Is this effort successful? _____

   _____

   _____

Note To The Teacher: Use with "Searching For Answers" on page 53.

Pattern

Use with "Six-Sided Search" on page 54.

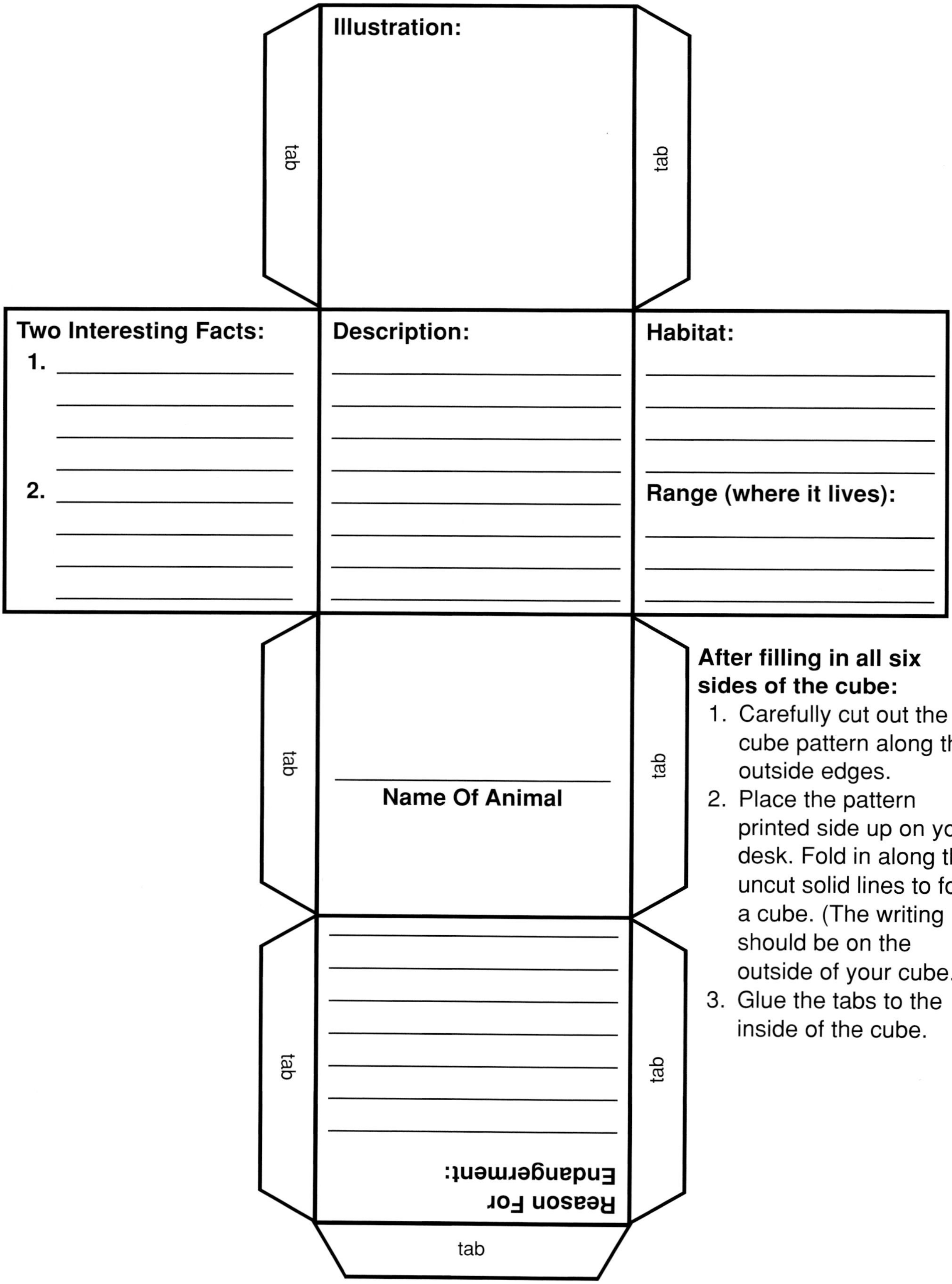

Illustration:

tab

tab

Two Interesting Facts:

1. _____

_____
_____
_____

2. _____

_____
_____
_____

Description:

_____
_____
_____
_____
_____
_____
_____

Habitat:

_____
_____
_____

Range (where it lives):

_____
_____
_____
_____

tab

_____
Name Of Animal

tab

After filling in all six sides of the cube:

1. Carefully cut out the cube pattern along the outside edges.
2. Place the pattern printed side up on your desk. Fold in along the uncut solid lines to form a cube. (The writing should be on the outside of your cube.)
3. Glue the tabs to the inside of the cube.

tab

_____
_____
_____
_____
_____
_____

Reason For Endangerment:

tab

tab

Buggy 'Bout Ecology

Ecosystems, homeostasis, biomes, food chains—put them all together and you've got a topic kids will go buggy over—ecology! Help students learn how plants and animals interact and depend on one another for survival with the following creative activities and reproducibles.

by Patricia Twohey

Ecosystems Everywhere!

Use this fun, hands-on activity to introduce students to ecosystems! *Ecosystem* describes how a habitat's plants and animals interact with one another and the nonliving parts of their environment. Draw a diagram of the very simple ecosystem (at the right) on the board, explaining each part to the class. Then divide students into groups. Assign each group an ecosystem: mountain, forest, rain forest, desert, savanna, wetland, beach, coral reef, or plains. Have each group research its ecosystem; then have group members prepare a skit—complete with simple costumes—that shows how the plants and animals in the ecosystem interact with one another. Invite each group to share what it learned by performing its skit for the class.

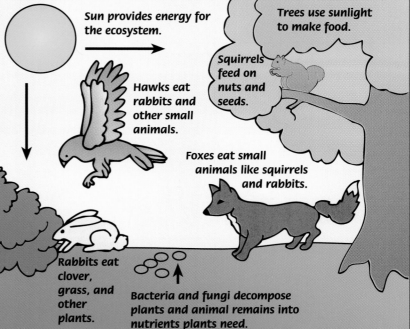

Sun provides energy for the ecosystem.

Trees use sunlight to make food.

Hawks eat rabbits and other small animals.

Squirrels feed on nuts and seeds.

Foxes eat small animals like squirrels and rabbits.

Rabbits eat clover, grass, and other plants.

Bacteria and fungi decompose plants and animal remains into nutrients plants need.

Keep The Balance

Turn to a fast-paced card game to teach students about homeostasis! The number of an ecosystem's plants and animals must stay in balance to survive. This balance is called *homeostasis*. Give each student four index cards; then divide the class into groups. Assign each group one of these ecosystems:

Ecosystem 1—plants, rabbits, foxes, hawks
Ecosystem 2—plants, mice, owls, foxes
Ecosystem 3—plants, deer, wolves, humans

Have the group follow the directions to play the game. Then have each student complete a copy of the reproducible on page 62.

To Play:
1. Print the name of a different organism from your ecosystem on each of your cards.
2. Combine your cards in a deck with your group members' cards and shuffle them.
3. Deal the cards to the group until there are none left.
4. Select one card from your hand to discard and pass facedown to the player on your right.
5. Pick up the card passed to you and look at it; then decide to keep or discard it.
6. Continue passing cards until a player has the four different members of the ecosystem and calls out, "Homeostasis!"

Who's For Dinner?

Challenge students to step up to the plate—the dinner plate, that is—and learn more about food chains. A *food chain* is a group of living things that form a chain in which the first living thing is eaten by the second, the second is eaten by the third, and so on. Write the name of each organism below on a paper plate. Give one plate to each student. Direct the student to research her organism; then have her write about how the organism gets energy on the plate's back and draw the organism on the plate's front.

After each student finishes her plate, have her find the two or three classmates whose organisms are members of her organism's food chain. Have each resulting group use tape and yarn to attach its plates in order to create a food-chain mobile.

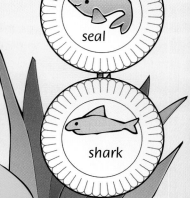

shrimp

mackerel

seal

shark

	desert	ocean	tropical rain forest	tundra	savanna	grassland
primary producer (mainly green plants)	mesquite tree	shrimp	rain tree	mosses and lichens	African grasses	prairie grasses and plants
primary consumer	kangaroo rat	mackerel	sloth	lemming	zebra	jackrabbit
secondary consumer (predator)	Gila monster	seal	harpy eagle	snowy owl	lion	coyote
tertiary consumer (predator)		shark				

Hibernation Pajama Party

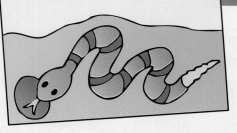

Winter's Coming, Mr. Snake!

Grab those blankets and come to a hibernation pajama party! Read aloud *The Happy Day* by Ruth Krauss (HarperCollins Children's Books, 1989). Then introduce the following terms to your class:

animal hibernation—a sleeplike state that protects an animal from cold or lack of food

animal estivation—a state of dormancy that protects an animal from heat or lack of water

torpor—a hibernation of only a few hours due to cold or lack of food.

Divide your class into groups. Have each group research the hibernating practices and other interesting facts of one of these animals: nighthawk, bat, chipmunk, snail, fat-tailed lemur, marmot, toad, lizard, snake, salamander, turtle, rufous hummingbird. Instruct each group to use the facts it finds to create a simple picture book.

When the books are finished, invite a primary class to your room. Spread out several blankets on your classroom floor. Divide the younger students equally among the blankets; then have each group share its picture book with one group of youngsters. You can bet that this will be a pajama party students won't soon forget!

Animals On The Go!

Travel the globe in a few short minutes with this animal migration activity. Some animals migrate because their environment becomes too harsh for survival at certain times of the year. Have students brainstorm a list of specific reasons that animals migrate *(food, climate, giving birth, breeding)*. Then have them list dangers migrating animals might face *(predators, hunting, fences, lack of food, injury, etc.)*. Next have students list ways people can help protect migrating animals from these dangers. Conclude by having each student complete a copy of page 63 as directed.

Chaparral—region with shrubs and small trees

Plants

People

Animals

Climate And Land

Other Cool Facts

Want to teach about the major land biomes? With this activity, it's in the bag! Write the name and definition of each major land biome (see the box) on a separate paper grocery bag. In each bag place five sheets of lined paper, each labeled with a different title—"Climate And Land," "Plants," "Animals," "People," or "Other Cool Facts"—along with a blank world map. Explain to students that a *biome* is a plant and animal community that covers a large geographic area. Then divide students into nine groups. Give each group one bag and research materials. Have each group mark and label its biome on its map; then have it fill in each titled paper with facts about its biome. Also have the group fill its bag with original pictures and prose about its biome. Conclude by having each group present its biome in a bag to the class.

- *Grassland*—region covered with short or tall grass
- *Savanna*—grassland with scattered trees and shrubs
- *Temperate Deciduous Forest*—region with trees that lose their leaves
- *Temperate Coniferous Forest*—region with pinecone-bearing evergreen trees
- *Tundra*—cold, dry region where trees cannot grow
- *Tropical Seasonal Forest*—warm region with climate both wet and dry
- *Tropical Rain Forest*—region with a forest of tall trees, year-round warmth, and lots of rain
- *Chaparral*—region with shrubs and small trees
- *Desert*—region with little plant life due to its scarce rainfall and dry soil

Where's The Wildlife?

Weave a little artistry into a lesson on animal adaptation with this colorful activity! Many animals blend in with their surroundings with the help of *camouflage*. Animals that use camouflage include chameleons, ptarmigans, killdeer, flatfish, butterflies, walkingsticks, ermines, and squids. Assign each student an animal that uses camouflage to research. Have the student describe the animal's habitat and camouflage on an index card. Then have each child illustrate his animal camouflaged in its natural habitat on a 12" x 18" sheet of drawing paper. Display the completed projects on a bulletin board titled "Where's The Wildlife?" Collect and shuffle the index cards. Read a card aloud; then challenge students to find the artwork that goes with it. Post each card beside its matching drawing.

Take Action!

Inspire your budding ecologists to apply their newfound environmental know-how in their daily lives. Provide each student with a copy of the contract on page 64 to complete as directed. Award the certificate on page 64 to each student who successfully completes the contract.

Walkingstick

Name _____

Keeping The Balance

Ecologists study how animals and plants interact with one another in their natural setting, or ecosystem. *Homeostasis* is the balance in the number of plants and animals in an ecosystem. When the different plants and animals compete for food, water, light, and other resources, they help to keep the balance. Sometimes natural events (like very cold weather) or man-made events (like the burning of trees) can disturb this natural balance.

Directions: Pretend that you and the members of your group are ecologists. Read each description. Brainstorm and list the possible effects the events taking place in the ecosystem could have on its homeostasis. Then list ways to help to keep the balance in each ecosystem.

ECOSYSTEM 1
Rabbits eat the plants that grow in a large meadow. Foxes eat the rabbits. Last year the weather was so good that there were lots of plants. Also many more rabbits than usual were born. Since there were more rabbits, the foxes had lots to eat and stayed healthy. The healthy fox population had many more babies than usual so their population grew even larger.

Effects On Homeostasis		Ways To Keep The Balance

ECOSYSTEM 2
In the tropical forests, people and animals have lived together with nature for many years. Lately companies have been buying the land. The companies cut down the trees for wood. Or they use the cleared land for farmland to grow crops for money.

Effects On Homeostasis		Ways To Keep The Balance

ECOSYSTEM 3
On a plateau, deer feed mostly on a small supply of grass. Coyotes feed on the deer. Hunters have been killing so many coyotes that very few remain.

Effects On Homeostasis		Ways To Keep The Balance

Bonus Box: On the back of this page, list three natural and three man-made events that can affect an ecosystem.

©The Education Center, Inc. • *The Best Of* THE MAILBOX® *Science • Intermediate* • TEC1475 •Key p. 159

Animals On The Go!

Some animals travel the same routes every year. This practice is known as *migration*.

Directions: Pretend that you are a travel agent for the migrating animals listed in the chart below. Your job is to map out each animal's travel route. First color the box to the left of an animal's name in the chart below. Then use the same color to draw a line on the map to show the animal's route. Finally calculate how far that animal travels during a round-trip.

Color	Traveler	Distance (Miles One Way)	Departs From	Destination	Round-Trip Mileage
	1. Arctic Tern	11,250	North Pole	South Pole	
	2. Bat	1,200	Canada	Bermuda	
	3. Golden Plover	9,500	Alaska/Canada	South America	
	4. Monarch Butterfly	1,000	U.S./Canada	Mexico	
	5. Short-Tailed Shearwater	10,000	Australia	Alaska	
	6. Atlantic Salmon	3,000	St. Lawrence River	Atlantic Ocean	
	7. Blue Whale	2,500	Indian Ocean	Antarctica	
	8. Dogfish	1,250	Canadian Coast	Mediterranean Sea	
	9. Fur Seal	4,500	Pribilof Islands, Alaska	California Coast	
	10. Green Turtle	1,500	South America	Ascension Island (Atlantic Ocean)	

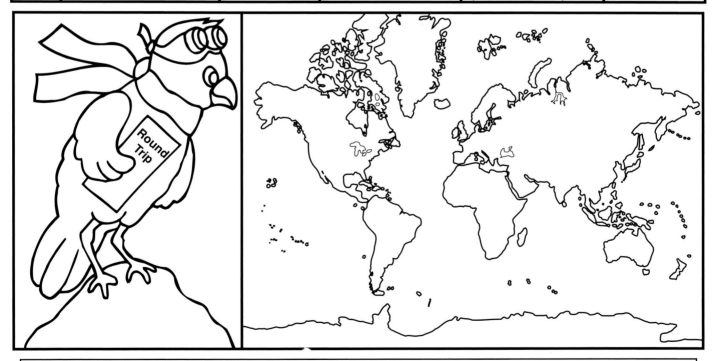

Bonus Box: Based on round-trip mileage, list the animals in order from the one that travels the farthest distance to the one that travels the least.

Note To The Teacher: Use with "Animals On The Go!" on page 60. Provide each student with colored pencils or crayons and access to a world map or globe. Explain to students that the routes they draw will not be exact, but only representative.

Take Action!

Directions: Select one ecology action plan to complete. Then fill in the contract at the bottom of this sheet.

① Water Conservation

- List the ways you use water.
- Make an action plan that explains how you can save water.
- Discuss your plan with your teacher.
- Record your water usage for one week.
- Tell how your plan worked.
- List three reasons people should conserve water.

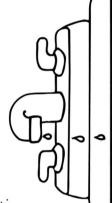

② Pollution And Waste Reduction

- List examples of pollution and waste found at your school or home.
- Make an action plan that explains how you can reduce pollution.
- Discuss your plan with your teacher.
- Record your pollution-fighting activities for one week.
- Tell how your plan worked.
- List three reasons people should reduce the amount of pollution in the world.

③ Ecosystem Preservation

- Diagram the plants and animals in the ecosystem around your home or school.
- Describe how the living and nonliving members of this system interact with one another.
- List five things that might cause an imbalance in the ecosystem.
- Observe the ecosystem for one week and list any changes that occur.
- List three ways you can help keep the ecosystem in balance.

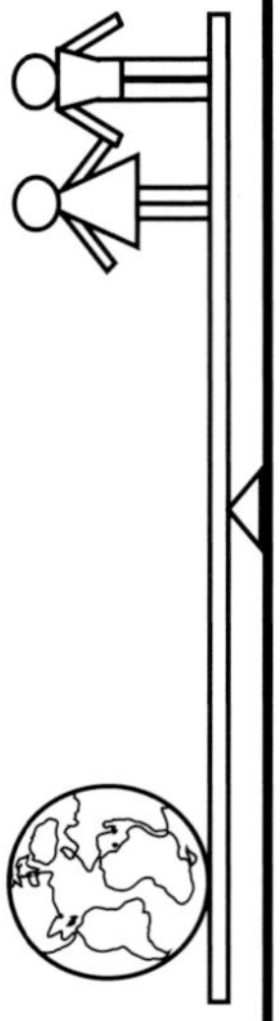

④ Endangered Plant Or Animal Conservation

- Research and record ten facts about an endangered plant or animal that lives near your home or school.
- Write an action plan describing how you can help to protect this animal or plant.
- Discuss your plan with your teacher.
- Record all of your animal- or plant-saving activities for one week.
- Describe what would happen if everyone were to follow your action plan.
- List three reasons people should protect endangered plants and animals.

I, _____, promise to care about the ecology of my planet by completing
name
action plan number _____ . I will complete all parts of the plan by
ecology action plan number
_____ .

Today's Date _____
date

Student Signature _____

ECO-EXPERT

Thanks!

_____

is awarded this Eco-Expert Award for successfully completing an Ecology Action Plan.
Our planet thanks you for caring!

Teacher's Signature _____   Date _____

FROM HEAD TO TOE

Creative Activities For Studying The Human Body

It's the most marvelous machine ever created, composed of highly specialized parts doing their jobs with amazing efficiency. No, it's not a Ferrari—it's the human body, a walking wonder that fascinates everyone. Help students take a closer look at some of the human body's wonders with the following creative activities and reproducibles.

by Beth Gress and Becky Andrews

Your skeleton has 206 bones.

Paper Dolls And People Parts

"Hey, did you know your heart pumps about 100,000 times a day?" As students study the human body, they'll come across tons of fascinating facts they'll want to share with others. Give them the opportunity to do just that by providing several copies of a paper-doll pattern as shown. Place the patterns at a center along with scissors, butcher paper, and reference books about the human body. Encourage students to use their free time to read through the books to find interesting information about the human body. When a student finds a fact he'd like to share, have him trace the pattern on butcher paper and cut out the tracing; then have him label the cutout with his fact. Tape the cutouts hand-to-hand on a wall to resemble a string of paper dolls. Challenge students to encircle your classroom with fact dolls. Or set an even bigger goal by challenging them to make a string of dolls that will stretch all the way from your classroom door to the principal's office!

Body Beautiful Flip Books

Review important vocabulary with a book-making activity that can double as an assessment tool. Write the letters of the alphabet vertically down a large sheet of chart paper. As you come across new vocabulary words during the course of the unit, list them beside the appropriate letter on the chart. At the end of the unit, have each student choose 25 words to include in a self-checking vocabulary flip book. Have students follow these steps to make their books:

Materials:
one 4" x 6" piece of cardboard   scissors   markers or crayons
twenty-five 4" x 6" index cards   hole punch   ruler
two metal rings   pencil

Steps:
1. Punch two holes in the top of the cardboard piece as shown.
2. Use a ruler and a pencil to divide the index cards in half vertically.
3. Punch two holes at the top of each card as shown, using the cardboard piece as a guide.
4. On the left side of each card, write a vocabulary word. On the right side, write the word's definition.
5. Cut the cards down the middle on the dividing lines.
6. Place the card halves containing the vocabulary words on top of the left side of the cardboard piece, aligning the holes; then insert a metal ring through the holes.
7. Place the card halves containing definitions on top of the right side of the cardboard piece, aligning the holes. BE SURE THAT THESE CARDS ARE IN A DIFFERENT ORDER FROM THE WORD CARDS. Insert a metal ring through the holes.
8. Flip the right side of your book to find the definition card for the first word on the left. On the back of both the word card and the definition card, write a 1.
9. Flip to the second word card on the left. Find the definition card for this word; then code the backs of both cards with a 2.
10. Continue labeling the backs of matching cards in this manner.
11. Swap books with a friend. Have your friend try to match each word card with its definition, looking on the backs of the cards to check his answers.

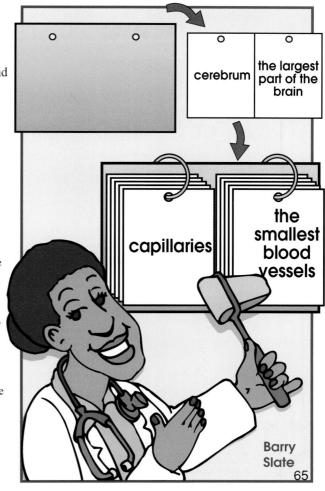

cerebrum | the largest part of the brain

capillaries | the smallest blood vessels

Barry Slate

65

The Match Game

Your students may already know that there are different blood types, but do they understand what those blood types may mean if they ever need a transfusion? Use the reproducible hands-on experiment on page 69 to help students understand transfusion reactions between different blood types. Divide the class into groups; then give each group the following materials:

clear plastic cup of water
clear plastic cup of water tinted with red food coloring
clear plastic cup of water tinted with blue food coloring
clear plastic cup of water tinted with red and blue food coloring (purple)
empty clear plastic cup (to use as a test cup)

eyedropper
copy of page 69
water for rinsing

Before beginning, explain to students that there are four main blood types, which are classified as A, B, AB, and O. In a blood transfusion, a person with one type of blood will become ill if he receives another type that doesn't match his. In this experiment, students will discover which blood types can be given in a blood transfusion to persons with any of the four blood types. They will also learn the type of blood that persons with any of the four blood types can receive. Be sure that students rinse the test cup and eyedropper thoroughly after each test. Also be sure students understand that clear water added to colored water doesn't represent a change; the color has only changed in shade, so the match is safe. But colored water added to clear does represent a change, indicating an unsafe match. See the answer key on page 159 to check students' results. After the experiment, have students identify the blood type that is a safe donor for any blood type *(O, the universal donor);* then have them identify the blood type that can safely accept blood from any donor *(AB, the universal recipient).* To check comprehension, ask questions such as "If you have B blood, to whom can you safely donate blood? *(people with B or AB blood)* If you have A blood and need a transfusion, from whom can you receive blood?" *(anyone with A or O blood)*

The "Blood Mobile"

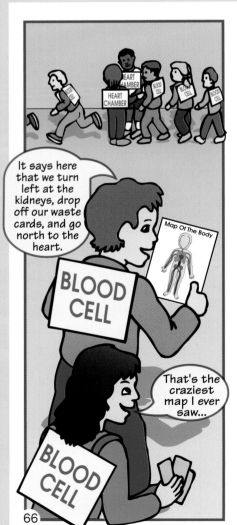

Students often have a difficult time understanding that the same blood that goes out from the heart and lungs to different parts of the body also returns to the heart and lungs to begin the journey all over again. Give students an unforgettable lesson on this concept with a "mobile" circulatory system simulation. To prepare, have a parent volunteer label 80 index cards with the word *food,* 80 with *oxygen,* 80 with *waste,* and 80 with *carbon dioxide.* Assign the following roles to students:

chambers of the heart: four students   **small intestine:** one student
lungs: two students   **body cells:** four students
kidneys: one student   **blood cells:** remainder of class

Have each student make and wear a large nametag labeled with his role. Give the food cards to the small intestine students, the oxygen cards to the lungs, and the waste and carbon dioxide cards to the body cells; then head to the gym. Arrange students according to the diagram on page 68. (Duplicate the card on that page and carry it with you for easy reference.) Once students are arranged, direct them through the following steps:

1. The blood cells begin at the star and circulate by passing between two of the heart chambers.
2. The blood cells proceed to the lungs where they each pick up an oxygen card.
3. The blood cells move on through the other two heart chambers toward the small intestine where they each receive a food card. *(Explain that particles of food actually enter the bloodstream through the walls of the small intestine.)*
4. Each blood cell goes to a body cell to provide it with food and oxygen. To simulate this, the blood cell exchanges his food card for a waste card; then he exchanges his oxygen card for a carbon dioxide card.
5. Each blood cell goes to the kidneys where he deposits his waste card.
6. Each blood cell returns to the heart chambers and the lungs, where he exchanges his carbon dioxide card for an oxygen card. Then the cycle begins again.

Let students exchange roles and repeat the simulation until each student has had the chance to be a traveling blood cell. For fun, ask students how long they think it would take for a blood cell to complete a round-trip through the body and back. They may be surprised to learn that the trip takes less than a minute!

"Dem" Bones

You don't need a life-size skeleton model to bone up on the skeletal system! Just purchase some inexpensive paper skeletons around the Halloween season. Laminate each skeleton; then give one to each cooperative group, along with a wipe-off pen and a list of important bones. Have groups label their skeletons, making notes of any inaccuracies. For free-time practice, place an unlabeled skeleton and self-sticking notes labeled with the names of important bones at a center. Have students post the notes correctly on the skeleton.

You Are What You Eat!

An apple a day may keep the doctor away, but what about zucchini, oat bran, and tuna? Focus on the importance of good nutrition with the following activity. Divide students into five teams: one team for each food group presented in the U.S. Department of Agriculture's Food Pyramid (see the chart below). Have one student from each team lie down on a large piece of butcher paper. Trace the student's body; then have team members cut out the tracing and mount it on a wall, door, or bulletin board. Next have each team research to identify specific foods included in its group, vitamins and minerals provided by those foods, and how those nutrients aid the body.

Once the research is completed, have each group cut out magazine pictures of foods from its group; then have team members glue the pictures onto their body cutout, positioning the pictures on the body parts those foods aid. For example, a glass of milk might be glued in the mouth area (teeth), while a carrot could be glued in the eye area. Have students post a description of each food's benefit(s) to the body—written on a small index card—around the perimeter of the cutout.

The Food Pyramid: A lecture by Dr. Tutankhamen

FATS, OILS, AND SWEETS
Use sparingly.

MILK, YOGURT, AND CHEESE GROUP (2-3 servings)

MEAT, POULTRY, FISH, DRY BEANS, EGGS, & NUTS GROUP (2-3 servings)

VEGETABLE GROUP (3-5 servings)

FRUIT GROUP (2-4 servings)

BREAD, CEREAL, RICE, & PASTA GROUP (6-11 servings)

Eating Out And Nutrition

As a follow-up to the "You Are What You Eat!" activity, discuss the group found at the top of the food pyramid: Fats, Oils, and Sweets. Explain to students that the message for this group is to "use sparingly." Brainstorm a list of fatty foods; then give each team used in "You Are What You Eat!" several menus gathered from local restaurants, including fast-food establishments. Have the groups discuss the types of foods offered in the restaurants and how they stack up in terms of the food pyramid and fat content.

Next give groups the following scenario: "You have been instructed by your doctor to eat healthier and cut down on fatty foods. But you travel in your job and often must dine in restaurants. Which restaurants will you visit and what will you order?" Have each group design a healthful one-week eating plan using the menus. Remind students of "tricks" a health-conscious diner can use, such as scraping fatty mayonnaise off a hamburger or substituting a baked potato for French fries (unless the menu forbids such substitutions). Have each group write its plan on a large piece of poster board to share with the class. Ask students questions such as "Which restaurants would you advise a health-conscious person to avoid? Why? Is it worth the health risks to eat a fatty food you just love? Why do you think the majority of Americans have poor eating habits?"

Come To Your Senses!

Let students become the experts on the five senses with a challenging group project. Give each of five groups a copy of page 71. Assign a sense to each group; then have its members work together to complete the projects listed on the reproducible. Allow students to develop their own activities to add to the list with your approval. After students complete their projects, have each group present its information to the class.

Fun puzzle

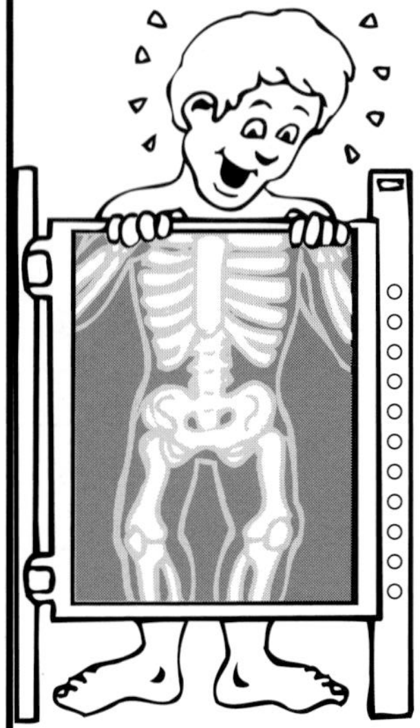

You're A Walking Wonder!

Did you know that you're a walking wonder? Well, you are! The human body is more amazing than any machine or computer. To prove that, look at the facts about your body below. Fill in each blank with a number from the box. Cross out each number as you use it. THIS ISN'T A TEST—it's just for fun!

60,000	40	100
9,000	106	22
4	100,000	600
90	300	20
206	13,000	100,000
500	85	32

1. You have _____ bones in your body.
2. _____ percent of your brain is water.
3. Your heart pumps _____ quarts of blood each day.
4. You have over _____ muscles in your body.
5. You use _____ muscles each time you take one step.
6. There are _____ miles of blood vessels in your body.
7. You have _____ bones in your feet and hands altogether.
8. Your heart beats over _____ times a day.
9. There are _____ miles of tiny tubes in each of your kidneys.
10. Your small intestine is _____ feet long.
11. You have _____ bones in your skull.
12. There are _____ million nerve endings in your skin that detect pain.
13. You have _____ taste buds in your mouth.
14. _____ percent of your blood is water.
15. Your mouth produces _____ milliliters of saliva every day.
16. You have about _____ trillion cells in your body.
17. You probably have about _____ hairs on your head.
18. You will have _____ teeth when you are fully grown.

The "Blood Mobile" Simulation
Reference Card

take a carbon dioxide card; give an oxygen card
give a food card
take a food card; give a waste card
take an oxygen card; give a carbon dioxide card
take a waste card

STUDENT ROLES:
Lungs:
Small Intestine:
Body Cells:

Kidneys:

CIRCULATION ROUTE

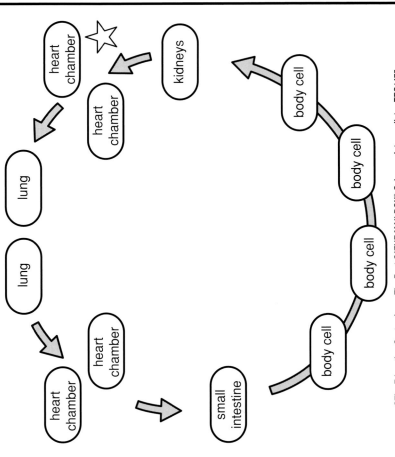

Note To Teacher: Use with "The 'Blood Mobile'" on page 66.

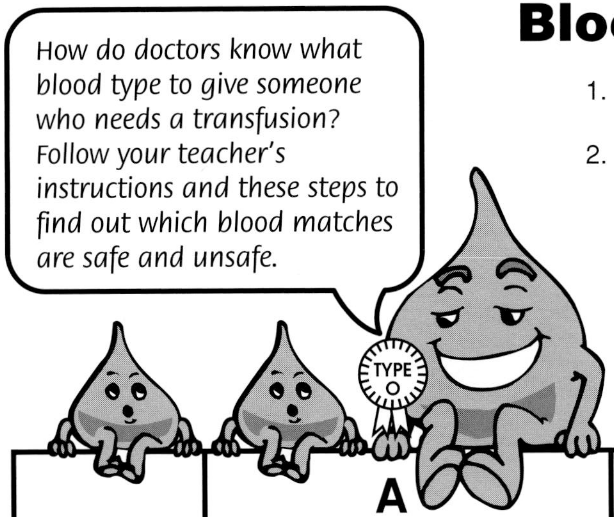

Blood-Typing: The Match Game

How do doctors know what blood type to give someone who needs a transfusion? Follow your teacher's instructions and these steps to find out which blood matches are safe and unsafe.

1. Put a few droppersful of receiver A's "blood" in a clear cup.

2. Add one dropperful of donor A's blood to the cup; then circle YES or NO/SAFE or UNSAFE on the chart. Use these guidelines:
   • If the color of the receiver's blood stays the same (a darker or lighter shade is considered the same), then the match is SAFE.
   • If the color of the receiver's blood changes, then the match is UNSAFE.
   • Clear water donated to colored water is **not** a color change. But colored water donated to clear water does indicate a color change.

3. Rinse out the eyedropper and cup; then repeat the test for donor B.

4. Continue until you have completed all 16 tests (each patient's blood is tested four times).

	A donor (red water)		B donor (blue water)		AB donor (purple water)		O donor (clear water)	
A receiver (red water)	color change? YES NO	SAFE or UNSAFE?	color change? YES NO	SAFE or UNSAFE?	color change? YES NO	SAFE or UNSAFE?	color change? YES NO	SAFE or UNSAFE?
B receiver (blue water)	color change? YES NO	SAFE or UNSAFE?	color change? YES NO	SAFE or UNSAFE?	color change? YES NO	SAFE or UNSAFE?	color change? YES NO	SAFE or UNSAFE?
AB receiver (purple water)	color change? YES NO	SAFE or UNSAFE?	color change? YES NO	SAFE or UNSAFE?	color change? YES NO	SAFE or UNSAFE?	color change? YES NO	SAFE or UNSAFE?
O receiver (clear water)	color change? YES NO	SAFE or UNSAFE?	color change? YES NO	SAFE or UNSAFE?	color change? YES NO	SAFE or UNSAFE?	color change? YES NO	SAFE or UNSAFE?

Note To Teacher: See "The Match Game" on page 66 for a list of materials and steps for completing this project. See page 159 for an answer key.

69

I've Got To Hand It To You!

Did you know that the human hand contains 27 different bones that are moved by 35 different muscles? And that no two hands are built exactly like yours? Complete the following activities to discover more about your one-of-a-kind hands. For each activity you complete, draw a one-of-a-kind ring on the correctly numbered finger.

① Handwriting Hoodwinks

Just like everyone's hands are different, so is everyone's handwriting. No one can duplicate someone else's signature exactly. (Police call this kind of copy a *forgery*.) Why? Because no one else has the signer's unique hands. Try this experiment to see how well you can copy someone else's signature. Ask a friend to sign two pieces of paper. Practice copying your friend's signature until you have what you think is a good copy. Next give one of your friend's signatures to another buddy to study. Show the buddy your forgery and your friend's original signature on the other piece of paper. Can your friend pick out the forgery?

② Free-Moving Fingers?

Can you move each of your fingers without the other ones moving? Try this experiment. Rest your elbow on a table with your arm pointing up. Extend all four fingers horizontally so that they are parallel to the table. Now try to raise each finger, one at a time, without moving any of the other fingers. Most people can't do this. Make a list of occupations or talents that someone who could do this might have (how about a concert pianist?). Try your other hand; then conduct the experiment on another friend or family member.

③ A Teeny Bit Tired

How fast do the muscles in your fingers tire out when you work them? Try this experiment to find out. Hold a pinch clothespin between your thumb and index finger. Have a friend use a stopwatch or watch with a second hand to find out how many times you can open and close the clothespin in 30 seconds. You must open the clothespin completely each time you squeeze the ends together. Do the experiment three times and record your data on a chart. Did you get better or worse with each test? Now switch places with your partner. Compare your data.

④ Lucky Lefty

As you probably know, most people in the world are right-handed. Left-handed people have had some problems living in a right-handed world. Interview ten people who are *southpaws* (a nickname for people who are left-handed). Ask them about the advantages and disadvantages of being left-handed. Make a list of conclusions you can draw about left-handedness from your interviews. Write your conclusions on a large piece of poster board to share with the class.

⑤ Thumbs-Up!

Just how important are your thumbs anyway? To find out, have someone tape your thumbs across your palms, leaving your other fingers free. Stay "thumbless" for one hour. Be sure to do all the things you would normally do. At the end of the hour, list the activities you tried to do and how being thumbless affected them. Draw some conclusions about what thumbless animals can't do that we humans can.

Name_____   Group projects

Sense(s) My Group Will Investigate: _____

It's Time To Come To Your Senses!

Complete _____ of the projects listed for the sense(s) your group will investigate.

The due date is _____.

SIGHT

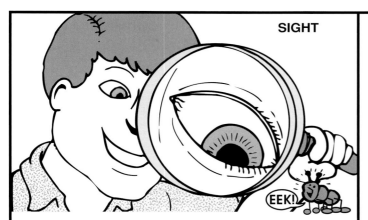

- Make a poster showing a diagram of the eye, with all parts labeled.
- List several diseases of the eye. Research to find out the causes of and treatment for each disease.
- Write and perform a public service announcement giving safety tips about the eye.
- Find examples of optical illusions to share with the class.
- Make a copy of the braille alphabet chart. Explain who Louis Braille was and what the braille system is all about.
- Gather data about the eye colors of students in your class; then make a graph illustrating the data.

HEARING

- Make a sound discrimination test. Tape-record a variety of sounds. Then play the recording for the class to see how many of the sounds can be correctly identified.
- Find out what a *decibel* is; then make a chart showing the decibel levels of at least ten sounds.
- Design a brochure that illustrates and explains the history of hearing aids.
- Be prepared to teach the class five words or phrases using the Single-Hand Manual Alphabet for the deaf.
- Make a poster showing a diagram of the ear, with all parts labeled.
- Perform a simulation that traces a sound's route when it enters the ear.

TOUCH

- Make a touch book for a young child that includes samples of various textures. Choose a theme for your book, such as the zoo or food. Use textures such as sandpaper, velvet, foil, Styrofoam®, etc. Share your book with the class; then give it to a local nursery school.
- Make a poster showing a diagram illustrating the layers of the skin.
- Interview a dermatologist to find out about his/her job and how people can care for their skin. Put your information in a magazine column of beauty tips.
- Find out how the FBI and other law enforcement agencies use fingerprints to solve crimes. Share your information on a chart.
- Cut off the foot of a tube sock; then pull the cut end over the top of a lidless oatmeal container and tape it around the container. Secretly put an object into the container; then have class members take turns putting a hand through the sock, feeling the object inside, and guessing what it is. Repeat with at least ten other objects.
- Find out what *skin grafting* is and explain it to the class.

TASTE AND SMELL

- Conduct a taste test in front of the class to determine the areas of taste on the tongue. Draw a large sketch of the tongue on the board. Use a toothpick to dab a bit of salt, sugar, cocoa (bitter), and unsweetened flavored drink mix (sour) on different areas of a volunteer's tongue. Label the areas on the sketch for salty, sweet, bitter, and sour.
- Take a survey to find out the favorite ice-cream flavors of students in your class. Make a graph to illustrate your results.
- Bring in ten items with distinctive smells. Place each item in a small paper cup; then cover the cup with foil. Poke holes in the foil. Number the cups and put them in a center; then have students try to identify each item. Provide an answer key.
- Draw a diagram that illustrates how smell relates to taste.
- Taste and smell are closely related. To demonstrate this to the class, have a volunteer taste an apple slice while you hold a cut onion by his nose. Ask the volunteer to describe the taste. Repeat the test with two other volunteers.
- Find the answer to this question: "Can the sense of smell get 'tired' or 'lost'?"

Note To Teacher: Use with "Come To Your Senses!" on page 67. Before duplicating, fill in the blanks concerning the number of required projects and the due date.

The Most Marvelous Machine

Creative Ideas For Studying The Human Body

Many wonderful inventions have been created throughout our history. But no invention can compare with the most marvelous machine of all time—the human body! Take your students on a guided tour through their amazing body systems with the following creative activities and reproducibles.

by Dana Sanders and Elizabeth H. Lindsay

A String Of Fascinating Facts!

Mesmerize your students with fascinating facts about the body's amazing systems. Duplicate the fact sheet and 12 copies of the pattern on page 75. Cut out each fact and glue it to a cut-out pattern as shown; then place the cutouts in a folder. Stretch a string from wall to wall in your classroom. Then, each day before beginning your body-systems unit, have each of several student volunteers pull one pattern from the folder. Have each student read his fact, then use a paper clip to hang it from the string.

To extend this activity, give your students the opportunity to share some facts of their own. Duplicate multiple copies of the pattern, placing them at a center along with scissors, colorful markers, and reference books about the human body. Encourage students to use their free time to read through the books to find interesting information about the human body. When a student finds a fact he'd like to share, have him write it on one of the cutouts and attach it to the string. Challenge students to fill the classroom with their fabulous facts.

If your intestines were uncoiled, you would be about 33 feet tall.

Thirteen pounds of skin are rubbed away each year by daily activity.

The Digestion Connection

Give your students a "taste" of the organs of the digestive system with this fun getting-to-know-you activity! Duplicate multiple copies of the nametags at the top of page 76 (one nametag per student). Cut out and mix up the tags. Give one tag to each student along with a copy of the "Digestion Connection Data Sheet" at the bottom of page 76. Direct each student to mingle with the other organs—her classmates—and fill in her data sheet with information about each organ listed (including her own). Afterward use the data collected to discuss the function of each organ in the digestive system.

Pam Crane

Body-Book Connections

Connect your students with the following exciting books for an inside view of the human body!

The Body Atlas by Mark Crocker; Oxford University Press, Inc.; 1991

The Body Atlas by Steve Parker; Dorling Kindersley Publishing, Inc.; 1993

The Human Body: An Amazing Inside Look At You by Steve Parker; Harry N. Abrams, Inc.; 1996

Inside The Body by Giuliano Fornari; Dorling Kindersley Publishing, Inc.; 1996

The Magic School Bus® Inside The Human Body by Joanna Cole; Scholastic Inc., 1992

I Wonder Why I Blink: And Other Questions About My Body by Brigid Avison; Larousse Kingfisher Chambers, Inc.; 1993

The Human Body (part of the What If...series) by Steve Parker; The Millbrook Press, Inc.; 1995

A Day In The Life Of A Heart

The heart is a tireless muscle that pumps as much as 2,000 gallons of blood and beats about 103,680 times every day! If this organ could talk, imagine the stories it would tell! Give the heart an opportunity to speak through the voices of your students. After a discussion of the heart's functions, have each student cut a large heart from red paper and use markers to decorate it with facial features. Next brainstorm with students the many things a heart might experience throughout a day, such as waking up to the sound of an alarm clock, running in a race at school, and watching a late-night scary movie. Record students' responses on the chalkboard. Next have each student choose one experience from the list (or create one of his own). Direct the student to write a quotation of what a heart would say in response to the experience on a cut-out speech bubble (for example, "When the alarm clock went off at 6:00 A.M., it made me skip a beat!"). Afterward have each student display his heart cutout and quotation on a bulletin board titled "All In A Day's Work."

When the alarm clock went off at 6 A.M., it made me skip a beat!

Dear Doctor "D,"
I was playing a game of basketball with my friends one day. All of a sudden, I got a really bad cramp in my calf. What is a cramp and why does it happen? What can I do the next time I have one?
Sincerely,
Charlie H.

Dear Charlie,
A cramp is a real pain—especially when it occurs in the middle of a ball game—isn't it? A cramp is when a muscle suddenly feels tight and painful. The muscle stops moving properly and feels stuck. This usually happens when you exercise too hard or for a long time. Doctors aren't exactly sure why a cramp happens, but it is probably from having too much or too little salt in the fluids surrounding the muscle's fibers. The next time you get a cramp, rest for a while and rub the sore spot.
Sincerely,
Dr. D

Ask The Experts

When you have a serious question, whom better to ask than an expert? Give your students the opportunity to become experts in the field of muscular health with the following creative activity. Write each question below on a different index card. Then pair students. Supply each pair with a question card and reference books about the human body. Direct the pair to research the answer to its question, then respond to it in advice-column style (see the example). Finally have each pair of experts share its question and response with its fellow "physicians."

- **Dear Doctor D:** My best friend just told me that I had muscles in my blood vessels! I bet him a soda that he's wrong. Do I win the bet, Doc? Sincerely, Will
- **Dear Doctor D:** What's the big deal about skeletal muscles anyway? Would it be so bad if I didn't have any? I'd think it would make me a more relaxed person, wouldn't it? Sincerely, Avery
- **Dear Doctor D:** I've heard that cardiac muscle is kind of special. What makes it any different from the muscles in my arms or legs? Sincerely, Mary
- **Dear Doctor D:** My sister tore a tendon while playing soccer. Why will this accident keep her on the sidelines for a while? How can I explain to her why it's important for her tendon to heal? Sincerely, Corinne
- **Dear Doctor D:** My neighbor's dad and mom are both bodybuilders. What about bodybuilding makes their muscles SO large? Sincerely, Nathan
- **Dear Doctor D:** I'm doing a report on muscle diseases. What can you tell me about muscular dystrophy and other muscle diseases? Sincerely, Maxie

No Bones About It!

About 206 bones make up the adult human skeletal system. They provide shape and support for muscles, nerves, and other soft parts of the body. Help your students remember the locations and functions of these bones by having them write a class rap. Duplicate the labeled skeleton on page 77. Display it on a wall with a large sheet of chart paper. Pair students; then assign each pair a bone or bone group, such as the skull, face, or shoulder area. Provide each pair with a colorful marker and a reference book about the human body. Direct the pair to write one line for the rap that includes information about the location and function of its assigned bone(s). Then, beginning with the frontal bone, have each pair use its marker to write its rap line on the blank chart. Perform the rap together as a class, having each pair read its own line aloud.

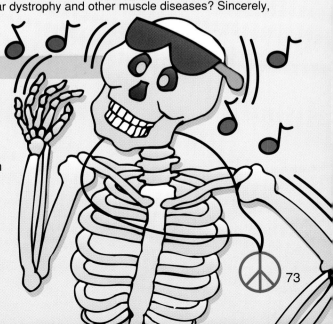

Beyond Belief!

Many of us have read or heard fascinating stories about people who wakened different from the way they were when they went to bed. Challenge your students to conjure up their own unbelievable stories—and review information they've learned about the human body—by using the journal prompts below. Write the prompts on a sheet of chart paper. Have each student choose a prompt and write a story beginning with the phrase "Would you believe that one day I woke up and…" Encourage students to include as much factual information about the human body in their stories as possible. After students have completed their stories, bind the pages between front and back covers. Display the book and invite students to read one anothers' "beyond-belief" stories.

Would you believe that one day I woke up and…
- I no longer had a skeleton!
- I had muscles the size of a bodybuilder's!
- my brain had doubled in size!
- my stomach was as large as a basketball!
- my heart was talking to me!
- I discovered I had lost my sense of taste!
- I found a note from my respiratory system pinned to my pajamas!

Body-Systems Flip Book

Your students will flip over this unique flip book! Divide students into groups of four. Supply each group with five copies of the pattern on page 78, reference books on the human body, markers or colored pencils, a stapler, and scissors. Direct each member of the group to draw, label, and color an illustration of a different body system on one of the patterns. On the fifth pattern, have one group member draw the outside of a person (face, hair, clothing, etc.). Then have the group compile the pages, putting the clothed drawing on top of the pile. Next direct the group to staple the pages together along the left side of the sheets. Once stapled, have the group cut each page along the dashed cut lines, being careful not to cut the pages apart completely. Finally have the group flip through the pages of its book, viewing the various parts of each system.

Deltoid
Pectoralis
Biceps
Femur
Kneecap (patella)
Fibula
Shinbone (tibia)
Anklebones (tarsals)
Foot Bones (metatarsals)
Toes (phalanges)

The Long And Short Of It

Help students learn more about the nervous system by investigating two types of memories stored by the brain. Explain to students that anything that you can remember for more than a few minutes is in your *long-term memory* (such as how to tie your shoe, how to find your way home from school, the time of your favorite television show, etc.). In fact, by the time a child is eight years old, his brain holds more information than a million encyclopedias! Nothing stays in your *short-term memory* for more than a few minutes. It can only store a maximum of nine things at one time. Most people can't remember more than seven items.

To test this fact, write the following sequence of letters on the board: I-S-O-F-B-A-L-M-E-T-U-P-N-Y. Have students look at the letters for a few seconds; then tape a large piece of paper over the letters. Have each child try to list the letters in order on his paper. (Most will only remember about seven letters.) Explain that you can get more in your short-term memory if you can group the facts to be stored into bigger units. Write this sequence of letters on the board: IS-OF-BAL-MET-UP-NY. Point out that now there are no longer 14 items to store, but only 6. Repeat the viewing and hiding steps above; then see if students do a better job of remembering the second set of letters.

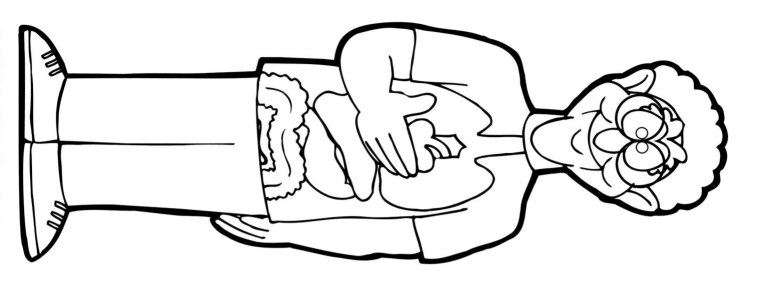

Fascinating Facts

Thirteen pounds of skin are rubbed away each year by daily activity.	If the main "thinking" part of your brain *(the cerebral cortex)* was ironed flat, it would be bigger than a large pillowcase.	If your intestines were uncoiled, you would be about 33 feet tall.
A full stomach holds more than a half-gallon of food and liquid.	When you grow up, you will have enough blood in your body to fill half a bucket. That would fill about five liter bottles of soda!	Babies are born with more than 300 bones, but adults have only about 200. The 100 extra baby bones don't just disappear; the smaller bones join to make bigger bones.
Different nerves in the body send out messages at speeds of up to 400 feet per second.	More than 640 muscles pull your bones so you can move. These muscles make up two-fifths of your body weight.	The average adult stomach processes about 1,100 pounds of food each year.
Your *funny bone* isn't really a bone. It is a nerve along the base of your arm. When you bang your elbow, this nerve may become pinched and create a not-so-funny tingling feeling in your arm.	Your biggest muscles are the ones you sit on.	When you sneeze, air rushes down your nose at over 100 miles per hour.

Nametags

Name: Mouth
Nickname: Jaws
Job: Mixer—
I chew food up into small pieces and mix it with liquid.
Hobbies: chewing, tearing, and grinding

Name: Esophagus
Nickname:
The Redneck
Job: Traffic Director—
I'm a muscular tube that makes sure food gets from the mouth down to the stomach.
Hobbies: squeezing, pushing, and swallowing

Name: Liver
Nickname:
Inspector #12
Job: Collector—
I'm a large organ that collects and sorts nutrients, storing them for use by the body. I also remove poisons and wastes from the blood.
Hobbies: collecting, sorting, cleaning, and storing

Name: Stomach
Nickname: The Mixer
Job: Food Processor—
I'm a *J*-shaped bag that blends food together and stores it for use by the body.
Hobbies: churning, mixing, and storing

Name: Small Intestine
Nickname: The Terminator
Job: Quality Control Manager—
I'm a tube that breaks down food more thoroughly. I pass on any food that isn't used to the large intestine.
Hobbies: digesting, absorbing, and transporting

Name:
Large Intestine
Nickname:
Big Snake
Job: Delivery Person—I'm a large tube that absorbs water and salt from undigested food. I also get rid of all the food the body can't use.
Hobbies: collecting, absorbing, and discarding

Name _____ The digestive system

Digestion Connection Data Sheet

Welcome to the "Digestion Connection," where meeting and mingling with organs in the digestive system is the name of the game! First fill in the space below with information describing the organ you are. Then "mingle" with the other organs in your class. Find and meet the organs listed in each box below. Fill in each box with the information you gather. Use the back of this sheet if you need more room.

1. **Name:** Mouth	2. **Name:** Esophagus	3. **Name:** Liver
Nickname: _____	**Nickname:** _____	**Nickname:** _____
Job: _____	**Job:** _____	**Job:** _____
_____	_____	_____
Hobbies: _____	**Hobbies:** _____	**Hobbies:** _____
_____	_____	_____
4. **Name:** Stomach	5. **Name:** Small Intestine	6. **Name:** Large Intestine
Nickname: _____	**Nickname:** _____	**Nickname:** _____
Job: _____	**Job:** _____	**Job:** _____
_____	_____	_____
Hobbies: _____	**Hobbies:** _____	**Hobbies:** _____
_____	_____	_____

Note To The Teacher: Use with "The Digestion Connection" on page 72.

A Fabulous Framework

The Human Skeleton

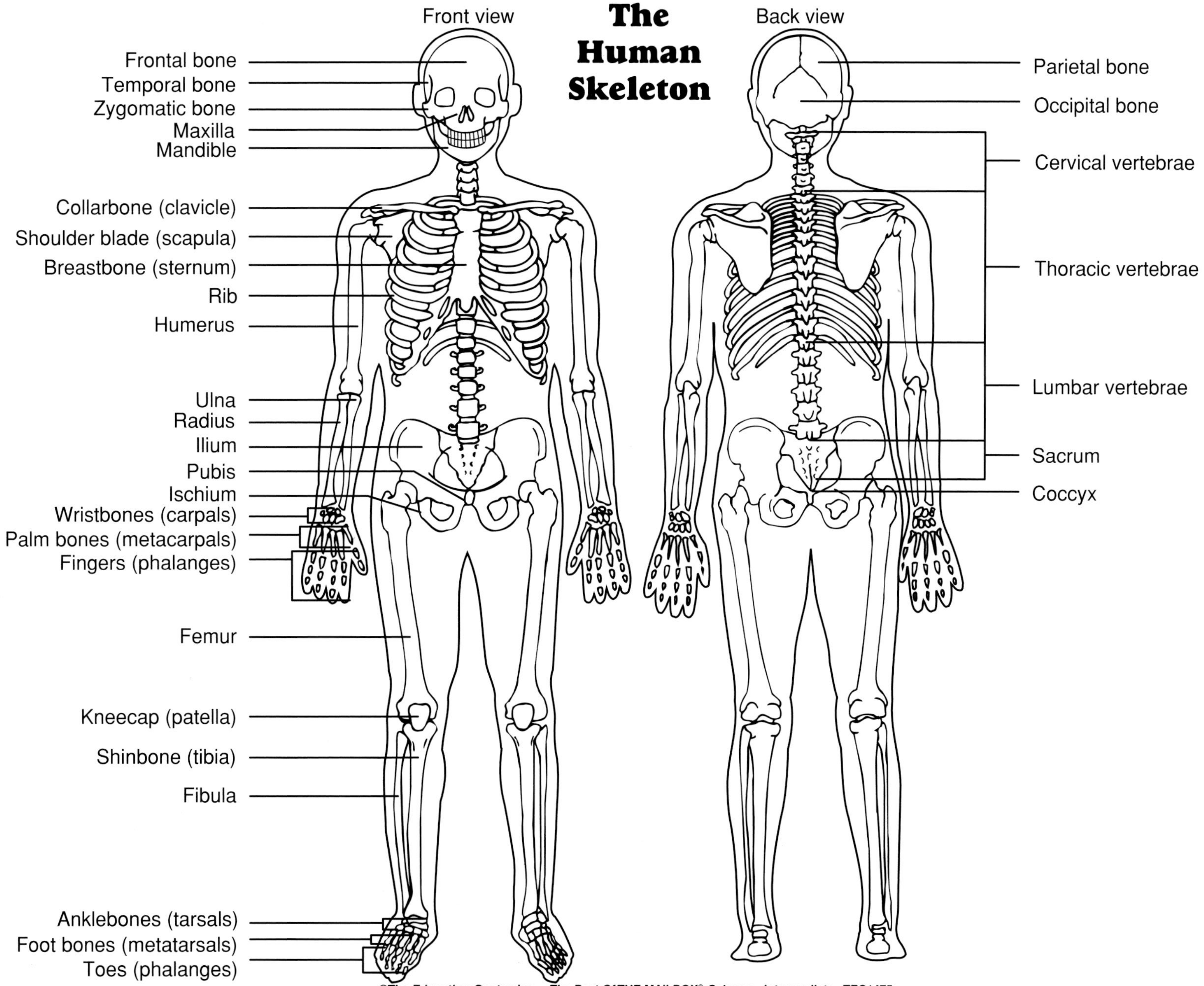

Front view

Back view

Back view labels:
- Parietal bone
- Occipital bone
- Cervical vertebrae
- Thoracic vertebrae
- Lumbar vertebrae
- Sacrum
- Coccyx

Front view labels:
- Frontal bone
- Temporal bone
- Zygomatic bone
- Maxilla
- Mandible
- Collarbone (clavicle)
- Shoulder blade (scapula)
- Breastbone (sternum)
- Rib
- Humerus
- Ulna
- Radius
- Ilium
- Pubis
- Ischium
- Wristbones (carpals)
- Palm bones (metacarpals)
- Fingers (phalanges)
- Femur
- Kneecap (patella)
- Shinbone (tibia)
- Fibula
- Anklebones (tarsals)
- Foot bones (metatarsals)
- Toes (phalanges)

Note To The Teacher: Use with "No Bones About It!" on page 73. Enlarge if desired.

Pattern
Use with "Body-Systems Flip Book" on page 74.

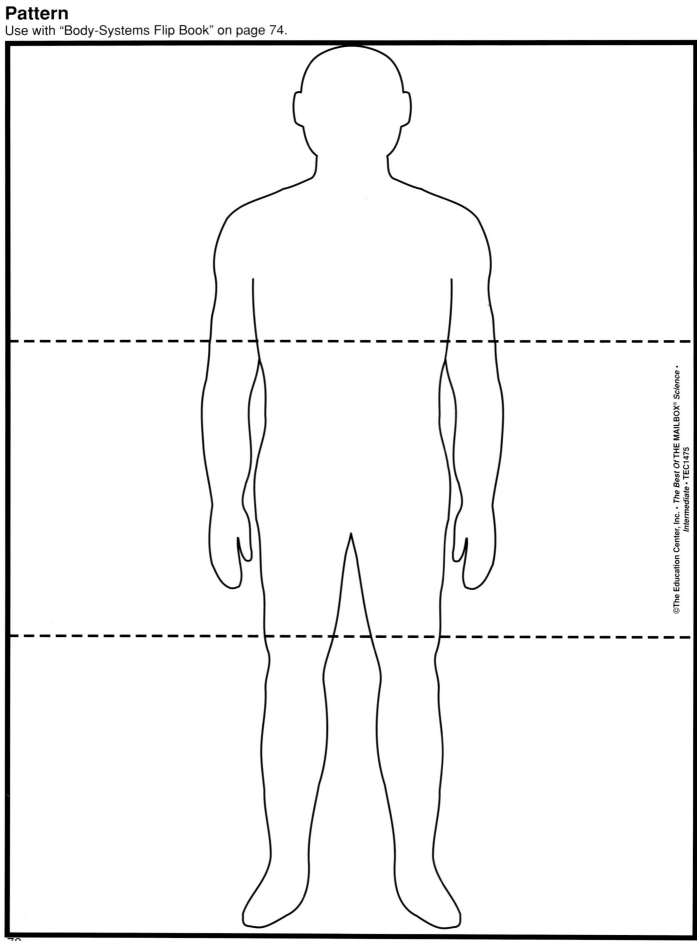

SPACE:
The Final "Fun-tier"
Thematic Activities On Space Exploration

Blast off into the study of space with the following
out-of-this-world activities!

by Christine A. Thuman

The Blue Planet

Although stars shine during the day, we have difficulty seeing them. Sunlight traveling to Earth reflects off the dust and water vapor in our atmosphere and prevents us from seeing all but the brightest planets at twilight. Simulate this effect with the following experiment.

Fill two identical glass jars with clear water. Dissolve a sliver of bar soap in one of the jars. Once the soap has dissolved, darken the room. Shine a flashlight horizontally through the jar filled with clean water. Note the color of the light as it passes through and out of the jar. Next shine the light through the soapy water. Again note the color of light as it passes through and out of the jar. What differences do you notice?

Light traveling through the soapy water bounces off the soap molecules. As a result, it is more difficult to see through the soapy water.

Out-Of-This-World Space Books

Boldly go in search of the best children's books about space—but not before reading the recommendations that follow!

- *Look Inside Cross-Sections: Space* by Moira Butterfield (DK Publishing, Inc.; 1994)
- *Black Stars In Orbit: NASA's African-American Astronauts* by Khephra Burns and William Miles (Harcourt Brace & Company, 1995)
- *The U.S. Space Camp Book Of Astronauts* by Anne Baird (Morrow Junior Books, 1996)
- *The Space Atlas: A Pictorial Guide To Our Universe* by Heather Couper and Nigel Henbest (Harcourt Brace & Company, 1992)

Blast Off!

A rocket needs a lot of energy to leave Earth's atmosphere. The rocket's thrust of power comes from gases bursting from an exhaust opening at its base. Have student groups mimic this process using simple materials.

Materials for each group of students: long, skinny balloon; binder clip; tape; scissors; drinking straw; spool of thread; ruler
Directions:
1. Cut two 2-inch lengths of straw. String a long length of thread through the straw sections.
2. Blow up the balloon and close the end with the clip. Tape the straw sections to the balloon as shown.
3. Securely tape one end of the thread to a desk or heavy object near the floor.
4. Draw the thread taut and tape the other end securely to the top of a door frame.
5. After positioning the balloon so that it slopes upward, remove the clip and hold the end of the balloon tightly.
6. Let go of the balloon's end and watch your rocket fly!

binder
clip

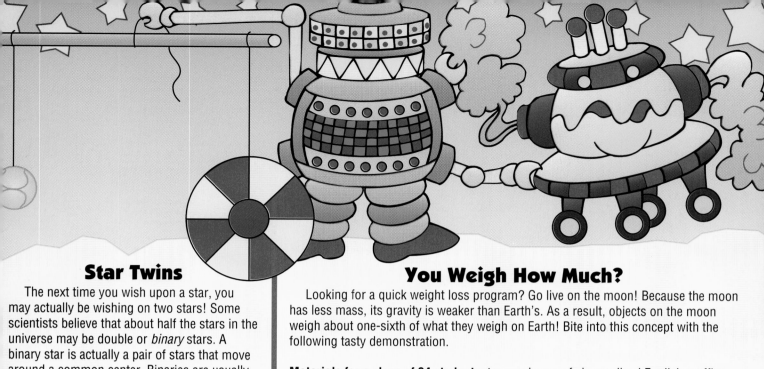

Star Twins

The next time you wish upon a star, you may actually be wishing on two stars! Some scientists believe that about half the stars in the universe may be double or *binary* stars. A binary star is actually a pair of stars that move around a common center. Binaries are usually so close together that you cannot see them as separate with the naked eye. Sometimes a small, brighter star is paired with a large, dimmer star. Viewed from Earth, this binary appears to blink or waver in brilliance depending upon which of the two stars is in front of, or *eclipsing,* the other. Demonstrate this concept using a tennis ball and a large, dark-colored beach ball. Tape each ball to the end of a different 12" piece of string. Tie the loose end of each string to an opposite end of a two-foot-long dowel. Tie another 12" length of string to the center of the dowel and balance the two balls like a mobile (see the illustration). As the class observes, rotate the two balls so that they take turns eclipsing each other. Discuss the following questions: When do you think the binary would appear the brightest? When would it appear the dimmest? What would this look like from Earth? What would it be like to live on a planet that revolves around a binary star system? Would you ever have a nighttime?

You Weigh How Much?

Looking for a quick weight loss program? Go live on the moon! Because the moon has less mass, its gravity is weaker than Earth's. As a result, objects on the moon weigh about one-sixth of what they weigh on Earth! Bite into this concept with the following tasty demonstration.

Materials for a class of 24 students: two packages of six presliced English muffins, 24 individually wrapped cheese slices, two 6-ounce jars of mild salsa, a bowl, two spoons, a toaster oven

Directions:
1. Before students arrive, remove five muffins from one package and set them aside. Close up this package. Next open one of the jars of salsa and spoon five-sixths of its contents into a bowl. Recap the jar.
2. Explain to students that objects on the moon weigh about one-sixth what they would on Earth. Invite a student to come to the front of the room and lift the opened muffin package in one hand while lifting the unopened package in the other hand. Have him compare the weight of the two packages and report his observations to the class.
3. Have two more students come up to the front of the classroom. Have one compare the weights of the opened and unopened jars of salsa. Have the other compare the weights of one cheese slice and six slices. Instruct both to report any observations.
4. Instruct every student to divide his own weight by six (rounding to the nearest pound) to discover how much he would weigh on the moon.
5. Finally celebrate this hypothetical weight loss by consuming man-on-the-moon muffins. Provide each student with a muffin half and a slice of cheese. Instruct each student to unwrap his cheese slice and carefully nibble off the corners to form it into a circle, and then place it on his muffin half. Pass around the salsa and spoons and have each student "shade" part of his moon muffin so that it resembles a particular stage of the moon (crescent, gibbous, half, or whole). If desired, have students toast their man-on-the-moon muffins before feasting on these lunar snacks!

Hey, you made crescent moons.

Pam Crane

How Far Is That Star?

Figuring out the distances of stars is as easy as a wink. The earth travels around the sun in an *elliptical,* or oval, path. When the earth is at one end of this ellipse, a scientist photographs the night sky. Six months later, when the earth reaches the other end of the ellipse, he photographs that same section of the sky. By comparing these two photographs, the scientist can spot any star that appears to have moved. The scientist measures this star's movement, or *parallax.* The closer a star is to Earth, the greater is its parallax.

To demonstrate this concept, paste 20 one-inch gold foil stars on different objects in the room; then have each student paste a star to the end of his right forefinger. Explain that the right eye represents the earth when it is at one end of its elliptical path, and the left eye represents the earth when it reaches the other end. Instruct each student to hold his star finger, pointing up, about a foot from his face. This placement of his finger represents a relatively close star. Closing his left eye, have him line up the star finger so that it covers one of the stars pasted around the room. Instruct him to open his left eye and close his right eye at the same time. His star finger will appear to move to the right. This movement represents the parallax of the star finger. Have him alternately wink his eyes several times to note the distance of the parallax.

Next have each student hold his star finger up at arm's length from his face. This represents a relatively distant star. Have him repeat the alternate winking procedure. Ask: "What differences did you notice in the movement of the star when it was held a foot away from your face and then at arm's length?" *(The student will notice that when the finger was held a foot from his face, its movement —or parallax—was greater than when the finger was held at arm's length. Stars that are closer to Earth have a larger parallax than more distant stars.)*

Death Star

What stellar spectacle inspires both dread and imagination? Why, a black hole, of course! Thought to be the result of a massive star's collapsed core, the gravitational pull of a black hole is so great that even light cannot travel fast enough to escape its clutches. Create a black hole model to demonstrate the pulling power of gravity. Stretch a piece of white, cottony material (like a piece of an old sheet) through a large embroidery hoop. Sprinkle a tablespoon of coffee granules in the center of the cloth. Turn on a vacuum cleaner; then hold its hose end under and near the very edge of the hoop. Making a small space between the vacuum cleaner hose and the fabric with your finger and thumb will cause the fabric to vibrate. The coffee granules will vibrate on the fabric and slowly be drawn toward the sucking vacuum hose. Similarly, a black hole attracts— but actually sucks up—nearby star fragments and gases. As a follow-up, have each student write a story describing what she thinks lies at the center of a black hole.

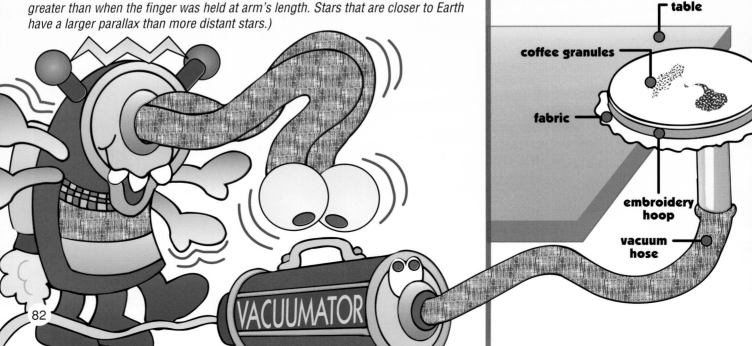

table

coffee granules

fabric

embroidery hoop

vacuum hose

VACUUMATOR

Getting The Dirt On Mars

In the 1970s two unmanned space probes, called the *Viking* landers, were sent to the surface of Mars. These sophisticated machines tested Mars's soil to determine if life existed on that planet. They did this by feeding nutrients to the soil and observing the soil for signs of life. Conduct a similar experiment right here on Earth!

Materials per group of students:

three 12-ounce glass jars   3 labels and a marker
clean sand   large pitcher
long-handled teaspoon   measuring cup
2 teaspoons salt   1/2 cup sugar
2 teaspoons yeast   2 cups warm water
2 teaspoons baking powder

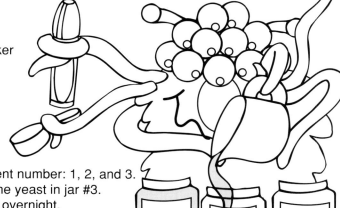

Directions:

1. Fill each jar 1/3 full of sand. Label each jar with a different number: 1, 2, and 3.
2. Mix the salt in jar #1, the baking powder in jar #2, and the yeast in jar #3.
3. Mars is a cold place, so store the jars in the refrigerator overnight.
4. Meanwhile mix the sugar and warm water in the pitcher. Set it aside.
5. The next day, pour 2/3 cup of sugar water into each jar. Set the jars aside.
6. Record any reactions. Which jar do you think contains life?

Feeding the soil with nutrients will cause chemicals in the soil to react quickly. However, living cells, if present, will react slowly and will continue to react as they multiply.

Note To The Teacher: Duplicate this experiment for a learning center or group activity. The jar containing salt will not react. The jar containing baking powder will react quickly, but then fizzle out. The jar containing yeast will react slowly and continuously because yeast contains living cells.

Why Does Mars Look Red?

By sending the two *Viking* landers to Mars, scientists discovered why that planet looks red from Earth. Conduct this experiment to find out why when we see Mars, we see red!

Don't go tracking that red Mars mud into this house!

Aw, Mom!

Materials for each group of students:

aluminum pie pan   heavy-duty scissors
sand   dishwashing gloves
steel wool pad   pitcher of water

Directions:

1. Half-fill the pan with sand.
2. While wearing the gloves, snip the steel wool into small pieces and mix them into the sand.
3. Carefully pour enough water into the pan to just cover the sand and steel wool mixture.
4. Set the pan in a safe place for several days. Replace any evaporated water daily.
5. Check the pan daily for any color changes. Record what you see. What does this tell you about the red soil of Mars?

When water mixes with iron, it creates rust. Although Mars is now desert dry, evidence exists that the planet once contained water. When this water mixed with iron compounds found in Mars's soil, the compounds rusted, making the soil look red.

Note To The Teacher: Duplicate this experiment for a learning center or group activity. After sitting in water for several days, the steel wool will rust, giving the sand a red tint.

Looking Good For Your Age!

Mercury, Venus, Earth, and Mars are called the *inner planets* because they are closest to the sun. How old would you be today if you had been born on an inner planet other than Earth? Use your division skills and a calculator to find out!

1. According to the chart, it takes 365.26 Earth days for Earth to make one trip, or *revolution*, around the sun. Each revolution is the same as a year. The chart shows that there are 88 Earth days in a Mercury year. How many Earth days are there in a Venus year? A Mars year?

   Number of Earth days in one Venus year: _____

   Number of Earth days in one Mars year: _____

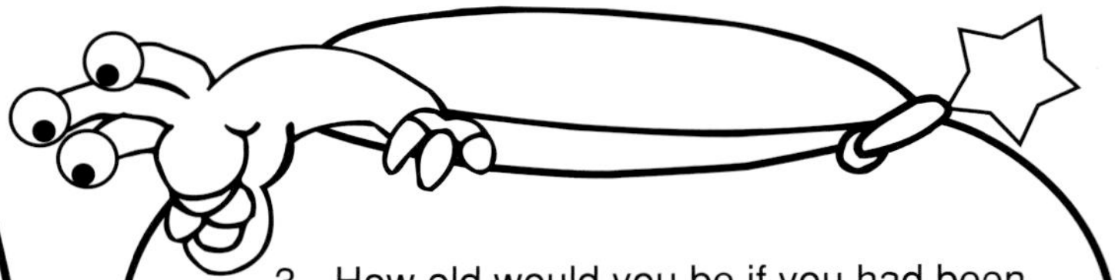

2. Write your age in years on the chart below. Then find your age in Earth days. To do this, multiply your age in years by 365; then add the number of days that have passed since your last birthday.

   Example: You are eight years old, and 28 days have passed since your birthday. Multiply 8 x 365; then add 28.

   (8 x 365) + 28 = days old
   2920 + 28   = days old
   2948   = days old

   Use the space below to calculate your age in Earth days.

   _____ x 365 + _____ =
   (age in years)   (days since birthday)

   *_____
   (age in Earth days)

3. How old would you be if you had been born on Mercury? Here's how to find out. Take the number of Earth days in a Mercury year (88). Divide this number into your age in Earth days (the * answer from Step 2).

   Example: If you are 2948 days old, divide 2948 by 88 to determine your age on Mercury.

   $$88 \overline{)2948.00}^{\,33.50}$$

   Wow! You'd be over 33 years old!

   Now find the answer using your age. Record the answer in the appropriate space on the chart below.

   (your age on Mercury)
   (number of days in Mercury's year)) (your age in Earth days)

4. Calculate your age as if you'd been born on Venus. Record your answer on the chart.

5. Calculate your age as if you'd been born on Mars. Record your answer on the chart.

	MERCURY	VENUS	EARTH	MARS
Revolution around the sun in Earth days	88 days	224.7 days	365.26 days	687 days
My age in Earth years				

Note To The Teacher: Provide each student with a copy of this page and a calculator.

A Pixel Is Worth A Thousand Words

Everyone knows that there's no camera store in the sky. So how do we get those fantastic photos from the space probes? Computers on the probes convert the photographs into many tiny squares called *pixels,* which are then sent through space as radio signals. Simulate this transmission by playing the following graphic game.

Materials for two students:

two copies of this page; three different colored pencils or markers (they should be different shades of the same color—for instance, a light blue, a medium blue, and a dark blue); a book

Directions:

1. You are the *transmitter.* Your job is to record the picture and send it back—in pixels—to Earth. Using the colored pencils or markers, draw a simple design on the graph below. Use only one color in each square. Leave some squares blank.

2. Fill out the KEY above the graph. To do this, leave box 0 blank. Color box 1 with the lightest shade of marker, box 2 with the next lightest shade, and box 3 with the darkest shade.

3. Fill out the KEY on the other copy of this page in the same way as in step 2.

4. Give your partner the three pencils and the copy of this page with only the key filled in. (DO NOT show him your design!) Sit across from your partner. Set a book upright between you and your partner to create a screen so that he cannot see your design.

5. Your partner is the *receiver.* His job is to correctly record the incoming pixels. Instruct your partner to call out the coordinates (for example: A1, B3, etc.) for each box on the graph, calling out one box at a time in order beginning with box A1 (followed by A2, A3, and so on).

6. Each time your partner names a box, respond by telling him the key code number: "0" if the box on your graph is blank, "1" if the box is the lightest shade, and so on with "2" or "3." After he's called out the coordinates for the entire graph, compare your design with his to see how accurately the design was transmitted and received.

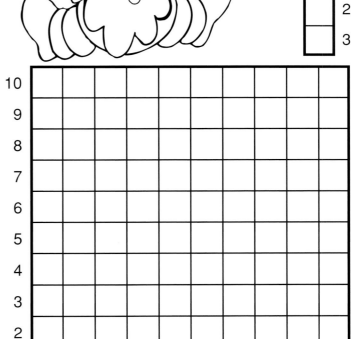

KEY

	0
	1
	2
	3

It's Greek To Me!

It may seem hard to believe, but the Greek philosopher Aristotle has traveled forward in time to the year 1996.

What to do: Research when and where Aristotle lived. Find out one of Aristotle's theories about space that was incorrect. Select one book from your school or classroom library that would explain space to Aristotle.

What to write: Write a story in which you meet Aristotle. Describe how you help him understand a modern truth about space.

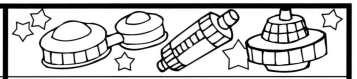

Living In Space

You have been selected to live on a space station. Although you are excited about your upcoming adventure, you know that life on a space station has its advantages and disadvantages.

What to do: Using books and current magazines, research what it's like to live in space for a long period of time.

What to write: Write a letter to a friend describing one day in the life of a space station astronaut.

Where's Columbus?

Oh no! Sally Ride's space shuttle has been caught in a time warp. She has traveled back in time to Europe in 1492.

What to do: Research to find out what Christopher Columbus believed about Earth and space before he set sail for the New World. Select an astronomy book from your school or classroom library that Sally Ride might recommend that Columbus read before his journey.

What to write: Write an adventure in which Sally Ride meets with Christopher Columbus before his first trip to the New World.

To Boldly Go...

The year is 2050. Because you were born on a Martian space colony, you have never been to Earth.

What to do: Read about Mars's atmosphere and land. Find out what humans would need to do in order to build a livable colony on that planet.

What to write: Write a letter to your pen pal on Earth describing your colony. Tell how you and your family get food and oxygen, and how you dispose of waste. Describe your educational and entertaining activities too.

Close Encounters?

For two nights in a row, you have seen strange lights in the sky. You suspect that they may be UFOs. But you wonder if there is another explanation.

What to do: Research the theories that both support and argue against the existence of UFOs.

What to write: Write a story in which you either encounter beings from another planet, or find out that the lights you have been seeing have another, more logical explanation. Weave facts from your research into your story.

Led By The Light

During the 1800s, many slaves managed to escape to the North by following the constellation known as the Big Dipper. They called this constellation "the drinking gourd."

What to do: Read several stories explaining how constellations have helped to guide people in the past.

What to write: Write an original story in which one of the characters has an adventure or solves a mystery with the help of one of the constellations.

Note To The Teacher: Duplicate this page for a learning center, group work, or an individual research/writing activity. Cut the cards apart; then mount them on tagboard and laminate them for durability. Give one card to each group or individual.

Weather Whys, Weather-Wise
Creative, Hands-On Activities For Learning About Weather

What's the best way to learn about weather? To watch it, of course! Help your students become weather-wise by having them create and use their own weather instruments. The following how-tos, hands-on demonstrations, and a few easy-to-find supplies—plus a class full of eager young meteorologists—guarantees that fun is in the forecast!

by Bonnie Pettifor

Getting Organized

The hands-on activities in this unit consist of reproducible student directions for making four weather instruments (pages 91–92), a reproducible wind speed chart and a guide to identifying clouds (page 93), and a reproducible weather log (page 94). On pages 88–90 are activities for introducing each weather instrument plus helpful information to share with your students.

Divide your class into groups of four to five students each. Provide *each group* with one copy each of pages 91 and 92. In addition, provide *each student* with copies of pages 93 and 94. Instruct each group to make all four weather instruments, then follow the directions outlined in the following activity for building a weather station. Enlist the help of students and their parents in securing the materials needed to make the instruments and weather stations.

In addition, supply each group with an outdoor thermometer and a pinwheel. The pinwheel will serve as an *anemometer,* or instrument for measuring wind speed. Although students won't be able to measure the exact speed of the wind, the pinwheel—plus the information provided in the chart on page 93—will help them observe, estimate, and record the intensity of winds.

Setting Up And Locating The Weather Stations

When each group has made its four weather instruments, share the following steps for setting up a portable weather station. Instruct each group to:

1. Cover the bottom and two sides of a plastic milk crate with burlap as shown (to create shade, yet still allow air to circulate).
2. Cover the top surface with a water-resistant piece of wood or a piece of strong plastic.
3. Use clay and duct tape to mount the weather instruments, including the thermometer and pinwheel, in and on the crate as shown.

Next instruct each group (with your assistance) to choose a safe location on your school grounds for its weather station. Make sure that the instruments have enough room to operate without interfering with each other, and that the rain gauge will not receive run-off rainwater from a building or tree. Place each station so that its thermometer faces north. (Students will have already identified north when making the weather vane described on page 91.)

Using The Weather Logs

Have each individual student make a weather log in which to record his observations at his group's weather station. Instruct each student to cut out the log (page 94) and paste it to the inside of a folder as shown. Next have the student cut out the wind speed chart and cloud identification chart from page 93 and paste them both inside the folder for easy reference.

On the first trip to make observations at the weather stations, accompany each group to its station to show students how to read their instruments and fill out their logs. Make sure that each station's weather vane is facing north as described on page 91. Have each group visit its weather station first thing in the morning and/or near the end of the school day—or at some other set time that is convenient. It's important to follow the same routine each day so that students can make valid comparisons of data. If it has rained overnight, be sure each group checks its rain gauge early in the morning—before the rainwater has time to evaporate.

So that students can fill out the last two columns on their logs each day, assign one student to either check a newspaper or listen to a weather report to find out the forecast for the next day. Have the student report his findings after everyone has had time to make a prediction in his log.

Before Making The Weather Vane: An Activity On Wind

Wind is simply air moving across the earth's surface. Wind may blow so gently that it's hardly noticeable, or it may blow hard enough to smash buildings. Winds are named according to the direction *from* which they blow. Thus an *east wind* blows from east to west and a *north wind* blows from north to south.

What's one way that wind affects weather? Answer that question by sharing the following demonstration with your students. Stack several books to resemble a mountain as shown below. Use a fan to create a strong wind a few feet from one side of the mountain. Next hold the end of a strip of tissue paper so that it extends out over the books as shown below. Ask students to observe what happens. *(On the side near the fan, the wind rises up. On the side away from the fan, the wind suddenly descends. Mountain ranges can change the temperature and direction of winds. Near a coast, they can keep ocean breezes from blowing into inland areas. In western Washington and Oregon, mountains block rain-filled winds from the Pacific Ocean. Thus the eastern side of these states is dry while the western side is wet.)*

Making A Weather Vane (Page 91)

Have each group make a weather vane for its station using the directions on page 91. Suggest that each group anchor an inexpensive compass in the modeling clay that holds the chopstick. This will make it easier for each group to place its weather vane correctly on its portable weather station. Remind students that the arrow of a weather vane will point in the direction from which the wind is blowing. A group doesn't necessarily have to use a chopstick. Any strong, thin item such as a knitting needle or sturdy wire will work. (Be sure to warn students about sharp points.) For a waterproof arrow, suggest that each group trace the arrow pattern on the flat side of a plastic milk carton and then cut out the tracing.

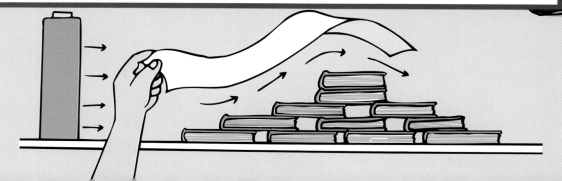

Before Making The Rain Gauge: An Activity On Precipitation

Produce rain in your classroom the same way that Mother Nature makes it! Fill a saucepan about one-quarter full with water. Place it on a heat source until the water comes to a complete boil. Next put several ice cubes into a frying pan and hold the pan several inches above the saucepan. Be sure to keep your hands from coming in contact with the steam. Soon drops of water will fall from the bottom of the frying pan. Ask students to hypothesize about why this rainfall occurred. *(The water vapor rose from the saucepan and hit the cold surface of the frying pan. There it collected as moisture. Soon the moisture became too heavy and fell as water droplets. In nature, a similar cycle occurs: Water evaporates from the earth, then the water vapor rises into the sky. There it's colder so the water collects into clouds. When the clouds become too heavy with water, raindrops fall to the earth.)*

Making A Rain Gauge (Page 91)

Have each group make a rain gauge for its station using the directions on page 91. Suggest that each group obtain an olive jar or any similar tall jar with straight sides. Assist the students in cutting the tops out of the two-liter pop bottles. If it happens to rain during the school day, have students note the times when the rain begins and ends. Then have them measure the amount of rainfall and compare it to the elapsed time to determine the rate of the rainfall.

What if it snows—how is a snowfall measured? Fill a two-pound coffee can (or any can that is about 12 inches tall with straight sides) with loose snow. Measure the depth of the snow. Place the can in a warm place and let the snow melt. Pour the resulting water into a rain gauge and see how many inches of water the snow made. *(It takes about one foot of snow to equal one inch of rain.)*

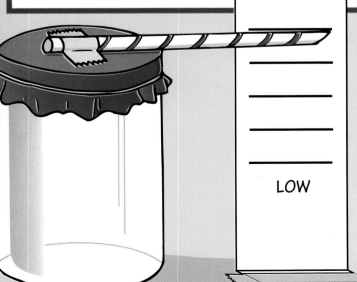

Before Making The Barometer: An Activity On Barometric Pressure

How strong is air pressure? The following demonstration will be an eye-opener for your students. Place a thin piece of wood (about two or three feet long and no more than one-eighth-inch thick) on a table so that nearly half of it extends over the edge. Lay three or four sheets of newspaper over the end of the stick that is resting on the table, smoothing them down carefully. Ask students what they think will happen when you hit the outer end of the stick with a hammer. Then, standing to one side, give the outer end of the stick a sharp hit with a hammer. *(The stick will break because its inner end has been held down by air pressure on the large sheets of newspaper.)*

Making A Barometer (Page 92)

Have each group make a barometer for its station using the directions on page 92. In order for the barometer to work well, the piece of balloon should not be stretched too tightly over the mouth of the jar. Have extra balloons on hand in case some balloons break as students stretch them. Cover the cardboard on which the scale is drawn with clear Con-Tact® paper to make it water-resistant. Encourage students to also keep track of the official weather report's barometric pressure readings and to watch for patterns that help them predict the weather. For example, low pressure often means bad weather, while high pressure usually means good weather.

Why does this barometer work? The greater the pressure, the more it pushes down on the balloon, causing the straw to point higher. The lower the pressure, the less it pushes down on the balloon, allowing the balloon to rise back up and the straw to point lower.

Before Making The Hygrometer: An Activity On Weather Indicators

For centuries, people whose livelihoods depend on the weather have known that nature gives all kinds of clues about the weather to come. Have students research weather lore to find out which signs are for real and which ones are little more than superstition—and no help at all for weather forecasting. Suggest the following:

- If the groundhog sees his shadow on Groundhog Day, the weather will remain cold for six more weeks.
- The scarlet pimpernel's tiny flowers open wide in sunny weather, but close tightly when rain is in the air.
- As the temperature rises, a grasshopper's chirping gets louder and louder.
- If you see cows lying down, rain must be on the way.
- If squirrels have very bushy tails in the fall, then a severe winter is coming up.
- If wool swells and straightens out, then rain is on the way.
- Wide-open morning-glory blooms mean fine weather.
- "If the oak flowers before the ash, we shall have a splash" (light rain for the next month or so).
- "If the ash flowers before the oak, we shall have a soak" (meaning very wet weather).
- When ants travel in a straight line, expect rain; when they scatter, expect fair weather.

Making A Hygrometer (Page 92)

Have each group make either a seaweed or a pinecone hygrometer using the directions on page 92. Students don't need to use both items in their weather stations; one will do. Use dried sheets of seaweed from an Asian grocery store if this is easier for you to obtain.

Why do these simple hygrometers work so well? The seaweed absorbs the moisture in the air, becoming limp when the humidity is high and rain threatens. The pinecone is one of nature's most reliable weather indicators. In dry weather, the scales on a pinecone open out. When the scales close up, it's a good sign rain is on the way.

It's gonna stay cold AND it's gonna rain!!!

Math For Meteorologists

Measuring carefully is one important facet of weather-data collecting, so incorporate various math skills into your weather unit. Try these suggestions:

- Compare metric and customary measures. Discuss how the metric system is easier to use in science.
- Introduce how to convert a Fahrenheit reading to Celsius. (Subtract 32 from the Fahrenheit reading; then multiply the difference by 0.55.)
- Show students how to convert a Celsius reading to Fahrenheit. (Multiply the Celsius reading by 1.8; then add 32 to the product.)
- Have students find the average temperature each week.
- Track the relative humidity included in the official weather reports. Convert percents to decimals.
- Graph the rainfall during a two-week or monthlong period.

Weather-Wise Literature

There are plenty of good books that focus on aspects of all kinds of weather. Here are just a few:

- Eyewitness Books *Weather* by Brian Cosgrove (Alfred A. Knopf, Inc.)
- *Weather: Mind-Boggling Experiments You Can Turn Into Science Fair Projects* by Janice VanCleave (John Wiley & Sons, Inc.)
- *Weather And Climate* by Barbara Taylor (Kingfisher Books)
- *The Science Book Of Weather* by Neil Ardley (Gulliver Books)
- *Storms* by Seymour Simon (Morrow Junior Books)
- *Weather Whys: Questions, Facts, And Riddles About Weather* by Mike Artell (Good Year Books)
- *It's Raining Cats And Dogs: All Kinds Of Weather And Why We Have It* by Franklin M. Branley (Avon Books)

Blowin' In The Wind

Keeping track of the direction from which the wind blows will help you notice weather patterns. Follow the directions below to make a weather vane.

Materials needed:

brick (with holes)   modeling clay   chopstick
4" x 8" piece of poster board   pen cap   masking tape
scissors   compass   arrow pattern (from page 93)
four cards labeled N, S, E, W   pinwheel   pencil

Procedure:

1. Cut out the arrow pattern and trace it on the poster board. Cut out the tracing.
2. Put clay into a hole in the brick.
3. Stick the chopstick into the clay.
4. Tape the pen cap to the middle of the arrow.
5. Balance the pen cap on top of the chopstick.
6. Place a small ball of clay near the point of the arrow to balance it.
7. Attach the four cards labeled E (east), N (north), W (west), and S (south) to the sides of the brick with masking tape as shown.
8. Place the weather vane in your weather station. Use a compass to help position the side labeled N so that it faces north.
9. Record the wind direction daily in your weather log. Remember: the arrow points to the direction from which the wind is blowing.
10. Tape the pinwheel to one corner of the station. Estimate the wind speed each day by observing the pinwheel. Use the wind speed chart in your weather log to help you.

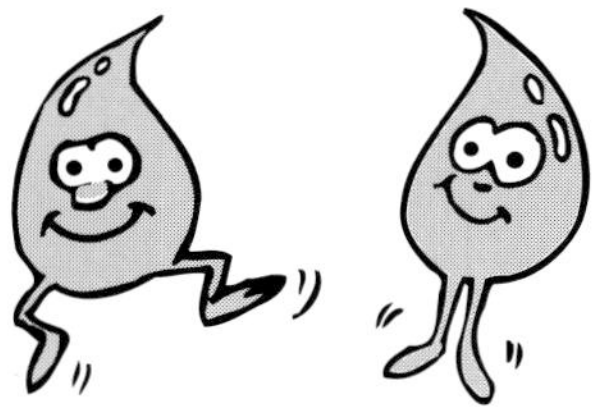

Save It For A Rainy Day

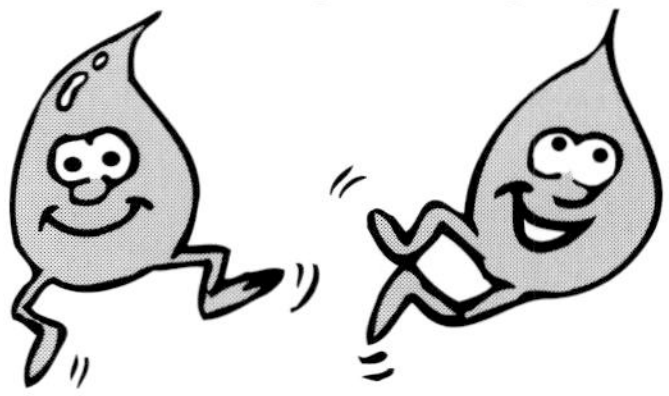

How is rain measured?
Follow the directions below to make a simple rain gauge.

Materials needed:

clear jar (with straight sides and a flat bottom)   empty, two-liter pop bottle
scale (from page 93)   modeling clay
clear Con-Tact® covering or wide transparent tape   scissors

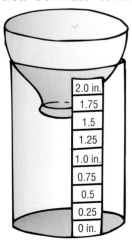

2.0 in.
1.75
1.5
1.25
1.0 in.
0.75
0.5
0.25
0 in.

Procedure:

1. Cut the top from the pop bottle.
2. Cut out the scale on page 93.
3. Attach the scale to the clear jar with clear Con-Tact® covering or wide transparent tape. Make sure that you line up 0 in. with the bottom of the jar.
4. Place the pop bottle top upside down in the clear jar to serve as a funnel.
5. Place your rain gauge in your weather station where it will receive rain directly from the sky. Secure it to the weather station with modeling clay.
6. Record how much water is in your rain gauge after each rainfall. Empty and dry out the gauge after you record the info in your weather log.

Note To The Teacher: See pages 88 and 89 for information on how to use this page.

Under Pressure

Falling pressure can mean that bad weather is on the way. How do you measure air pressure?
Follow the directions below to make a barometer, an instrument that measures air pressure.

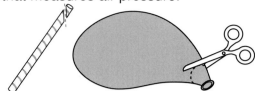

Materials needed:

plastic or glass jar	piece of cardboard	balloon
strong rubber band	drinking straw	scissors
tape	marker	ruler

Procedure:

1. Cut the balloon as shown and stretch the larger part across the mouth of the jar—but not too tightly.
2. Secure the balloon in place with a rubber band.
3. Cut the straw to make a pointed end as shown. Tape the opposite end of the straw to the balloon.
4. Have one group member hold the cardboard next to the jar. Make a mark and then draw a line across the cardboard where the straw now points.
5. Add three lines above and three lines below today's line, each 1/4 (0.25) inch apart. Label the top line "high" and the bottom line "low."
6. Place your barometer in your group's weather station. Tape the cardboard piece to the inside of the station so that the pointed end of the straw is aligned with the middle mark. Record high or low pressure each day in your weather log.

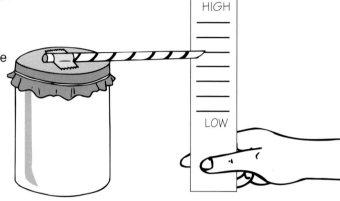

Nature's Hygrometers

Nature provides two things you can use as hygrometers. A *hygrometer* is a gauge of relative humidity.
See how seaweed or a pinecone can tell you how much moisture is in the air.

Materials needed:
dried seaweed or a pinecone
string

Procedure:

1. Hang the seaweed or pinecone inside your group's weather station. Make sure it is sheltered from rain.
2. Observe the seaweed (or pinecone) every day:
   a. If the seaweed is dry and stiff, record "low" on your weather log sheet in the "relative humidity" column.
   b. If the seaweed is limp and flexible, record "high" on the log sheet.
   c. If the pinecone scales are open, record "low" on the sheet.
   d. If the pinecone scales are closed, record "high" on the sheet.

Note To The Teacher: See pages 89 and 90 for information on how to use this page.

Wind Speed Chart

Use the chart below to help you determine wind speed for your weather log.

Wind Speeds

name	mph	effect on land
calm	less than 1	calm; smoke rises straight up
light air	1–3	weather vanes don't move; smoke drifts
light breeze	4–7	weather vanes active; wind felt on face
gentle breeze	8–12	leaves and small twigs move
moderate breeze	13–18	small branches sway; dust and loose paper blow about
fresh breeze	19–24	small trees sway
strong breeze	25–31	large branches sway; umbrellas difficult to use
moderate gale	32–38	whole trees sway; difficult to walk against wind
fresh gale	39–46	twigs break off trees
strong gale	47–54	slight damage to buildings; shingles blow off
whole gale	55–63	trees uprooted; considerable damage to buildings
storm	64–73	widespread damage; very rare occurrence
hurricane	74 and above	violent destruction

Scale

Use this scale with "Save It For A Rainy Day" on page 91.

2.0 in.
1.75
1.5
1.25
1.0 in.
0.75
0.5
0.25
0 in.

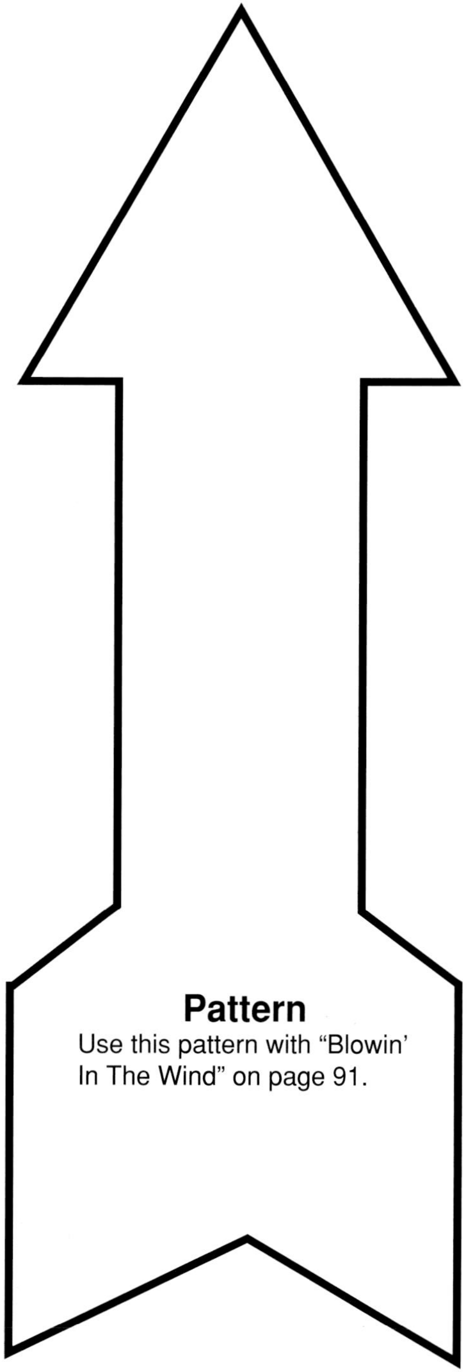

Pattern

Use this pattern with "Blowin' In The Wind" on page 91.

Types Of Clouds

Use the chart to help you determine cloud types for your weather log.

Clouds

Study the shape, size, and height of clouds to help you predict what the weather will be like.

nimbostratus
(gray layer; often dark; blots out the sun; rain or snow)

cumulonimbus
(dense, dark thundercloud; storms coming)

cirrus
(wispy, high-level clouds; made of ice crystals; weather is about to change)

cumulus
(mounds of clouds with flat bases; bright white in the sun; fine weather)

stratus
(thick, gray, low-level sheet; similar to fog; can cover high ground)

Weather Log

Meteorologist: _____

date and time	temperature	relative humidity	barometric pressure	precipitation (rain? snow?)	wind speed	wind direction	cloud type	my forecast for tomorrow	the official forecast for tomorrow	Was my forecast accurate?

94

©The Education Center, Inc. • *The Best Of THE MAILBOX® Science • Intermediate* • TEC1475

Note To The Teacher: See page 88 for information on using this reproducible.

Dive In To
THE SCHOOL OF OCEANOGRAPHY

Oceanography is the study of anything about the oceans—from their physical features to their inhabitants. Keep your students fishing for information about life under the sea—even if they're landlubbers at heart—with the creative ideas in this unit!

with contributions by Judith Brinckerhoff, Elizabeth H. Lindsay, and Mary Lou Schlosser

Fishing For Facts

Your students will dive into this research activity hook, line, and sinker! Label a fishbowl or other large container "Fishy Or For Real Facts." Next copy the fish pattern on page 99 for each student. Direct each student to find a fact about the ocean or one of its inhabitants, then write a true/false statement about the fact on her fish pattern. Have students place their fish patterns in the fishbowl when done. Post these fish on a bulletin board titled "Fishing For Facts."

Next instruct each student to use her free time to research one or more of the facts on the board to determine if it is true or false. Have the student copy the fact, her answer *(true* or *false),* and her name on a slip of paper, and then place the slip in the now-empty fishbowl. At the end of the week, pull a slip from the bowl and read aloud its answer. If it's correct, reward that student with a small treat for being the first to correctly identify that particular fact. Then pull out another slip until all the facts have been identified as true or false.

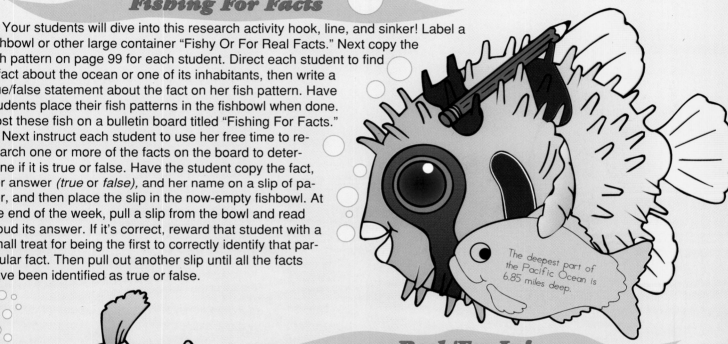

The deepest part of the Pacific Ocean is 6.85 miles deep.

Reel 'Em In!

Looking for just the right bait to catch your students' interest during your study of the ocean? Try the following motivating ideas:

- Decorate your room with items such as a nautical flag, a fishing net, a windsock, or even a small dinghy to create a marine atmosphere.
- Fill a small aquarium with various fish, coral, rocks, and plant life. Use this as a springboard for writing or art activities.
- Invite students to bring in their collections of seashells. Schedule time for show-and-tell, or obtain a field guide and have students identify and classify the shells.
- Place cassettes with sounds of the ocean or songs of the humpback whale at a listening center. Allow students to listen to the tapes for brief periods of rest and relaxation.
- Set the scene for some ocean-related reading. Fill a small wading pool, barrel, or seaworthy-looking trunk with books such as those suggested in "Literature Link" on page 98.
- Set up a marine research center. *Janice VanCleave's Oceans For Every Kid* (published by John Wiley & Sons, Inc.) is filled with easy activities and projects for hands-on student learning. Equip the center with the materials needed for one or more of the book's activities. Have students experiment during free time, or make the center a part of your lesson plans.

Budding Marine Botanists

A *marine botanist* is a scientist who specializes in the study of ocean plant life—from free-floating microscopic plankton to giant kelp. Millions of these plants form the base of the sea's food pyramid. If plants were to disappear from this pyramid, other life would be affected—including our own.

To help your students understand the unique characteristics of marine plants and their effects on other sea life, turn an area of your classroom into a plant research center. Supply the center with multiple copies of the pyramid pattern on page 99, a copy of the directions below, and reference materials. Have each pair of students research marine plants; then have the pair follow the directions for constructing a plant pyramid. Display each pyramid by attaching a string to the top and hanging it from the ceiling above the center.

Directions for making the plant pyramid:

1. On the base of the pyramid, write the names of three marine plants and draw a picture of each.
2. On one side of the pyramid, describe what the plants look like.
3. On a second side of the pyramid, describe how marine plants produce food.
4. On a third side of the pyramid, describe how plants are important to the marine food chain.
5. On the fourth side of the pyramid, describe other uses of marine plants.
6. Cut out the pyramid. Fold the sides and tabs at the dotted lines; then glue the sides to the tabs to construct the pyramid.

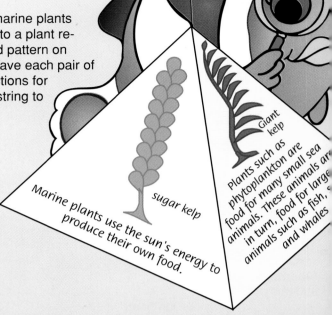

Animal Adaptation Wheels

It's not mere coincidence that ocean animals have special color patterns, shapes, body parts, and senses. These adaptations help ensure the survival of each animal within its ocean environment.

Challenge each of your students to take on the role of a marine biologist and research an ocean animal's adaptations. Give each student two sheets of light-colored construction paper and a brad. Direct each student to cut out two paper-plate-size circles, then use a pencil and a ruler to divide each circle into four equal sections. Next have the student cut out a section on one of the circles, then label each of the other sections on the two circles and put the wheel together using the diagrams below as a guide. Finally direct each student to write the animal's characteristics on the appropriate sections, then illustrate and color the project. Display the wheels on a wall or bulletin board titled "Animal Adaptation Wheels." Have students learn about one another's findings by turning the wheels.

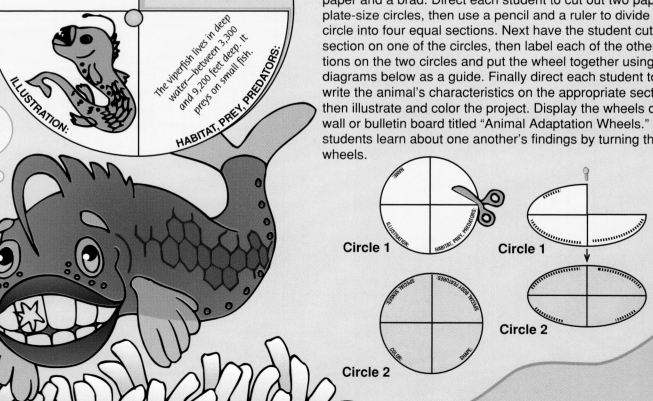

Zoning Out, Ocean-Style!

Ocean-animal habitats are divided into layers or zones according to the amount of sunlight each receives. (See the diagram below.) As depth increases, the amount of light decreases. The only light in the midnight zone is produced by *bioluminescence,* a process by which organisms produce their own light. There are also differences in temperature and pressure. All of these differences affect the types of animal life that can survive in each zone.

Help your students visualize the depth differences as well as the amazing variety of organisms that inhabit each zone by completing this hands-on activity.

Directions:

1. Divide students into groups of three. Distribute the following materials to each group: three pieces of yarn—one yellow, one blue, and one black; three 4-inch white circle cutouts; three crayons—one yellow, one blue, and one black; scissors; a ruler; tape.
2. Draw and label the diagram shown on the board (if you're not an artist, use labels for the animal drawings). Discuss the zones, asking students to identify the differences in the depths relative to the first zone. *(The first zone extends to a depth of 600 feet. The depth of the second zone is four times greater than the first, and the depth of the third zone is 20 times greater than the first.)*
3. Instruct one member of each group to cut a three-inch piece of yellow yarn to represent the depth of the sunlight zone. Tell students that the blue yarn represents the twilight zone and the black yarn represents the midnight zone. Ask students what the measurements should be for each of the two other pieces of yarn. *(The blue yarn should measure 12 inches and the black yarn should measure 60 inches.)* Have the other two members of each group measure and cut the blue and black yarns.
4. Direct each group to research other characteristics of each zone such as temperature, pressure, and animal life. Instruct the group to label each of the circles with a zone and its facts (including differences in depth and the amount of light received).
5. Finally have students connect (with tape) as shown, illustrate, and color the circles, putting the illustrations on the back of each. Hang the completed projects from the ceiling in your room or in a hallway.

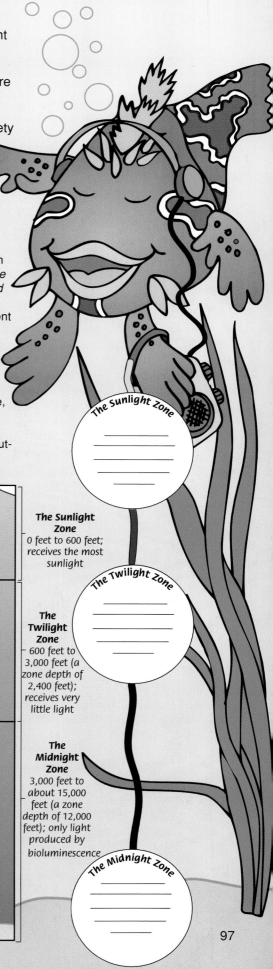

The Sunlight Zone

The Sunlight Zone
0 feet to 600 feet; receives the most sunlight

The Twilight Zone

The Twilight Zone
600 feet to 3,000 feet (a zone depth of 2,400 feet); receives very little light

The Midnight Zone
3,000 feet to about 15,000 feet (a zone depth of 12,000 feet); only light produced by bioluminescence

The Midnight Zone

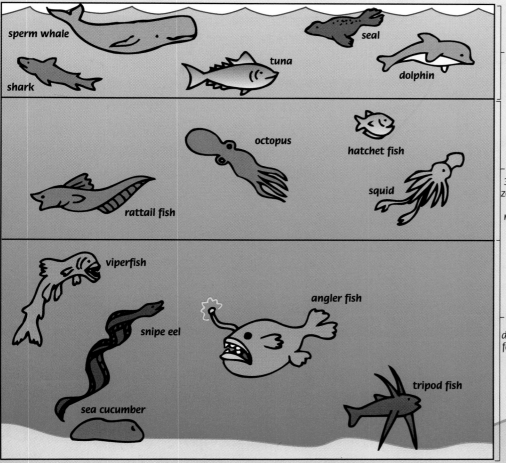

sperm whale

seal

tuna

dolphin

shark

octopus

hatchet fish

squid

rattail fish

viperfish

angler fish

snipe eel

tripod fish

sea cucumber

97

Ocean-Floor Field Trip

Imagine yourself on a field trip crossing the ocean floor. What do you think you would see? The same things you would see if you journeyed across the earth—mountains, valleys, and plains! Challenge each of your students to become *marine geologists*—scientists who study the geographic features of the ocean. Display and discuss the diagram of the ocean floor shown below. Then put students into groups of four and have each group use the following recipe to create a physical map of the ocean floor.

Materials per group:

transparent dish or pan (about 3 inches deep)
10–15 toothpicks
10–15 1" x 2" strips of paper
marker
transparent tape
spoon

4 cups flour
1 cup salt
1 1/2 cups water
food coloring (if desired)
large bowl

Directions:

1. Combine the flour and salt in a large bowl. Add the water and food coloring to the mixture, stirring until it forms a sticky dough. Knead the dough. (If the dough mixture is too sticky, add more flour.) The dough is ready to use when you can shape it into a smooth ball.
2. Place the dough mixture into the pan. Spread the mixture so that it touches each side of the pan.
3. Shape the dough, showing the contours and features of the ocean floor.
4. Using the marker and paper strips, label and define each ocean-floor feature. Tape each strip to a toothpick; then place the toothpicks in the dough mixture to identify each feature.
5. Let the dough dry; then share your group's physical map of the ocean floor with the class.

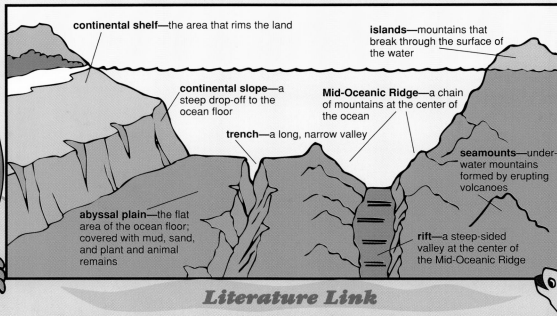

continental shelf—the area that rims the land

islands—mountains that break through the surface of the water

continental slope—a steep drop-off to the ocean floor

Mid-Oceanic Ridge—a chain of mountains at the center of the ocean

trench—a long, narrow valley

seamounts—underwater mountains formed by erupting volcanoes

abyssal plain—the flat area of the ocean floor; covered with mud, sand, and plant and animal remains

rift—a steep-sided valley at the center of the Mid-Oceanic Ridge

Literature Link

Fishing for some fascinating information about the ocean? Hook students into your ocean studies with these seaworthy books:

Fearsome Fish by Steve Parker; Raintree Steck-Vaughn Publishers, 1993
I Wonder Why The Sea Is Salty by Anita Ganeri; Larousse Kingfisher Chambers, Inc.; 1995
Hidden Treasures Of The Sea edited by Donald J. Crump; National Geographic Society, 1988
The Magic School Bus On The Ocean Floor by Joanna Cole; Scholastic Inc., 1992
Monsters Of The Deep by Norman S. Barrett; Franklin Watts, Inc.; 1991
Ocean: The Living World by Barbara Taylor; Dorling Kindersley, Inc.; 1994
Seas And Oceans by David Lambert and Anita McConnell; Facts On File, Inc.; 1985

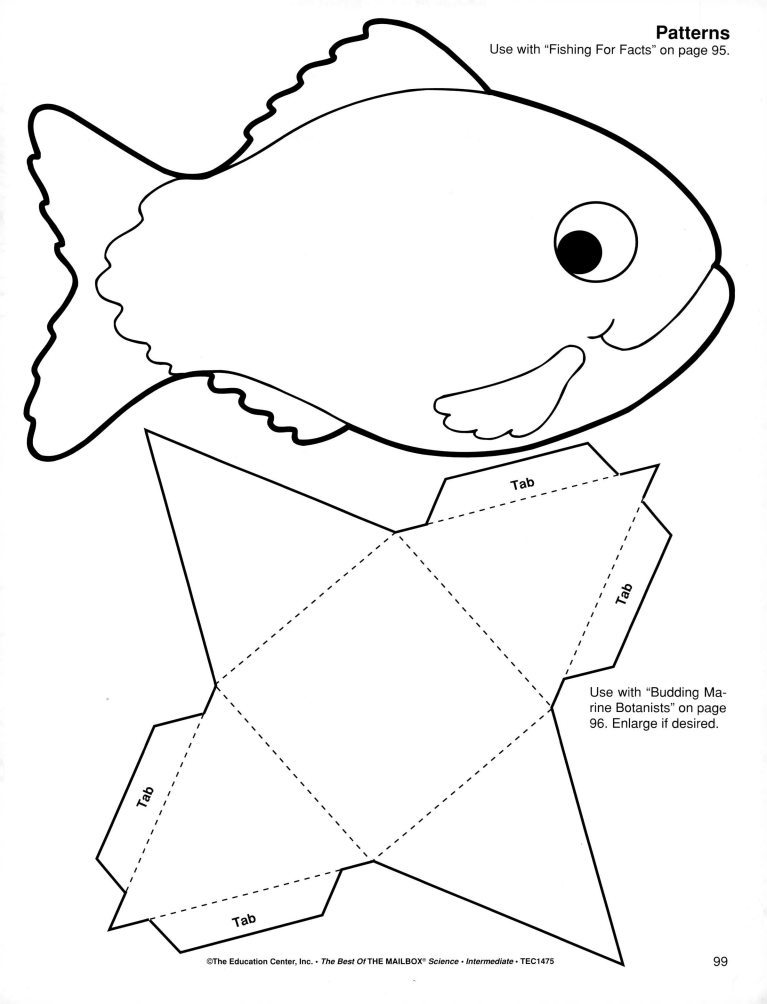

Tab

Tab

Tab

Use with "Budding Marine Botanists" on page 96. Enlarge if desired.

Tab

Something's Fishy!

Fish are found in an incredible variety of shapes, sizes, and colors. So how does an *ichthyologist* (a scientist who studies fish) keep track of them all? One way is to categorize fish. Fish can be put into groups based on their unique characteristics.

Professor Ich, a world-famous ichthyologist, needs an assistant to help him classify his fish. Study the characteristics of each fish; then group the fish into different categories based on their similarities and differences. (Each group should have at least two fish in it.) Glue the fish onto another sheet of paper showing the groupings. Label each group; then, on another piece of paper, tell why you included each fish in its group.

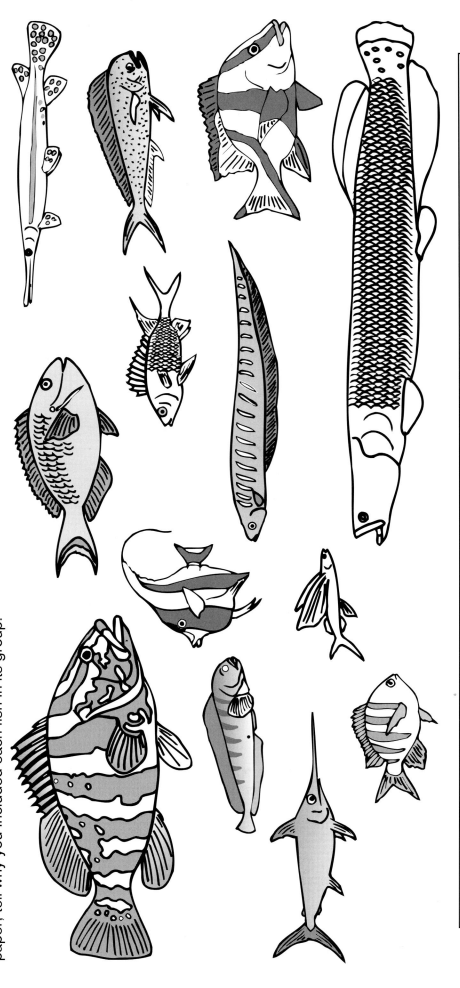

©The Education Center, Inc. • *The Best Of* THE MAILBOX® *Science • Intermediate* • TEC1475

Bonus Box: Compare your groupings with those of a classmate. In a paragraph in your journal, explain how your groupings were similar and different.

UNDERSEA TREASURE HUNT

Long ago, pirates used to scavenge the seas in search of treasures such as gold, jewels, and other precious cargo. Today we realize the sea has other treasures—its plants and animals.

Become a modern-day treasure hunter and learn more about these creatures of the sea. Answer the questions below on the back of this sheet. Use resource books and encyclopedias to help you. Color each coin yellow when you locate the answer to its question.

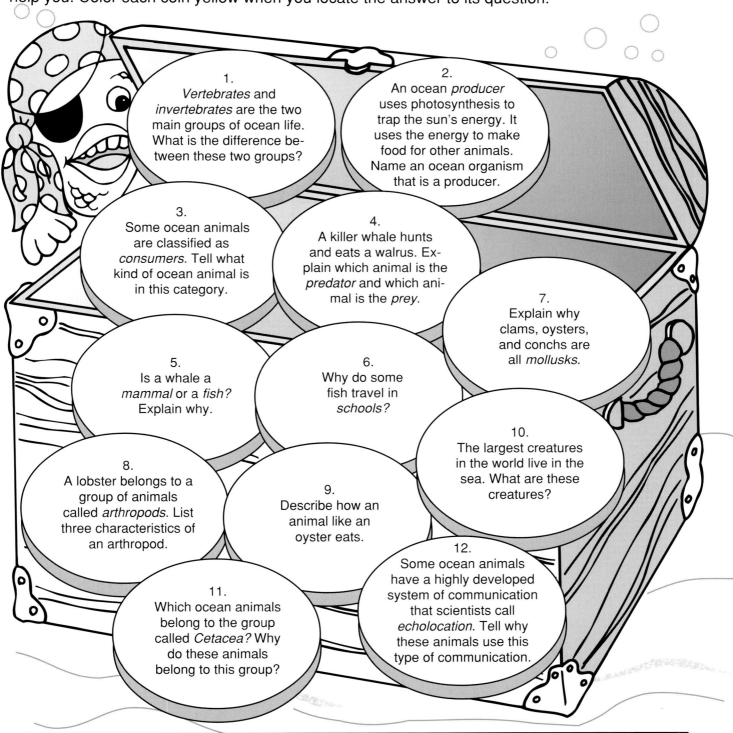

1. *Vertebrates* and *invertebrates* are the two main groups of ocean life. What is the difference between these two groups?

2. An ocean *producer* uses photosynthesis to trap the sun's energy. It uses the energy to make food for other animals. Name an ocean organism that is a producer.

3. Some ocean animals are classified as *consumers*. Tell what kind of ocean animal is in this category.

4. A killer whale hunts and eats a walrus. Explain which animal is the *predator* and which animal is the *prey*.

5. Is a whale a *mammal* or a *fish?* Explain why.

6. Why do some fish travel in *schools?*

7. Explain why clams, oysters, and conchs are all *mollusks*.

8. A lobster belongs to a group of animals called *arthropods*. List three characteristics of an arthropod.

9. Describe how an animal like an oyster eats.

10. The largest creatures in the world live in the sea. What are these creatures?

11. Which ocean animals belong to the group called *Cetacea?* Why do these animals belong to this group?

12. Some ocean animals have a highly developed system of communication that scientists call *echolocation*. Tell why these animals use this type of communication.

Bonus Box: On a large sheet of paper, draw and color a picture of an ocean-animal habitat. Include as many of the plants and animals listed above (with labels) as you can.

Aqua Tricks

Getting Your Feet Wet With Water Concepts

"Everything that's icy, moist, or wet, from the ocean to a drop of sweat..."—that's water! Flowing freely from our taps, water is something we tend to take for granted. Complete the following activities to instill in your students a deeper appreciation for this unique and vital resource.

by Christine Thuman

Water Is...

Treat your class to a visual journey of water images by reading aloud *Water* by Ken Robbins (Henry Holt and Company, Inc.) or *Water, Water Everywhere* by Mark J. Rauzon and Cynthia Overbeck Bix (Sierra Club Books for Children). Follow up by having each student describe and illustrate her most memorable water image by completing the sentence "Water is...." Bind these reflections into a class book by the same title.

Water, Water Everywhere?

Water covers nearly three-fourths of the earth's surface. Nevertheless, our watery planet contains very little drinkable, or *potable,* water. Human existence depends upon how we treat this fragile resource. Illustrate the scarcity of potable water using this introductory demonstration.

Provide each student with a 3 3/4-inch circle cut from construction paper. (Or duplicate the earth pattern on page 105 for each student.) As you model, have each student follow these directions:

1. Fold and cut the circle into four quarters.
2. Lay three of the quarters aside. *The remaining quarter represents the portion of the earth's surface that is NOT covered with salt water.* Cut this quarter in half to make two eighths. Set aside one eighth to represent all the land that is either too dry, hot, cold, or wet for people to live upon. *The remaining eighth represents the land that IS suitable for human habitation.*
3. Cut this last eighth into four equal pieces. Lay aside three of these pieces. *The remaining piece shows the part of the earth that is presently used for farming, supplying us with our food and clothing. This portion is not occupied by cities or highways.*
4. Cut a very small slice from this last piece. *This tiny sliver represents the 3/100 of 1% of the earth's surface which contains potable water.*

> That's all?

Aqua Maze

Did you know that every time you draw yourself a bath or pour a glass of lemonade you are using the same water that the dinosaurs used? For millions of years, our water recycled and cleansed itself through the amazing *hydrologic cycle.* Nevertheless, pure water is seldom found in nature. That's because water is an excellent *solvent.* Other substances dissolve readily into water. This means that as water travels up into plants, it carries with it minerals and nutrients. However, when harmful chemicals dissolve into water, they pollute the water, endangering plants, animals, and people.

Use the "Aqua Maze" game on page 106 to demonstrate the predicaments that water faces as it makes its way around the water cycle. Follow the directions on the page to complete the gameboard. After students have played the game, divide your class into groups to research the various water hazards they encountered.

Raindrops Keep Falling On My Head!

Drench your classroom in water wisdom by creating a rain shower of water facts. Cut a supply of raindrop shapes from light blue construction paper. Each time a student learns a new fact about water, have him write it on a raindrop. Suspend each raindrop from the ceiling with a length of fishing line.

Elise Nash—Gr. 5, Delaware Academy, Delhi, NY

Water Storage And Distribution

Imagine that you woke up one day to find your town's water supply shut down due to pollution. After solving the problem, you'd want to find ways to prevent that situation from reoccurring. In countries where water is scarce, people face these problems daily. Even in water-rich nations, cities and towns benefit from carefully planning how to store and use their limited supply of water.

Invite a representative from the water or health department to your class to discuss water storage and distribution in your community. Obtain a topographical map of your town; then have students trace your town's path of water distribution.

Planning A Water-Safe Community

What would a water-safe community look like? As a class, brainstorm the components of an imaginary community including roads, schools, shopping malls, parks, residential areas, business and downtown areas, factories, a landfill, a water source (reservoir, aquifer, river, etc.), a water treatment plant, and a sewage treatment plant. Discuss ways to safely and logically place these components within the community to ensure protection of the water supply.

Working in cooperative groups, have students design and draw plans for a water-safe community. Give each group a large sheet of newsprint to use for a rough draft. Once each group has sketched an acceptable plan, have the group transfer its plan to a sheet of 18" x 24" poster board or construction paper using markers or crayons. After completing the final drawing, have a representative from each group explain their plan, including how they arranged the community components and their rationale. Post the completed projects on a bulletin board under the heading "Planning A Water-Safe Community."

Finally discuss the group planning process with your students. How did working as a group help or hinder the planning process? How did group members feel when their ideas were accepted or rejected? What kinds of problems might a group of community planners face when working together?

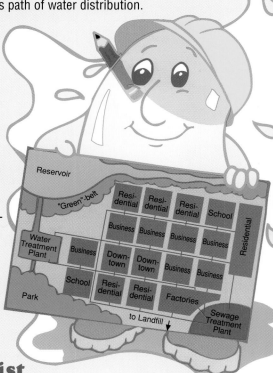

Literature/Resource List

The Magic School Bus At The Waterworks
Written by Joanna Cole; Illustrated by Bruce Degen
Published by Scholastic Inc.

The Water Cycle
Written by David Smith; Illustrated by John Yates
Published by Thomson Learning

The Sierra Club Kid's Guide To Planet Care & Repair
Written by Vicki McVey; Illustrated by Martha Weston
Published by Sierra Club Books for Children

Wonderful Water
Written and Illustrated by Bobbie Kalman and Janine Schaub
Published by Crabtree Publishing Company

Hands-On Experiments With H₂O

Dip into these simple experiments designed to illustrate some of the basic principles of water.

Water has a high surface tension. As insects skate over the surface of a pond, their feet make small depressions in the water's surface. Why don't they fall through? Water molecules are strongly attracted to each other. This property, called *cohesion,* causes the surface of water to act like a strong elastic membrane. As a result, water has a high *surface tension.* To demonstrate this concept, fill a small bowl half-full with water. Hold a small paper clip horizontally over the water. Carefully lower the clip so that it rests on the top of the water. Let go gently. The clip will float. You may need a couple of tries. Next add a drop of dishwashing liquid to the water. What happens? Soap inhibits the surface tension of water. This is useful when you want to clean dishes. However, what happens to animals if soapy waste water is dumped into a stream or river?

Water is upwardly mobile. If an object has tiny tubes in it, water will quickly move into those tubes because the air pressure inside the tubes is less than the pressure outside. This *capillary action* enables water and nutrients to travel up the trunks of trees. Demonstrate capillary action with these two experiments:

- Fill a cup one-quarter full with water. Use several drops of food coloring to darken the water. Trim off the bottom end of a celery stalk with a knife. Stand the cut end of the stalk in the water overnight. Observe the color of the stalk's upper leaves. The colored water has moved up through the leaves, pushed upward by the air pressure in the room.
- Think your paper towel is the "quicker picker upper"? Test your favorite brand against another. Cut a 2" x 6" strip from two different brands of paper towels. Designate one end of each strip as the dipping end; then draw a pencil mark a half-inch from the bottom of that end. Fill two small bowls with colored water. Dip the ends of each strip into the water up to the pencil line. Measure the distance that the colored water travels up the strip in 30 seconds. Which towel demonstrates better capillary action?

Water has a high specific heat. *Specific heat* is the amount of heat needed to raise the temperature of one gram of a substance by one degree Celsius. Substantial energy is required to break apart the strong hydrogen bonds of water. Consequently a large amount of heat is needed to raise the temperature of one gram of water one degree Celsius. The specific heat of water, measured as 1, is higher than that of any other substance. Water's high specific heat enables it to absorb large amounts of heat with little change in temperature. If you have ever been to the beach, you know that the ocean water in June is much cooler than the water in August. Furthermore, you can return to the beach in September and still find that the waters are relatively warm. This property makes water useful in cooling car engines and in circulating heat in home hot-water heating systems.

Demonstrate this property with the following experiment. Fill a paper cup half-full with cool tap water. Use a Celsius thermometer to measure the temperature of the water. Tell students that you are going to ignite the cup. Have them predict what will happen. Use a match to light the rim of the cup. The cup will burn down to the level of the water, but then the flame will go out. Measure the temperature of the water again. Has it changed?

Water clings. The following experiment demonstrates that water clings to water *(cohesion)* and to other objects *(adhesion)*. Have plenty of paper towels handy. This experiment—which works best with groups of two to four students—is sure to be a splash hit!

Soak a length of cotton string (about one meter) in water. Stretch the string between a beaker filled with colored water and the center of an empty cup (see the illustration). Holding the string taut, with one end always in the beaker of water, raise the beaker so that the angle of the string is about 30 degrees. Slowly pour the water out of the beaker. With a little practice and some adjustment to the angle, the water should move down the string and into the empty cup!

I say, old bean!

Water moves into objects. Water swells objects. Wet a dry sponge or take a long bath and notice your prunelike skin to observe this property known as *imbibition*. To demonstrate imbibition, measure the length and width of a dry kidney bean. Record these measurements. Place the bean in a cup half-filled with water and let it sit overnight. Take the bean out of the water the next day and measure its length and width. Compare your measurements. Water has soaked into *(or imbibed)* the bean, causing it to swell.

Pattern
Use with "Water, Water Everywhere?" on page 102.

Aqua Maze

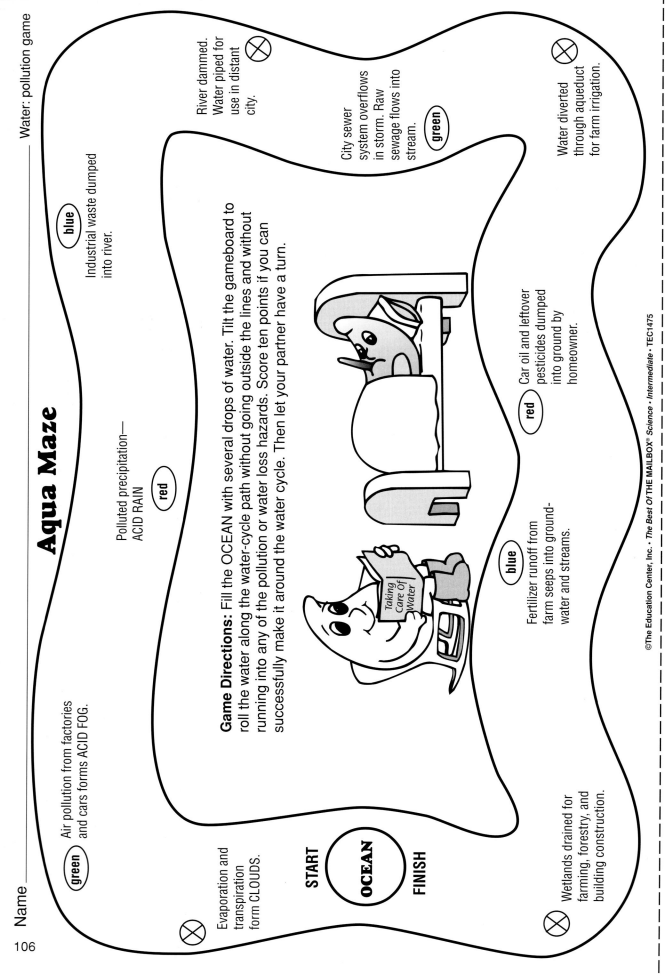

green Air pollution from factories and cars forms ACID FOG.

Evaporation and transpiration form CLOUDS.

red Polluted precipitation—ACID RAIN

blue Industrial waste dumped into river.

River dammed. Water piped for use in distant city.

City sewer system overflows in storm. Raw sewage flows into stream.

green

Water diverted through aqueduct for farm irrigation.

red Car oil and leftover pesticides dumped into ground by homeowner.

blue Fertilizer runoff from farm seeps into groundwater and streams.

Wetlands drained for farming, forestry, and building construction.

START

OCEAN

FINISH

Taking Care Of Water

Game Directions: Fill the OCEAN with several drops of water. Tilt the gameboard to roll the water along the water-cycle path without going outside the lines and without running into any of the pollution or water loss hazards. Score ten points if you can successfully make it around the water cycle. Then let your partner have a turn.

Preparing the gameboard: See "Aqua Maze" on page 102. Duplicate page 106 for each pair of students onto tagboard or white construction paper. Color the pollution hazards ◯ with markers as indicated. Laminate each gameboard; then punch a hole in each water loss hazard ⊗. Give each pair of students a gameboard, an eyedropper, and a small paper cup of water.

AIN'T NOTHING BUT A ROCKHOUND!

ROCKS AND MINERALS ACTIVITIES THAT CAN'T BE BEAT

Treat students to a rock 'n' rolling science experience with these hands-on activities about rocks and minerals!

by Cindy Mondello

MOVIN' ON:
TEACHER DEMONSTRATION

Erosion is the wearing away and moving of rock materials by natural forces. The main cause of erosion on the earth's surface is running water. To help students understand erosion, pour a mixture of half sand and half soil in an empty aquarium. Pile the mixture high on one end of the aquarium to form a steep hill with a flat top. Use a watering can to sprinkle "rain" softly on the soil. Have students watch what happens. *(The running water carries away some of the soil as it travels down the slope.)* Then have students observe what happens when you make it rain harder. *(More of the soil and sand mixture will be carried down the slope.)* Next plant some grass or plant clippings on the hilltop and hillside, and repeat the sprinkling. Ask students how the plants change the erosion process. *(Plants are the best protection against soil erosion. Plants, grass, trunks of trees, and exposed roots help slow the speed of runoff. When water travels slowly, it has less carrying force.)* As a follow-up activity, have students research to find other causes of erosion.

MAKIN' DEPOSITS:
STUDENT ACTIVITY

Bank on the fact that students will understand the concept of deposition with the following activity. *Deposition* is the settling of materials carried by the agents of erosion—water, wind, and ice. Have students predict what will happen to rock particles of different sizes when they are deposited by water. Then divide students into groups of four to complete the following experiment:

Materials for each group: equal amounts of sand, gravel, and pebbles; large jar with lid; water

Procedure:
1. Mix together the sand, gravel, and pebbles in the jar.
2. Add water until the jar is about three-fourths full.
3. Secure the lid on the jar.
4. Shake the jar carefully until the contents are thoroughly mixed.
5. Allow the contents to settle.

Have students observe how long it takes for the materials to settle. Then ask: "What happened to the jar's contents when it was set down? Do you see different layers on the bottom? What is different about them? How do you think materials settle in rivers or streams?" Conclude by having each student make a sketch of the jar, labeling each layer correctly.

MATERIALS LIST

- soil
- sand
- watering can
- grass clippings or clippings from a plant or bush
- water
- newspaper
- waxed paper
- dark bread (two slices)
- white bread (one slice)
- scissors
- glue sticks
- gravel
- pebbles
- large jars with lids (one for each group of four)
- plastic drinking straws (one per child)
- modeling clay
- white vinegar
- glass jars (one for each group of four)
- unglazed ceramic tile
- large aquarium (empty)
- marble chips (found at a plant nursery)
- assortment of minerals (collected from nature or purchased at a hobby store)
- rock-and-mineral field guides

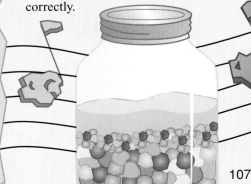

ROCK SANDWICH, ANYONE?: TEACHER DEMONSTRATION

One of the three types of rocks is *metamorphic rock*. Help students discover how metamorphic rock is formed with the following demonstration. Place several sheets of newspaper on the floor. Position a sheet of waxed paper on top of the newspaper. Stack three pieces of bread on the waxed paper—a white slice between two dark slices. Cover the bread with another sheet of waxed paper. Walk across the "rock sandwich" several times. Then cut the sandwich in half with scissors. Have each student describe the inside of the sandwich. Follow up the demonstration by having students define the three types of rocks (*igneous, sedimentary,* and *metamorphic*) in their science journals. *(The three slices of bread represent three layers of sedimentary rock. When pressure was applied to the rock, it changed into metamorphic rock. Metamorphic rocks are formed by changes in igneous or sedimentary rocks. These rocks may be changed to metamorphic rocks by extreme heat and pressure. Metamorphic rocks are found beneath the earth's surface and are generally the hardest and densest of the three types of rock.)*

BREAKING UP IS HARD TO DO: STUDENT ACTIVITY

New rocks are formed while others are broken apart and changed. This breakup and change of rocks and minerals is called *weathering*. There are two main types of weathering: *physical weathering* and *chemical weathering*. The simple experiments below will help your students understand the differences in the two.

Physical Weathering: How does freezing water break up rocks?
Materials for each student: 1 plastic drinking straw, modeling clay, water
Procedure:
1. Seal one end of the drinking straw with clay. Make sure the clay does not extend past the end of the straw.
2. Fill the straw with water.
3. Seal the other end of the drinking straw with clay.
4. Place the straw in a freezer for 24 hours.
5. Observe the straw the next day. What has happened? How does this relate to physical weathering? *(The clay plugs have been pushed out of the straw and a column of ice is extending past the ends of the straw. Water expands when it freezes. When water gets into cracks in and around rocks, it can actually move or break the rocks when it freezes.)*

Chemical Weathering: How does rain chemically weather rocks?
Materials for each group of four students: marble chips, glass jar, white vinegar
Procedure:
1. Place marble chips in the glass jar.
2. Fill the jar with white vinegar, a mild acid.
3. Observe and record the effect of the vinegar on the rocks for one or two days. *(Raindrops dissolve small amounts of carbon dioxide from the air. When water and carbon dioxide combine,* carbonic acid *is formed. Rocks can be weathered by acidic rain. Rocks containing limestone weather more quickly than others. Minerals such as calcite, gypsum, and halite are also dissolved by the carbonic acid in rainwater.)*

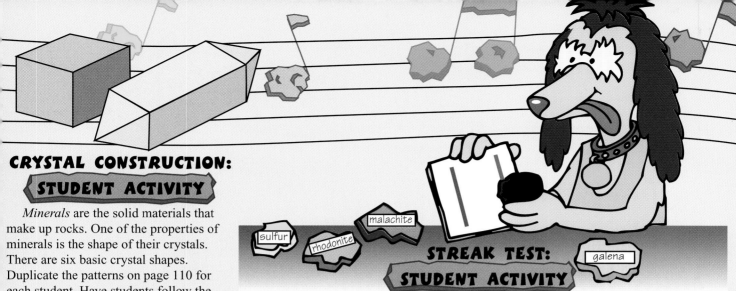

CRYSTAL CONSTRUCTION:
STUDENT ACTIVITY

Minerals are the solid materials that make up rocks. One of the properties of minerals is the shape of their crystals. There are six basic crystal shapes. Duplicate the patterns on page 110 for each student. Have students follow the directions on the page to make models of *cubic* and *tetragonal* crystals. Encourage students to use rock-and-mineral guides to find the names of the other four crystal systems and examples of each one. *(The six basic crystal shapes and examples of minerals are* cubic *[halite, galena],* tetragonal *[zircon, chalcopyrite],* hexagonal *[quartz, calcite],* orthorhombic *[sulfur, staurolite],* monoclinic *[mica, gypsum], and* triclinic *[feldspar, rhodonite].)*

STREAK TEST:
STUDENT ACTIVITY

Another way of identifying a mineral is by the colored mark it makes when rubbed against a piece of unglazed porcelain. This color is known as the mineral's *streak.* Make a streak test kit with an assortment of minerals and an unglazed ceramic tile. Ask several student volunteers to rub the edge of each mineral along the ceramic tile. Have students compare the colors of the different minerals with the colors of the streaks that were made. *(Color cannot always be used as a clue to the identity of an unknown mineral. Some minerals are always the same color, but the colors of other minerals may vary. A streak test is more reliable than a mineral's color. For example, malachite is a green mineral that makes a green streak, and sulfur is a yellow mineral that makes a yellow streak. Hematite, on the other hand, is a mineral that can be either black or red, but always makes a red streak.)* Have each student or group use a rock-and-mineral field guide to make a streak chart as a reference for further mineral studies.

DIGGING UP ROCKS AND MINERALS

Dig up rocks and minerals for the activities in this unit by contacting the geology departments of local colleges and universities for information. To purchase rocks and minerals that don't occur naturally in your area, check the Yellow Pages for local rock-and-mineral shops or teacher supply stores. The following stores carry rocks and minerals and are located in many areas. To find the stores nearest you, call the home offices listed below:

The Nature Company
750 Hearst Avenue
Berkeley, CA 94710
(510) 644-1337

The Discovery
Channel Store
750 Hearst Avenue
Berkeley, CA 94710
(510) 644-1337

The Nature
Of Things Store
10700 W. Venture Drive
Franklin, WI 53132
(800) 283-2921

World Of Science, Inc.
900 Jefferson Road, Bldg. 4
Rochester, NY 14623
(716) 475-0100

REFERENCE BOOKS FOR ROCKHOUNDS

Rocks And Minerals by Alan Woolley (EDC Publishing, 1992)

The Magic School Bus Inside The Earth by Joanna Cole (Scholastic Inc., 1987)

Adventures With Rocks And Minerals, Book II: Geology Experiments For Young People by Lloyd H. Barrow (Enslow Publishers, Inc.; 1995)

The New York Public Library Incredible Earth: A Book Of Answers For Kids by Ann-Jeanette Campbell and Ronald Rood (John Wiley & Sons, 1996)

Rocks And Minerals edited by Lisa Miles (EDC Publishing, 1997)

Patterns

Use with "Crystal Construction" on page 109.
Provide students with scissors and glue sticks.

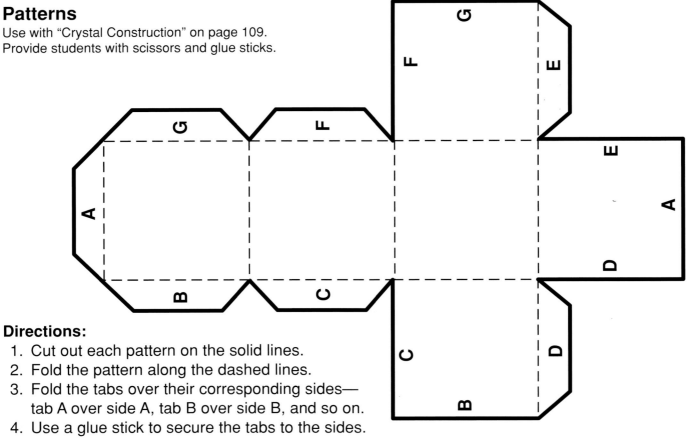

Directions:

1. Cut out each pattern on the solid lines.
2. Fold the pattern along the dashed lines.
3. Fold the tabs over their corresponding sides—tab A over side A, tab B over side B, and so on.
4. Use a glue stick to secure the tabs to the sides.

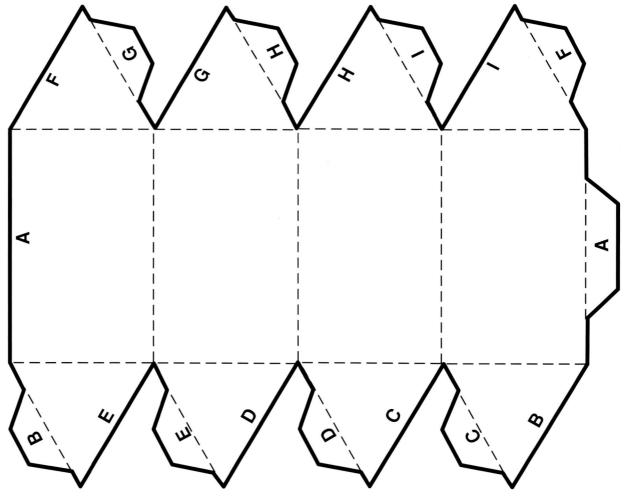

Name_____ Experiment

MINING FOR MMM-GOOD MINERALS

Some rocks contain large amounts of minerals. These rocks are called *mineral deposits.* A mineral deposit that can be mined for profit is called an *ore.* Silver, gold, and asbestos are examples of ores. However, there can be problems with the mining of ores. A mine may cover a very large area and may reach deep into the earth's surface. This digging up of very large areas of land can cause environmental problems.

Complete the following activity to help you understand the difficulty in reaching ores. You will also discover how land is lost during mining.

Materials for each student: 1 chocolate-chip cookie, toothpick, plastic drinking straw, paper towel, centimeter ruler, clock

MINING RULES
1. Your mine will earn $1,000 for every 2 cm of straw that is filled with chocolate pieces.
2. The value of your chip mine goes down $100 just for mining it.
3. You will be charged $100 for every five minutes it takes to mine the chocolate.
4. You will be fined $100 for each cookie piece that breaks off. The more damage you cause, the more money you lose.

PART I: MINING & PROCESSING
1. Examine the chocolate-chip cookie mine (your cookie). How many "minerals" (chocolate chips) can you see on the surface? _____
2. Record your starting time: _____
3. Use the toothpick to carefully dig out the minerals. You may *look* at the bottom of the cookie, but you may only mine it from the top.
4. To process your minerals, separate the crumbs from the chocolate you have mined.
5. Record your ending time: _____
6. Record your total mining and processing time: _____ minutes
7. Total Mining & Processing Fee ($100 per every five minutes): $ _____

PART II: LAND DAMAGE
1. Chip Mine Fee: $100
2. Land Damage: Count the cookie pieces that broke off as you worked: _____
   # of cookie pieces x $100 = $ _____
3. Total Land Damage + Chip Mine Fee: $_____

PART III: MEASURE MINERALS
1. Pick up the mined chocolate pieces with the straw.
2. Measure the amount of chocolate in the straw: _____ cm
3. Record the value of your minerals ($1,000 for every 2 cm of straw filled): $ _____

PART IV: COMPUTE PROFIT
Total Mining & Processing Fee $_____ +

Total Land Damage Fee $_____ =

Total Cost $_____

Value of Minerals $_____ −

Total Cost $_____ =

Total Profit $_____

PART V: CONCLUSIONS
Write your answers on the back of this sheet.

1. How is your chip mine like a real one?
2. How is it different?
3. What happened to the land while you were mining?
4. How could you repair the land?

A Vanishing Treasure

A Thematic Unit On The Tropical Rain Forest

Two hundred years ago, 20 percent of the earth's land was covered with rain forests. Today, that figure has dropped to an alarming seven percent. What has caused the devastation, and why should we be concerned? Explore these questions with the following creative activities, reproducibles, and ready-to-use booklet project.

by David Yeager and Susan Barnett

Background For The Teacher

Peer into the thick, leafy canopy of a tropical rain forest and what will you see? Over half of the world's species of plants and animals. Oxygen suppliers and a crucial link in the water cycle. Tribal groups who live in much the same way as their Stone Age ancestors. Huge trees holding soil in place, preventing floods and erosion. Rare plants that provide vital ingredients for medicines. A vast array of irreplaceable riches—that's what you'll see.

But the tropical rain forest is fast becoming a vanishing area. At a rate of 100 acres per minute, rain forests are being cut down to make room for cash crops, dams, farms and cattle ranches, and logging operations. Because of recent conservation efforts, your students may already know a thing or two about the rain forest. Start your journey into the rain forest by posting these trivia:

Tropical Rain Forest Trivia

- Scientists estimate that a rain forest area the size of a football field is destroyed *each second*.
- Tropical rain forests have up to 80 and as much as 240 inches of rain a year. It rains more than 200 days a year.
- About 3,000 rain forest plants can be used to make medicines that fight cancer.
- A few acres of rain forest in the Amazon River Basin have more species of plants than in all of Europe.
- An estimated 50 species of plants and animals become extinct *every day*.
- In a Central American rain forest, you could find 950 different kinds of beetles on one large tree!
- Rain forests grow in more than 50 countries. Most are found in Brazil, Indonesia, and Zaire.

Teeming With Life: An Experiment

To convey to students just how much life there really is in the rain forest, try this simple experiment. Give each student a three-foot length of yarn. Have the student tie the ends of the yarn together to make a large loop. Head outdoors; then have each child place his loop on a small area of your school grounds. Have students look very carefully and count/record all the different kinds of plants and animals inside their loops. After five or ten minutes, call students back together and have them share their results. Then tell them that the same amount of space in a rain forest would have *ten times* as many kinds of life!

Going, Going, Gone!

When rain forests are destroyed, so are the habitats of many living things. Particularly at risk are *endemic* species—plants or animals that are found only in one area. For example, gorillas are limited to central Africa. Destroying the habitat of endemic species easily results in extinction.

Highlight the awesome variety of animal life in the rain forest by challenging students to become rain forest zoologists. Have each student choose an animal to research from the list below. Challenge students to find out not only about their animals' physical characteristics but also about how they are specially suited to survive in the rain forest and why they should be protected from extinction. Let your young zoologists share their information on some of the most widely read items in the world—cereal boxes! To make a boxed report, have a student use rubber cement to cover an empty cereal box with butcher or construction paper. Instruct him to glue his facts (written on index cards) and captioned illustrations to the box. Display the finished boxes on a table, grouping them according to the rain forest layer (canopy, understory, or floor) in which each animal is found. Encourage sharing by letting students check out a boxed report overnight to read at breakfast the next morning!

Rain forest animals to research:

jaguar	woolly spotted monkey
tiger	bird of paradise
lemur	tapir
okapi	black vulture
scarlet ibis	poison arrow frog
three-toed sloth	anaconda
gecko	black caiman
tarsier monkey	mynah bird
giant otter	Asian rhinoceros
mountain gorilla	golden lion tamarin
orangutan	toucan
harpy eagle	red-eyed tree frog
iguana	leaf-cutter ant
ocelot	Morelet's crocodile

A New Species

Add an exercise in creative thinking to your rain forest study. Scientists believe that most of the plants and animals in the rain forest have not even been discovered yet. Instruct students to pretend that they have just encountered an unknown rain forest animal or plant. Have each child draw a picture of his discovery, labeling parts that make it adaptable to life in the tropics. In addition to his drawing, have the student write a diary entry naming his discovery and describing how he encountered it, in what rain forest layer his discovery lives, and the role it plays in the interdependent life of the rain forest. Bind the pictures and entries in a class book entitled *New Rain Forest Residents*.

Build A Forest Floor

Unlike many of the forests of North America, the tropical rain forest cannot recover once it is cut. The soil beneath the rain forest is very weak and not fertile enough to support the thick growth of trees and plants. Rather, forest plants and trees are fed by a top layer of decaying leaves and other vegetable materials.

Create your own rain forest floor and watch as it grows. Provide each student with a quart-sized, plastic freezer bag. Head outdoors and have each student collect one or two handfuls of drying leaves and twigs. Have each student break the leaves and twigs into small pieces; then have him place the pieces into the bag. Add a tablespoon of water and two pinches of blood meal (available at most garden shops and hardware stores) to the bag. Label each bag with a student's name and the date; then place the bags in a warm place, such as near a sunny window.

Check the bags every three days, watching for signs of growth. After several days, students should begin to notice the rapid decomposition of the plant material and the growth of bacteria. Some of the samples may even begin growing mushrooms (which are *not* edible). As students observe and record the growth in their science journals, ask questions such as:

- Do you notice any change in your sample from the previous observation?
- What color changes have occurred?
- Are there any signs of new growth? How would you describe the appearance of this new growth? Is it light or dark in color?
- Does this new growth look like it will grow to become a green leafy plant or a fungi?

Once the decomposition process is complete, drop a seed into each bag and begin a second round of observations. The seed should sprout and grow quickly. Explain to students that it is the nutrients from the "forest floor" that contribute to the life of the seed.

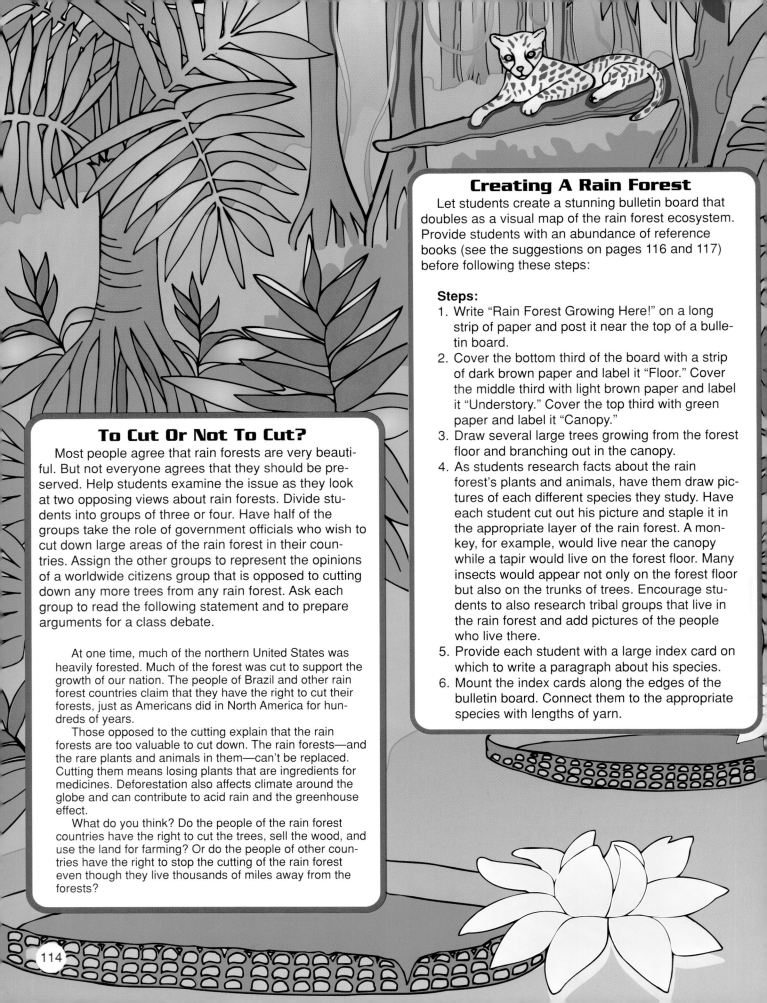

Creating A Rain Forest

Let students create a stunning bulletin board that doubles as a visual map of the rain forest ecosystem. Provide students with an abundance of reference books (see the suggestions on pages 116 and 117) before following these steps:

Steps:
1. Write "Rain Forest Growing Here!" on a long strip of paper and post it near the top of a bulletin board.
2. Cover the bottom third of the board with a strip of dark brown paper and label it "Floor." Cover the middle third with light brown paper and label it "Understory." Cover the top third with green paper and label it "Canopy."
3. Draw several large trees growing from the forest floor and branching out in the canopy.
4. As students research facts about the rain forest's plants and animals, have them draw pictures of each different species they study. Have each student cut out his picture and staple it in the appropriate layer of the rain forest. A monkey, for example, would live near the canopy while a tapir would live on the forest floor. Many insects would appear not only on the forest floor but also on the trunks of trees. Encourage students to also research tribal groups that live in the rain forest and add pictures of the people who live there.
5. Provide each student with a large index card on which to write a paragraph about his species.
6. Mount the index cards along the edges of the bulletin board. Connect them to the appropriate species with lengths of yarn.

To Cut Or Not To Cut?

Most people agree that rain forests are very beautiful. But not everyone agrees that they should be preserved. Help students examine the issue as they look at two opposing views about rain forests. Divide students into groups of three or four. Have half of the groups take the role of government officials who wish to cut down large areas of the rain forest in their countries. Assign the other groups to represent the opinions of a worldwide citizens group that is opposed to cutting down any more trees from any rain forest. Ask each group to read the following statement and to prepare arguments for a class debate.

At one time, much of the northern United States was heavily forested. Much of the forest was cut to support the growth of our nation. The people of Brazil and other rain forest countries claim that they have the right to cut their forests, just as Americans did in North America for hundreds of years.

Those opposed to the cutting explain that the rain forests are too valuable to cut down. The rain forests—and the rare plants and animals in them—can't be replaced. Cutting them means losing plants that are ingredients for medicines. Deforestation also affects climate around the globe and can contribute to acid rain and the greenhouse effect.

What do you think? Do the people of the rain forest countries have the right to cut the trees, sell the wood, and use the land for farming? Or do the people of other countries have the right to stop the cutting of the rain forest even though they live thousands of miles away from the forests?

Destroying A Rain Forest

Use the student-created bulletin board described in "Creating A Rain Forest" on page 114 to illustrate the reasons for rain forest destruction. Replace the title at the top of the board with a new title strip labeled "The Disappearing Rain Forest." Remove one section of the bulletin board at a time over several days, beginning with the canopy and ending with the floor. As a section is removed, transfer the students' drawings to a wall space which you've labeled "In Danger Of Extinction." As the board finally becomes bare, discuss with students the causes of rain forest deforestation: shortage of land for crops, logging, farms and cattle ranches, cash crops, shortage of fuel wood, mining, and new towns and dams. Let students draw pictures of such items as bulldozers, livestock, and farm implements to depict the causes of deforestation. Mount these on the bare board for a stark visual display of a rain forest's demise.

Want More Information?

If you and your students want more information about the rain forest or suggestions on how you can get involved in saving this precious resource, contact the following organizations. (Please: only one request per class.)

Rainforest Action Network
221 Pine Street, Suite 500
San Francisco, CA 94104

Rainforest Alliance
65 Bleecker Street, 6th Floor
New York, NY 10012-2420

Earthwatch Headquarters
680 Mount Auburn Street
P.O. Box 1904
Watertown, MA 02471

Around The World

Exactly where are these rain forests we keep hearing about? Use the following activities to weave a strand of geography into your rain forest unit:

• Most of the remaining tropical rain forests are located in the region between the Tropic of Cancer and Tropic of Capricorn. Provide each student with a copy of the outline map on page 118. Have students use wall maps, globes, or a student atlas to identify and label the countries in which tropical rain forests are found.

• Have students write to the United Nations ambassador of each country, asking for information on that country's rain forest policy. Send letters to: U.N. Ambassador for (name of country), United Nations, New York, NY 10017.

• Arrange the class into teams of three or four students each. Assign a rain forest country to each group. Provide resource materials on the countries. Have each team locate five of the most fascinating facts it can find about its country. Have team members illustrate their facts on a piece of poster board, adding illustrations. Display the posters for several days; then have the class vote on the five most fascinating facts from all of the posters.

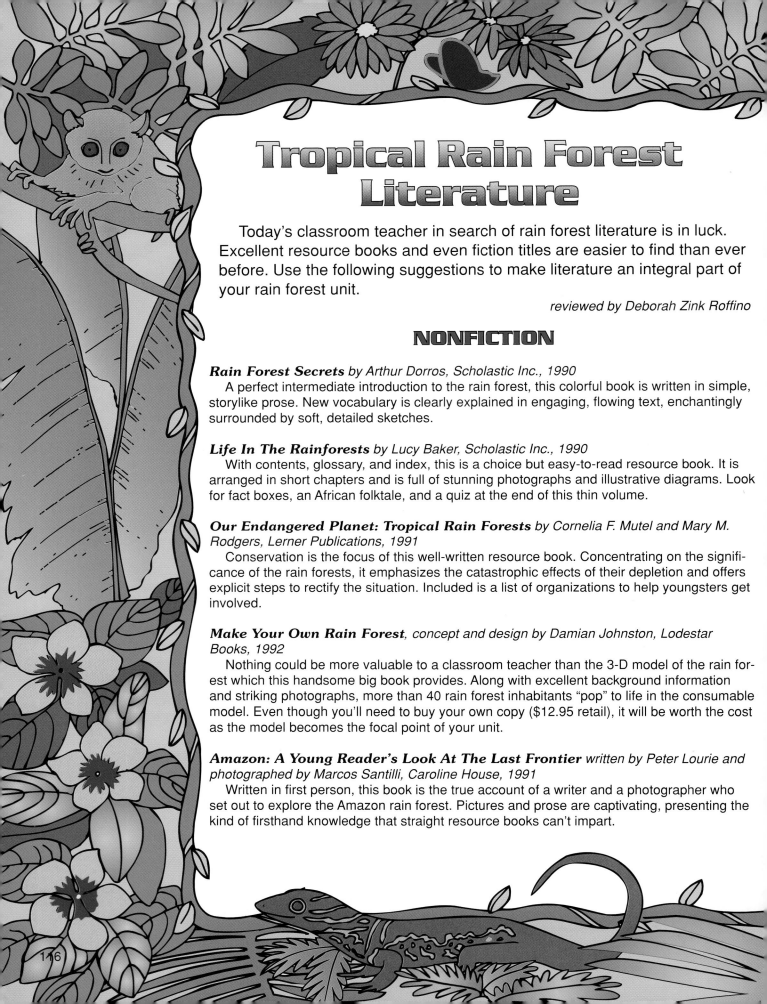

Tropical Rain Forest Literature

Today's classroom teacher in search of rain forest literature is in luck. Excellent resource books and even fiction titles are easier to find than ever before. Use the following suggestions to make literature an integral part of your rain forest unit.

reviewed by Deborah Zink Roffino

NONFICTION

Rain Forest Secrets by Arthur Dorros, Scholastic Inc., 1990
   A perfect intermediate introduction to the rain forest, this colorful book is written in simple, storylike prose. New vocabulary is clearly explained in engaging, flowing text, enchantingly surrounded by soft, detailed sketches.

Life In The Rainforests by Lucy Baker, Scholastic Inc., 1990
   With contents, glossary, and index, this is a choice but easy-to-read resource book. It is arranged in short chapters and is full of stunning photographs and illustrative diagrams. Look for fact boxes, an African folktale, and a quiz at the end of this thin volume.

Our Endangered Planet: Tropical Rain Forests by Cornelia F. Mutel and Mary M. Rodgers, Lerner Publications, 1991
   Conservation is the focus of this well-written resource book. Concentrating on the significance of the rain forests, it emphasizes the catastrophic effects of their depletion and offers explicit steps to rectify the situation. Included is a list of organizations to help youngsters get involved.

Make Your Own Rain Forest, concept and design by Damian Johnston, Lodestar Books, 1992
   Nothing could be more valuable to a classroom teacher than the 3-D model of the rain forest which this handsome big book provides. Along with excellent background information and striking photographs, more than 40 rain forest inhabitants "pop" to life in the consumable model. Even though you'll need to buy your own copy ($12.95 retail), it will be worth the cost as the model becomes the focal point of your unit.

Amazon: A Young Reader's Look At The Last Frontier written by Peter Lourie and photographed by Marcos Santilli, Caroline House, 1991
   Written in first person, this book is the true account of a writer and a photographer who set out to explore the Amazon rain forest. Pictures and prose are captivating, presenting the kind of firsthand knowledge that straight resource books can't impart.

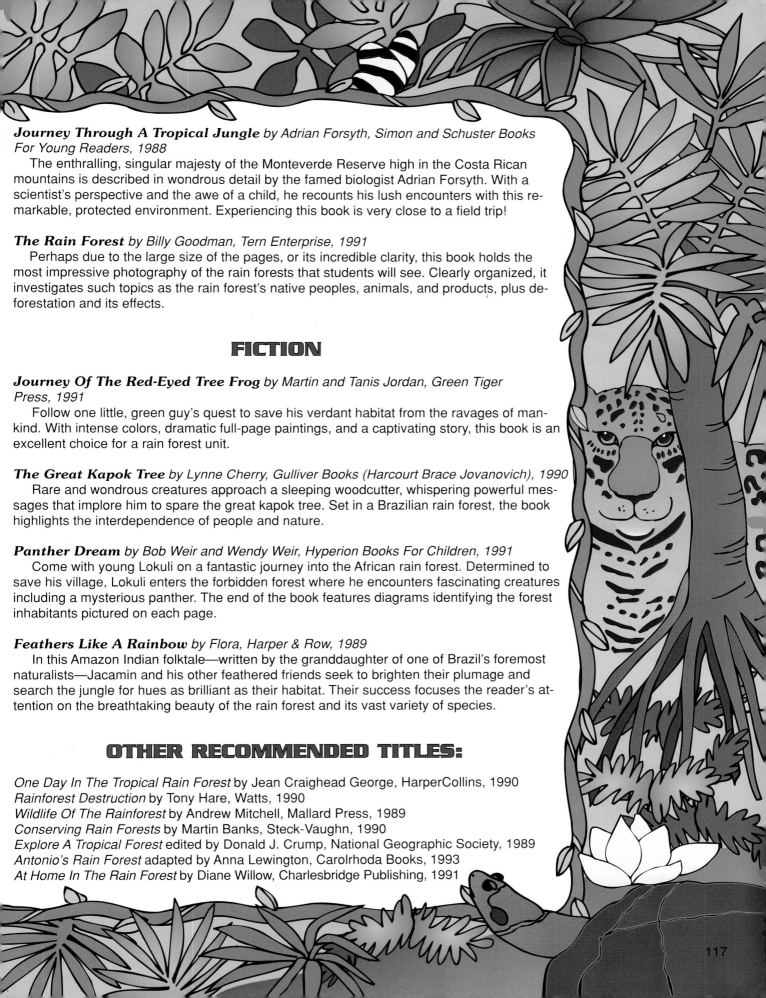

Journey Through A Tropical Jungle by Adrian Forsyth, Simon and Schuster Books
For Young Readers, 1988
    The enthralling, singular majesty of the Monteverde Reserve high in the Costa Rican
mountains is described in wondrous detail by the famed biologist Adrian Forsyth. With a
scientist's perspective and the awe of a child, he recounts his lush encounters with this re-
markable, protected environment. Experiencing this book is very close to a field trip!

The Rain Forest by Billy Goodman, Tern Enterprise, 1991
    Perhaps due to the large size of the pages, or its incredible clarity, this book holds the
most impressive photography of the rain forests that students will see. Clearly organized, it
investigates such topics as the rain forest's native peoples, animals, and products, plus deforestation and its effects.

FICTION

Journey Of The Red-Eyed Tree Frog by Martin and Tanis Jordan, Green Tiger
Press, 1991
    Follow one little, green guy's quest to save his verdant habitat from the ravages of man-
kind. With intense colors, dramatic full-page paintings, and a captivating story, this book is an
excellent choice for a rain forest unit.

The Great Kapok Tree by Lynne Cherry, Gulliver Books (Harcourt Brace Jovanovich), 1990
    Rare and wondrous creatures approach a sleeping woodcutter, whispering powerful mes-
sages that implore him to spare the great kapok tree. Set in a Brazilian rain forest, the book
highlights the interdependence of people and nature.

Panther Dream by Bob Weir and Wendy Weir, Hyperion Books For Children, 1991
    Come with young Lokuli on a fantastic journey into the African rain forest. Determined to
save his village, Lokuli enters the forbidden forest where he encounters fascinating creatures
including a mysterious panther. The end of the book features diagrams identifying the forest
inhabitants pictured on each page.

Feathers Like A Rainbow by Flora, Harper & Row, 1989
    In this Amazon Indian folktale—written by the granddaughter of one of Brazil's foremost
naturalists—Jacamin and his other feathered friends seek to brighten their plumage and
search the jungle for hues as brilliant as their habitat. Their success focuses the reader's attention on the breathtaking beauty of the rain forest and its vast variety of species.

OTHER RECOMMENDED TITLES:

One Day In The Tropical Rain Forest by Jean Craighead George, HarperCollins, 1990
Rainforest Destruction by Tony Hare, Watts, 1990
Wildlife Of The Rainforest by Andrew Mitchell, Mallard Press, 1989
Conserving Rain Forests by Martin Banks, Steck-Vaughn, 1990
Explore A Tropical Forest edited by Donald J. Crump, National Geographic Society, 1989
Antonio's Rain Forest adapted by Anna Lewington, Carolrhoda Books, 1993
At Home In The Rain Forest by Diane Willow, Charlesbridge Publishing, 1991

Name _____

Tropical Rain Forests Of The World

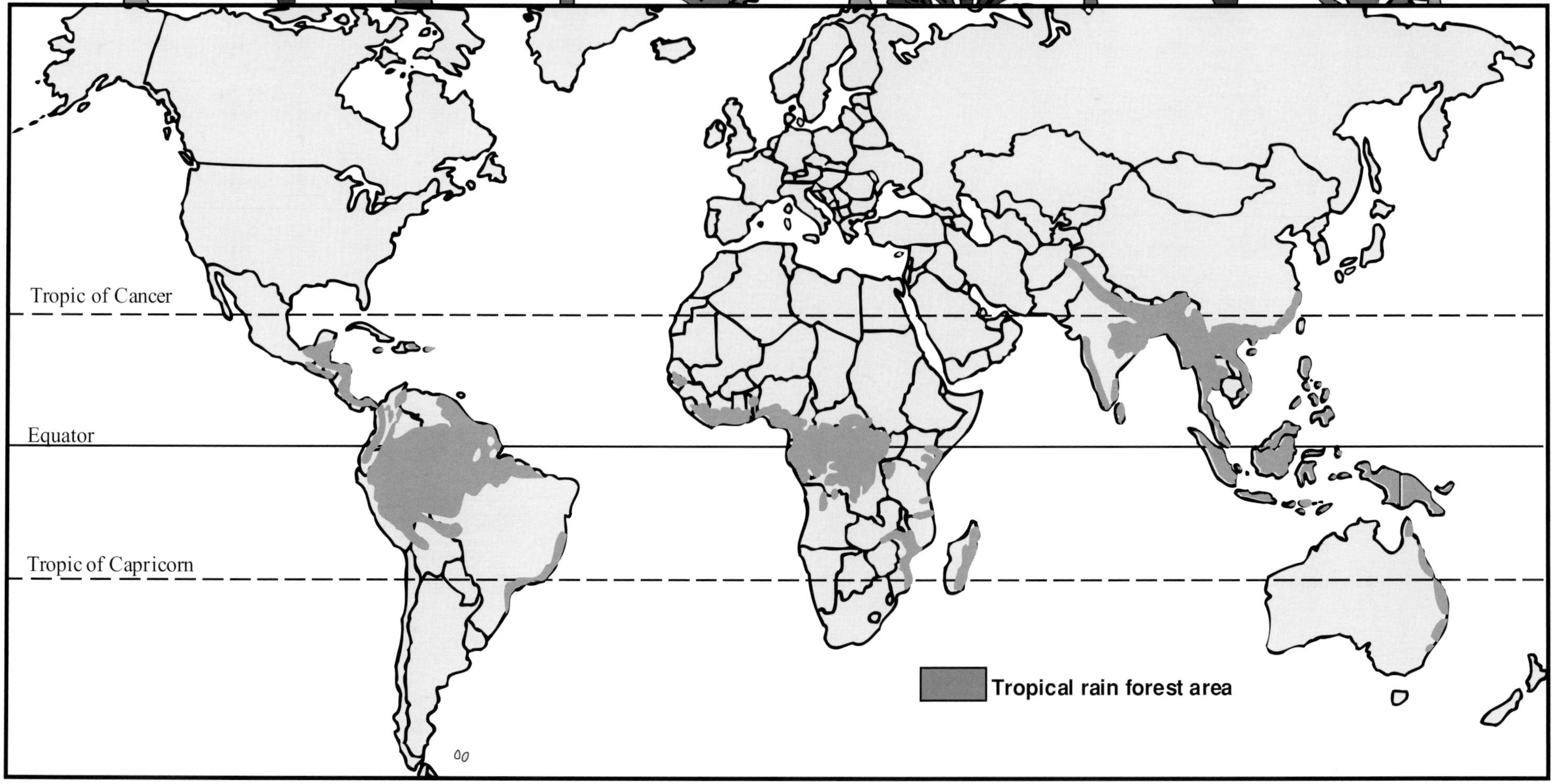

Tropical rain forest area

Tropic of Cancer

Equator

Tropic of Capricorn

118

Note To Teacher: Use this map with the half-page activity sheet on page 119.

Name _____

Tropical Rain Forests Of The World Activity Sheet

Use a world map or globe to help you complete these activities on the map on page 118.

1. Label these six continents: North America, South America, Australia, Europe, Asia, Africa.

2. Label these oceans: Atlantic, Pacific, Indian.

3. Below are some of the countries which have tropical rain forests. Label each country on the map.

Costa Rica	Panama
Colombia	Ecuador
Brazil	Guyana
Zaire	Nigeria
Cameroon	Congo
Gabon	Madagascar
India	Thailand
Indonesia	Papua New Guinea

4. Label the Amazon River in Brazil.

Bonus Box: On the back of this page, list ten countries in which there are no tropical rain forests.

Note To Teacher: Use with the reproducible map on page 118.

©The Education Center, Inc. • *The Best Of* THE MAILBOX® *Science • Intermediate* • TEC1475

Name _____

Worth Saving?

Below are reasons why tropical rain forests should be saved. Discuss each reason with your group or partner. In the blank, write the number that best expresses your opinion about each reason.

> **1**=very important to me
> **2**=important to me
> **3**=somewhat important to me
> **4**=not very important to me
> **5**=not important to me at all

____ Rain forests have unique plants for new foods, medicines, and other products.

____ The rain forest is home to many rare animals and plants. Destroying rain forests could make these species extinct.

____ Cutting rain forests causes problems such as soil erosion and water pollution in the rain forest countries.

____ Rain forest products (bananas, nuts, wood, etc.) will become scarce and more expensive if rain forests are destroyed.

____ Many birds migrate to the rain forest in the winter. Losing rain forests could endanger these species.

____ The rain forest is home to different peoples. No one has the right to destroy these peoples' homes and ways of life.

____ The rain forest helps clean our planet's air.

____ Destroying the rain forest could change weather patterns. Deforestation could cause more droughts and deserts.

____ The rain forest is a beautiful place with many awesome plants and animals.

Now design a "Save The Rain Forest" poster that illustrates the reasons that you marked with a 1 or a 2.

©The Education Center, Inc. • *The Best Of* THE MAILBOX® *Science • Intermediate* • TEC1475

Name ____

Made In The Rain Forest

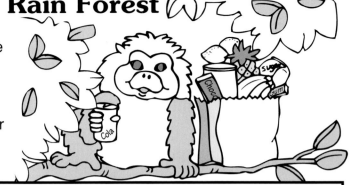

Did you know that many of the items in your home probably came from the rain forest? Take this checklist home; then check any item that you find in your home. Don't forget to read the labels on food products and other items to see if any of their ingredients come from the rain forest or near the rain forest.

FRUITS/VEGETABLES

___ avocado
___ banana
___ grapefruit
___ guava
___ lemon
___ lime
___ mango
___ orange
___ papaya
___ pineapple
___ plantain
___ potato
___ sweet potato
___ tangerine
___ tomato
___ yam

SPICES

___ allspice
___ black pepper
___ cardamom
___ cayenne
___ chili pepper
___ chocolate/cocoa
___ cinnamon
___ cloves
___ ginger
___ mace
___ nutmeg
___ paprika
___ turmeric
___ vanilla

OTHER FOODS

___ Brazil nuts
___ cashew nuts
___ chicle (chewing gum)
___ coconut
___ coffee
___ cola
___ macadamia nuts
___ peanuts
___ rice
___ sesame seeds
___ sugar
___ tapioca
___ tea

HOUSEHOLD ITEMS

___ African violet
___ aluminum plant
___ bay rum lotion
___ camphor (insect repellent, medicine)
___ coconut (lotions and soaps)
___ copal (varnish, printing ink)
___ lime (soap, bath oil)
___ patchouli (perfume, soap)
___ rubber (balloons, erasers, foam rubber, hoses, balls, rubber bands, rubber gloves, shoe soles, tires)

WOODS, CANES, FIBERS
(cabinets, doors, furniture, floors, models, paneling, toys)

___ balsa
___ bamboo
___ jute (rope, burlap, twine)
___ mahogany
___ rattan
___ teak

After you've completed the checklist: Meet with two or three classmates. Compare your checklists; then combine your data. Make a graph to illustrate your data *by category* (such as HOUSEHOLD ITEMS). Here are the types of graphs you can choose from:

- bar graph
- circle graph
- pictograph

 Note To Teacher: Divide the class into groups of three or four students each for the graphing activity.

Pollution, Pollution— What's The Solution?

With pollution, the sky's no longer the limit! Mother Earth's fragile water and land are increasingly threatened by humankind's activities. Examine the causes and consequences of pollution with the following hands-on investigations and reproducible activities.

by Bill O'Connor

Air Pollution

We need clean air to breathe. But it seems that everything we do adds pollution to the air—even breathing! Like all animals and many microorganisms, we exhale carbon dioxide gas. A small amount of carbon dioxide is normal in the atmosphere, but too much may be absorbing the sun's heat and causing global warming.

Teacher-Directed Student Activity: *Limewater* is a diluted solution of calcium hydroxide and is used to detect the presence of carbon dioxide in a substance. Use lime-water to detect carbon dioxide in breath. Obtain calcium hydroxide from a secondary science teacher or order it from a science-supply company. A small jar will last for years! Just mix one-fourth teaspoon per gallon of water; then stir vigorously, allow to settle, and pour off the clear liquid for students to use for testing. Pour this liquid into small paper cups and provide students with drinking straws. Have students blow their breath into the liquid and observe the changes that occur. *(The clear liquid turns into a milky-white solution, meaning that carbon dioxide is present.)*

Teacher Demonstration: Make a cone with a file folder, forming the cone so that one end is large enough to fit over a car's exhaust pipe. Make the opposite end small enough so that the opening of a balloon will stretch over it. With the engine running, place the free end of the cone over a car's exhaust pipe and inflate the balloon. Next squirt the gases from the balloon into lime-water. Students will be amazed at how much carbon dioxide there is in car exhaust!

Student Activity: Another form of air pollution is *particulates:* particles of smoke, soot, and grime in the air. Make particulate detectors by taping small squares of waxed paper on index cards. Lightly coat the waxed paper with petroleum jelly to which particles in the air will stick. Place the detectors around your school to see if some areas have dirtier air than others. (Be sure to protect the detectors from rain.) Make detectors to take home and monitor particulates in the different areas of your community. After a set period of time, examine the detectors with a magnifying glass or microscope. Count and compare the number of particles within a fixed area.

Student Activity: If it snows in your area, try this simple activity to monitor particulate pollution. Collect some freshly fallen snow in a clean plastic container. Allow it to completely melt; then pour the resulting water through a white, paper coffee filter. You should observe plenty of particulate pollution on the filter. Examine the particles with a magnifying glass or microscope. Can you identify any of them?

Teacher Demonstration: All kinds of stuff gets into the air. We can even have pollution in our homes! Ask your school custodian for used air filters from a forced-air heating system. Or bring in a filter from your own home. Ask students to speculate where the material on the filter might have come from. Have volunteers examine some of the material with a magnifying glass or microscope.

Susan Hodnett

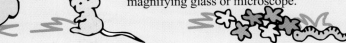

Water Pollution

We enjoy clean water for bathing and swimming. We also need clean drinking water to live. Many people in the world don't have safe sources of drinking water. Animals that live in lakes and streams need clean water too. Yet every time we use water, we pollute it. Natural systems can purify water, but sometimes we overload nature's ability to recover.

Teacher Demonstration: Pour clean tap water into several numbered jars of the same size. To each jar, add a small amount of one of the following substances: soap, motor oil, paint thinner, salt, metal polish, soil, raw egg yolk, etc. Leave one jar with clean water. Ask students to guess what has been added to each jar. Caution students not to drink any of this water, or any water that is not from a source known to be safe. Discuss substances that, like salt, may not be visible or have an odor.

Teacher Demonstration: Even after treatment, much wastewater contains nutrients that can cause algae and bacteria to grow. Waste from food processing, farming, and homes may contain so many nutrients that bacteria use up all the oxygen, causing fish and other water animals to die. To demonstrate this problem, fill two large, clear glass jars with tight-fitting lids with water; then let them stand for 24 hours. Add just enough methylene blue (available in pet stores or from a biology teacher) to both jars to turn the water a very pale blue. Next drop a small handkerchief containing organic matter (leftover fruit or vegetable) into one jar. Cap both jars tightly and have students observe them for several days. Ask students, "Which jar loses its blue color? Why?" *(Decomposition of organic matter uses up oxygen. Methylene blue will lose its color if there is no oxygen in the water.)*

Student Activity: Put a handful of dry grass or hay in a jar of water. (Timothy or clover works best, but grass from a ditch where water collects will work fine. Pond water is ideal, but you can use tap water if you let it stand for 24 hours.) A few days after adding the dried grass, the water will turn cloudy and develop an odor. Examine a drop of the water under a microscope. You'll see many one-celled organisms swimming around madly! The Golden Guide *Pond Life* will help you identify them. Water pollution endangers these organisms, which are an important part of the food cycle in our natural waters.

Teacher Demonstration/Student Follow-Up Activity: Divide one student's water from the student activity at the bottom of this page into several small jars. In each jar, place a small amount of a foreign substance. In addition to those listed in the teacher demonstration to the left, use a pesticide or garden chemical. Have students examine drops of water from the jars daily with microscopes. Challenge students to count the number of organisms that they see at one time in each of five drops of water from each jar. Have students graph their results to determine the effect of the different substances on pond life.

Class Activity: Most towns and cities are eager to educate their citizens about water supplies. Arrange a field trip to a local sewage or drinking-water treatment plant. These places are especially interesting to children. Obtain information before your trip and have the class prepare a list of questions. Provide each student with a piece of corrugated cardboard, a "trip sheet" with questions and space for drawing, and two large rubber bands to hold the sheet to the cardboard. Upon your return to school, divide students into small groups to plan and prepare a mural.

Class Activity: Evaluating water quality by checking for the presence or absence of species known as *environmental quality indicators* is a widely used monitoring technique. Groups like Stream Watch check populations of aquatic plants and animals regularly. Ask secondary science teachers, members of environmental groups, or your local wildlife or park ranger if there are any such groups working in your area. They would probably welcome the chance to visit your class and talk about the condition of local waters. Your students may even want to "adopt" a stream or pond in your area.

Land Pollution

Once polluting substances get into the soil, it's very hard to remove them. These substances can have adverse effects on plants and animals. How do plants react to various substances in the soil?

Student Group Activity: Plant about 10 easy-to-grow plants—such as beans, corn, marigolds, or radishes—in small plastic pots. Once the plants are well established, add about one-half cup of a substance such as soap, motor oil, salt, vinegar, or used floor-cleaning water to each pot. (With your teacher's assistance, add paint thinner and metal polish to two of the pots.) Water the plants normally for a week or two. Which substances seem to have the most effect on the plants? Do different substances have different effects? Keep a record of your observations.

What about substances that get into plants, which are then eaten by animals? Many pesticides, such as the now banned DDT, accumulate in plant and animal tissues. Predators, which eat contaminated prey, can develop high concentrations of the substances. This is a big problem with game fish, which can have large amounts of mercury, lead, and other toxic substances collected out of the water from plants and animals below them in the food chain. How does this happen? Try the simulation game to the right with your students to find out.

Teacher-Directed Student Activity: Provide each student with 40 small objects (dry beans, popcorn, paper squares, etc.) that represent food. The objects should be the same color except for four. Do not explain why to the students. Cheese-flavored and plain popcorn work well, especially if you play the game outdoors.

Divide the class into grasshoppers, mice, and owls, or any three animals that form a food chain. Assign three students as owls; then assign two-thirds of the rest of the class as grasshoppers and one-third as mice. Give each student a small bag, which represents her "stomach." Collect all of the "food"; then scatter it around a defined area. First give the grasshoppers one minute to gather food. Then give the mice one minute to catch the grasshoppers—any that they catch must surrender their "food." Finally, allow the owls one minute to chase and catch mice.

Ask the grasshoppers how many have obtained food. Those who have not been eaten by mice will have survived. Those mice that successfully caught grasshoppers have also survived, unless their bags contain three or more pieces of colored food. Explain that the food eaten by the grasshoppers was sprayed with pesticides (represented by the colored pieces) and that three pieces is a lethal dose for a mouse! Finally, ask the owls how well they did. Since owls are larger animals, only those who have ten or more pieces of contaminated food are at risk. Tell the owls that they will not die! However, the pesticide has affected their reproductive system and their eggs will not hatch. Discuss what might happen to the food chain if the owls could not reproduce.

Great Books On Caring For The Environment:

- *Global Warming* by Laurence Pringle
- *Brother Eagle, Sister Sky: A Message From Chief Seattle* illustrated by Susan Jeffers
- *Cartons, Cans, And Orange Peels: Where Does Your Garbage Go?* by Joanna Foster
- *Living Treasure: Saving Earth's Threatened Biodiversity* by Laurence Pringle
- *My First Green Book* by Angela Wilkes
- *Windows* by Jeannie Baker
- *Going Green: A Kid's Handbook To Saving The Planet* by John Elkington, Julia Hailes, Douglas Hill, and Joel Makower
- *Save The Earth: An Action Handbook For Kids* by Betty Miles
- *At Home In The Rain Forest* by Diane Willow

Music To My Ears (Not!)

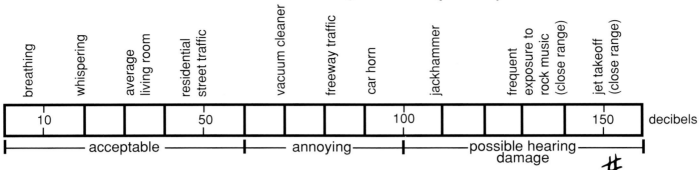

breathing	whispering	average living room	residential street traffic	vacuum cleaner	freeway traffic	car horn	jackhammer	frequent exposure to rock music (close range)	jet takeoff (close range)	

10   50   100   150   decibels

├─────── acceptable ───────┤├──── annoying ────┤├──── possible hearing ────┤
                                                          damage

Noise pollution can be a problem, especially in urban areas. People in and near cities are often exposed to loud noise. Airplanes, automobiles, buses, motorcycles, trains, trucks, construction projects, and industries all produce noise. Noise causes discomfort in some people. Loud noise can damage hearing or even cause deafness.

Noises are measured in units called *decibels.* The chart above shows the approximate decibel level from some sources of noise.

What kinds of noise do you hear? Listen for different noises in your environment. In the graph, draw a horizontal bar for each noise, showing how loud you think it is. In the blank boxes, include four other noises you often hear.

Place/Activity	20	40	60	80	100	120	140	160
mowing the lawn								
in my bedroom								
listening to music								
in a park								
on a bus								
at a ball game								

20   40   60   80   100   120   140   160
decibels

Caution: Pollution Passing Through

Water pollution reduces the amount of pure, fresh water for drinking and cleaning, and for activities such as swimming and fishing. One type of pollutant is solids found in water. By filtering water, many of the solids can be removed.

Even though water is filtered, some of it is still not safe to drink. Chemicals and bacteria cannot be completely filtered out.

Pair up with a partner and complete the following experiment.

Purpose: Find out which water contains the most solids.

Hypothesis: Which water do you think contains the most solids? _____

Materials: 5 white coffee filters, 5 large paper cups, 1 cup of water from each of 5 different places (ponds, puddles, streams, tap water, etc.), tape, magnifying glass or microscope

Procedure:
1. Tape a coffee filter inside each large cup. (See illustration.)
2. Label the paper cups to match the five different sources of water.
3. Slowly pour the water through the filters of the paper cups.
4. Allow the water to completely pass through the coffee filter.
5. Carefully remove each filter.
6. Examine the particles on the filters with a magnifying glass or under a microscope. Can you identify any of the solid materials?

Observations:
1. Which water contained the most solids? _____
2. What do you think is(are) the source(s) of the solids? _____
   _____
3. Which water is the cleanest? _____
   Why do you think this water is so clean? _____
   _____
4. Is each cup of filtered water now safe to drink? _____ Explain. _____
   _____
   _____

Conclusions: What have you learned about filtering water? _____
_____
_____
_____

Bonus Box: Filter the water a second time. Compare the coffee filters and the filtered water.

Take A Stand—Save The Land!

Choose one project from each sign below. Your projects are due on _____.

Create And Present

- Invent a use for plastic, six-pack rings. Make a poster describing the advantages of your new product. Attach a sample of your invention to the poster and label its parts.

- Make a before-and-after photo poster. Take photographs of three or four environment problems that you would like to help solve (a leaky faucet, litter, items not being recycled, etc.). Attach each photo to the top of the poster. Below each photo, list the steps that you will take to solve that problem. Take an "after" photograph of each problem to show the improvements you made and attach it below the list of steps.

- Many environmental problems are caused by things that help people. Make a "good-news, bad-news" booklet that describes some of these problems. For example: On one page, write about and illustrate how cars provide transportation. Then on the opposite page, write about and illustrate how cars are the major cause of most of our air pollution.

Research And Read

- Read *50 Simple Things Kids Can Do To Save The Earth* by The EarthWorks Group. Choose one of the 50 chapters to share with the class. Use posters, graphs, and other visuals to help you teach the class about the topic that you chose.

- Research and write a report on Rachel Carson. Find out why she is called the "founder of modern ecology."

- Research laws and ordinances in your community and state that have been passed to protect the environment. Contact your city and state's environmental health departments. Rewrite the laws in your own words and share them with your classmates.

Perform And Persuade

- Write a 60-second public service announcement for television to persuade people not to litter. Direct your commercial to a first-grade audience. Use props, posters, costumes, etc., in your presentation. After sharing it with your classmates, share it with a primary class.

- Pretend that you are a Styrofoam® hamburger container, glass bottle, aluminum can, or newspaper. Write a *monologue* telling your audience where you came from, the energy and materials that were used to make you, and how you can be recycled. Make a costume for your character and present your story to the class.

- Make a large poster of a stream and its banks. Cut a round hole the size of your face in the middle of the poster. Next pretend that you are a stream and write a 30-second commercial to convince someone or some group to adopt you. Hold the poster in front of your face when you present your commercial to the class.

Note To Teacher: Write a due date in the blank before duplicating this page for your class.

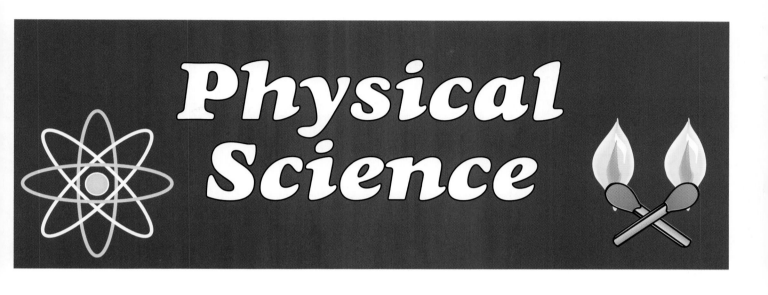

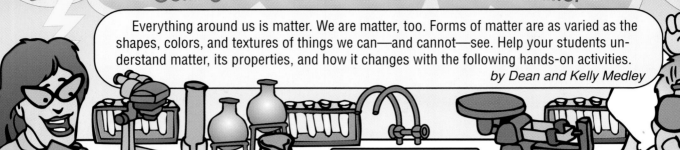

What's The Matter? Everything!
Getting A Grasp On The Basic States Of Matter

Everything around us is matter. We are matter, too. Forms of matter are as varied as the shapes, colors, and textures of things we can—and cannot—see. Help your students understand matter, its properties, and how it changes with the following hands-on activities.

by Dean and Kelly Medley

Chalk It Up!
Small-Group Activity

Materials per group: 1 plastic liter bottle, 2/3 cup vinegar, chalk, balloon, string, paper towel, measuring spoons, hammer, balance, weights or jumbo paper clips (1 clip equals 1 gram)

Directions:

1. *Mass* the empty balloon by placing it on the balance and using the weights to measure it. Record the mass on notebook paper.
2. Wrap the chalk in a paper towel and break it into pieces with a hammer.
3. Pour approximately one tablespoon of chalk into the soda bottle.
4. Pour the vinegar into the bottle.
5. Quickly place the balloon over the mouth of the bottle.
6. When the balloon has expanded, tie it off with the string and remove it from the bottle.
7. Mass the balloon again. What is the difference in mass? What caused the change?

   The chalk and vinegar create carbon dioxide gas through a chemical change. The students should notice that a gas has volume *(takes up space)* and has mass *by the change in the appearance and mass of the balloon.*

It's In The Bag!
Whole-Class Activity

Materials: large mixing bowl, measuring cup, mixing spoon
For each student: 1 quart-size zippered freezer bag, 1 pint-size zippered freezer bag, 1 pint ice, 1 pint rock salt, spoon
Ice-cream ingredients: six 12-ounce cans of orange soda, four 14-ounce cans of sweetened condensed milk, four 14-ounce cans of water, a dash of vanilla flavoring (This recipe will make approximately 34 two-thirds cup servings.)

Directions:

1. Mix the ice-cream ingredients together in a large bowl.
2. Give each student one large bag almost filled with equal amounts of ice and rock salt.
3. Give each student one small bag filled with 2/3 cup of the ice-cream mixture.
4. Place the sealed, small bag inside the large bag.
5. Seal the large bag and shake it until the ice-cream mixture is firm to the touch.
6. Grab a spoon and eat orange ice cream right out of the bag!

   While the students enjoy their ice cream, discuss the physical change *that has taken place. By changing the temperature, students have turned a liquid into a solid. Discuss what would happen if the students left their ice-cream bags at room temperature for a time.*

Literature Matters Too!

Add the "element" of literature to your studies on matter with the following books:

How To Think Like A Scientist: Answering Questions By The Scientific Method by Stephen P. Kramer (Thomas Y. Crowell, 1987)

Chemically Active! Experiments You Can Do At Home by Vicki Cobb (J. B. Lippincott, 1985)

Eyewitness Science: Matter by Christopher Cooper (Dorling Kindersley, Inc.; 1992)

Adventures With Atoms And Molecules: Chemistry Experiments For Young People by Robert C. Mebane and Thomas R. Rybolt (Enslow Publishers, Inc.; 1985)

The Alchemists: Magic Into Science by Thomas G. Aylesworth (Addison-Wesley, 1973)

Thousand Island
Teacher Demonstration

Materials: 1 bottle of each of the following salad dressings: Italian, Ranch, French, oil-and-vinegar; large mixing bowl; large spoon

Thousand Island dressing ingredients: 3 cups mayonnaise, 1 cup ketchup, 6 tablespoons sugar, 6 tablespoons pickle juice

Directions:

1. List the Thousand Island dressing *ingredients* on the board. Do not include the label "Thousand Island dressing."
2. Have a student volunteer pour the Thousand Island ingredients into the bowl and mix them together.
3. Tell the class that the student has made a *solution.*
4. Have students guess the identity of the solution. Tell them it is Thousand Island salad dressing. They will use it with the activity below, " 'Lettuce' Make A Mixture."

Discuss the meaning of *solution.* Ask the students if there is any way to separate the salad dressing into its original, independent parts. Explain to students that a solution cannot be broken down into its original parts. Show students the other bottles of dressings. Have students decide which of the other dressings are solutions. What about the Italian and the oil-and-vinegar dressings? Tell students that in the next activity (" 'Lettuce' Make A Mixture") they will learn about mixtures.

Meltdown
Teacher Demonstration

Materials: 3 saucepans, 3 hot plates, 3 candy thermometers, 3 oven mitts, 3 stirring spoons, 1/2 cup peanut butter, 1/2 cup chocolate morsels, 1/2 cup marshmallows, cookies

Directions:

1. Have students estimate the melting temperatures of the peanut butter, chocolate morsels, and marshmallows. Record their estimates on the board. Have them give reasons why they chose each temperature. Prompt discussion by asking students to consider what kinds of factors could affect the melting points of the three foods.
2. Place the peanut butter, chocolate, and marshmallows in separate saucepans.
3. Place each pan on a hot plate and set the heat at MEDIUM.
4. Have volunteers stir each food continuously.
5. Have other volunteers use the mitts to hold the thermometers in the foods so that they do not touch the bottom of the saucepans. Each volunteer should announce the temperature as soon as he sees that his food has thoroughly melted.
6. Record the melting point temperatures on the board.
7. Discuss how successful the students were in estimating the melting points.
8. Culminate the experiment by allowing the students to dip the cookies into the different liquids they created and eat their yummy treats!

As students learn about the transitions from solid to liquid to gas, they should be aware that different solids require different temperatures to change to liquids. Many substances have different evaporation points and boiling points as well. The melting points of these foods are: peanut butter—approximately 100° F, chocolate—approximately 130° F, marshmallows—approximately 170° F.

"Lettuce" Make A Mixture
Whole-Class Activity

Materials: lettuce and other assorted salad vegetables, croutons, bacon bits, serving bowls (1 per salad vegetable), 1 large salad bowl, small kitchen knives, 2 large forks to toss and serve salad, 1 small bowl and 1 fork for each student, salad dressings listed in "Thousand Island" above

Directions:

1. Under close supervision, have students cut the vegetables into bite-sized pieces and place each type in a separate serving bowl.
2. List each salad ingredient on a chart.
3. Toss all the ingredients together in the large bowl to make a super salad.
4. Serve each student a bowl of salad.
5. Have students list the ingredients they can see in their bowls.
6. Use the dressings from the activity above to top the salads.
7. Have students grab their forks and dig in!

Students will be able to see each ingredient clearly and will even be able to pick out individual vegetables. Point out that the salad is an example of a *mixture. The parts of a mixture—once combined—can then be separated again into individual elements.* Students should now understand that the Italian and the oil-and-vinegar dressings are mixtures. Have students list other foods that are mixtures.

Barry Slate

Spaced-Out
Small-Group Activity

Materials per group: tall jar with lid, 1 cup water, measuring cup, water-based marker, 1/2 cup Cheerios®, 1/2 cup uncooked rice, paper towels

Directions:

1. Pour the water into the tall jar.
2. Use the marker to mark and label the water level on the outside of the jar.
3. Pour out the water and dry the jar.
4. Measure 1/2 cup of Cheerios® and add it to the jar.
5. Measure 1/2 cup of rice and add it to the jar.
6. Place the lid on the jar and shake it for several seconds.
7. After the contents have settled, mark and label the food line level on the outside of the jar.
8. Compare the two marks. Which one is higher? Why is one mark lower if you used equal amounts of water and food?

The mark for the water level will be higher, because the water molecules have no spaces between them. Many forms of matter have spaces between their molecules. Even body tissues have spaces between the cells to allow smaller molecules (like oxygen) to pass through the tissues. In this activity, the cereal represents molecules with open spaces between them. The rice fills in the spaces between the pieces of cereal. Therefore the combined food takes up less space than the water.

Pass The Peas
Teacher Demonstration

Materials: 15 dried peas; clear, glass dessert plate; cross-stitch hoop; overhead projector

Directions:

1. Explain to students that you will demonstrate the movement of atoms in each state of matter.
2. To demonstrate the movement of atoms in a **solid**, place the peas in one layer on the glass plate. Place the plate on the lighted overhead projector. Move the plate slightly so that the peas *vibrate* without changing their positions in the group.
3. To demonstrate the movement of atoms in a **liquid**, place the hoop on the overhead projector. Pour the peas in one layer inside the hoop. Move the hoop gently so that the peas bounce off the inside edges randomly.
4. To demonstrate the movement of atoms in a **gas**, move the peas in the hoop so fast that they fly out of the hoop.

Remind students that even the atoms in solids move, but because the atoms are so small and close together, the movement is slight and unnoticeable. On the other hand, liquids take the shape of the container in which they are placed. The molecules in a liquid move faster than those in a solid, but stay within an area together. Finally, atoms in a gas move very quickly, spreading out to fill a space randomly.

To check comprehension, divide students into groups of three. Have the groups move like each state of matter.

Chemical And Physical Changes
Teacher Demonstration

Materials: 2 tablespoons sugar, 1 cup water, 2 pie pans, spoon, hot plate, oven mitt

Directions:

1. Pour one cup of water and one tablespoon of sugar in a pie pan.
2. Stir until the sugar has completely dissolved.
3. Heat the pan on a hot plate set on HIGH until the water evaporates. Crystals of sugar will appear. Use the oven mitt to remove the pan before the crystals burn, and allow the crystals to cool.
4. Allow students to taste the crystals.
5. Ask students if the sugar underwent a physical or a chemical change.
6. Next heat one tablespoon of dry sugar in the other pan. Allow the sugar to burn.
7. When the sugar has cooled, let the students taste the burnt sugar.
8. Ask students if the sugar underwent a physical or a chemical change.

In steps 1–3, the sugar changed from a solid to a liquid and back to a solid without changing its molecular structure. These changes were only physical. *Not only did the sugar start out and end up in crystal form, but it also retained its sweet taste.*

In steps 6 and 7, the sugar underwent a chemical *change. The change in structure should have been immediately apparent to students. The burnt sugar left a carbon residue, and the sweet property was no longer evident.*

Name _____

Do your skills of observation really matter when it comes to describing and classifying matter? You bet they do! Scientists rely heavily on their senses and reasoning abilities as well. Conduct the following thinking activities as you explore the properties of matter.

Describing Properties

1. Gather the following **materials:** ice cube; samples of M&M's® candy, maple syrup, grape soda, lemon extract.
2. Using your five senses, explore each item.

3. Record your observations in the chart below. Use a *simile* to describe each item. For example, to describe a feather, you might say it feels as "soft as cotton."

	ice cube	M&M's®	maple syrup	grape soda	lemon extract
Looks as...					
Smells as...					
Tastes as...					
Sounds as...					
Feels as...					

Classifying By Property

1. Read the list of solid objects below. Explore each item in your imagination using your five senses.
   paper   grass   desk   kite   chair   lettuce   leaf   stick   broom

2. Next read the five properties listed below. One *descriptive category* that could be written for the property of color is "as green as an emerald." Which of the solid objects listed above could you place in this category? You might have said, "Grass, lettuce, and leaf," because they are all green objects.
   COLOR   SIZE   SHAPE   WEIGHT   TEXTURE

3. On the back of this page, write a descriptive category for each of the five properties. Then list objects, from the list above, that would fit under that description.

4. Share and compare your categories with those of your classmates.

- -

Note To The Teacher: Provide small samples of the items listed in "Describing Properties" for each student or small group of students. The list of items includes *solids* (ice and candy), *liquids* (syrup and soda), and a *gas* (lemon extract). The essence of lemon is concentrated in an alcohol base. Alcohol is very volatile and evaporates quickly. Therefore, the students are experiencing the gas, not the liquid.

Beach Ball Blowup!

Does air have mass and take up space? Try the following activity with some beach balls and find out!

Materials: 3 identical inflatable beach balls, 1 balance, standard weights, lots of air

Directions:
1. Use the weights and balance to mass each empty beach ball. Record each beginning mass in the chart below.
2. Blow up one beach ball until it's half full of air. Blow up one beach ball completely. Leave one ball empty.
3. Mass each ball again and record your results in the chart.
4. Subtract to find the mass of air for each ball.
5. Answer the questions below.

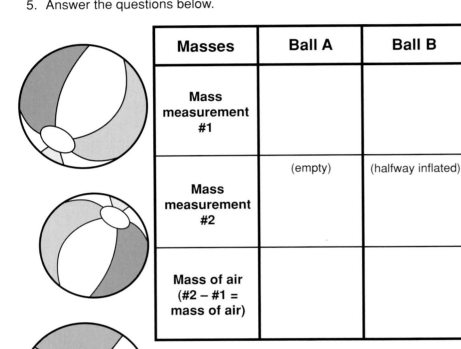

Masses	Ball A	Ball B	Ball C
Mass measurement #1			
Mass measurement #2	(empty)	(halfway inflated)	(completely inflated)
Mass of air (#2 – #1 = mass of air)			

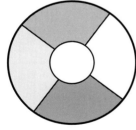

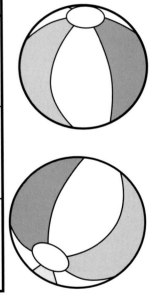

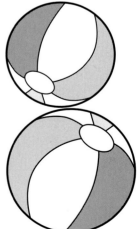

Questions:
1. Which ball did not change in mass? _____
   _____

2. Which ball had the largest change in mass? _____
   _____

3. What did you do differently to each ball? _____
   _____
   _____

4. How did the ball that was completely inflated look different from the other balls? _____
   _____

Note To The Teacher: Gases are often odorless and colorless. While it may be difficult to see most gases, we can notice their effects. This activity demonstrates that air, which is made up of many different gases, has both mass and volume. Therefore, air is matter.

Speeding Molecules

Can we really see molecules move? Keep your eye on the color and the clock, and you'll find out!

Materials for each pair of students:

2 labels	2 drinking glasses
2 eyedroppers	2 thermometers
hot and cold water	food coloring
measuring cup	2 stopwatches or watches with second hands

Directions:

1. Fill one glass with 1/2 cup of cold water. Fill the other glass with 1/2 cup of hot water. Label the first glass "cold" and the second glass "hot."
2. Use a thermometer to find the temperature of the water in each glass. Record the temperatures in the table below.
3. Fill each eyedropper with the same amount of food coloring.
4. Squeeze all the food coloring into each glass at exactly the same time, while your partner starts both stopwatches.
5. Observe the glasses to determine when the food coloring has completely colored the water.
6. Stop each stopwatch when the water is completely colored.
7. Record the time for each glass in the table.
8. Answer the questions below. Use the back of this sheet if you need more space.

	HOT	COLD
TEMPERATURE		
TIME		

Questions:

1. Which glass of water became colored first? _____

2. Why do you think that glass of water became colored first? _____

3. What do you think would happen if you added ice to the cold water? _____
_____

4. What do you think would happen if you heated the hot water? _____
_____

5. How does temperature affect the movement of molecules? _____

- -

Note To The Teacher: A *molecule* is a group of atoms that move together as one. This experiment shows the movement of food coloring molecules in water molecules. Molecules in any state of matter move faster as the temperature increases. The students should be able to observe the more rapid movement of food coloring molecules in the hot water.

To adapt this activity as a teacher demonstration, place two clear Pyrex® dishes on an overhead projector. Complete the activity as described. The class will be able to observe and time the movement of the food coloring molecules in each dish.

SIMPLE MACHINES... MADE SIMPLE!

Hands-on Activities For Exploring Basic Machines

Simple machines help us do work by trading force for distance. It's that simple! And no matter how complex a machine may be, it is based in some way on one or more of the six types of simple machines: the lever, wheel and axle, pulley, inclined plane, wedge, and screw. Help students discover how simple machines make things work with the following creative, hands-on activities.

by Dean and Kelly Medley

THE SIMPLICITY OF SIMPLE MACHINES

Simple machines came into being because they made work easier for early humans. Although a simple machine has few or no moving parts, it can help us maximize our strength and motion. The learning activities in this unit provide students with opportunities to work hands-on with every-day examples of simple machines.

Many of the activities and demonstrations are best suited for completing outside, using common playground equipment. However, the concepts can be presented just as effectively with alternative materials. Books are recommended as weights. Use comparable materials—or real weights—to complete the activities that require them.

EASY DOES IT! (WARM-UP ACTIVITY)

Materials needed: 30 thick textbooks, 1 toy wagon, 2 jump ropes, 2 stopwatches

Directions:

1. Use the jump ropes to mark start and finish lines about 30 feet apart.
2. Divide the books into two equal stacks. Place the stacks a few feet apart behind the start line.
3. Place the toy wagon beside one of the stacks.
4. Choose a pair of students to stand behind each stack of books. Try to choose pairs that are fairly equal in strength. Also choose a timer for each pair.
5. Instruct each pair to move its stack of books across the finish line. For safety reasons, each pair may move only three books at a time. The pair with the wagon may load three books at a time into the wagon, then pull the wagon across the finish line. The other pair must carry three books at a time across the finish line, then return for more until all of the books have been moved.
6. When you signal, "Begin!", each timer times his team until all books have been moved across the finish line.

Discuss the results of this activity with your class. Allow other pairs to complete the race too. Students should see that using the wagon was quicker and required less physical energy than running back and forth carrying the books. Ask students how they could make the wagon an even better machine. (Answers might include adding a motor to the wagon or making the wheels bigger.)

A MACHINES MINIPOSTER

Provide each student with a copy of the miniposter on page 137. Use the poster in one of these ways:

- Have each student keep it in his science notebook as a ready reference.
- Have each student cut page 137 into six sections, then glue each section onto a separate page in his science journal.
- Have each student create an accordion book by folding a 6" x 24" piece of white construction paper into sixths. Then have him cut and paste each simple machine onto a section as shown. The student uses the blank sections of the book for his notes.

PLAYGROUND PLANE
(SMALL-GROUP ACTIVITY)

Materials needed: playground slide (or a board placed on an incline), 5 large books, 1 long jump rope

Directions:

1. Tie one end of the rope snugly around the stack of books.
2. Place the stack of books at the bottom of the slide's steps.
3. Have students take turns climbing to the top of the slide and pulling the books straight up by the opposite end of the rope.
4. Next place the stack of books at the bottom of the slide. Have each student pull the books up the slide to the top. Remind students to try to use the same amount of force when pulling the books up the slide as they did when pulling the books straight up in step 3.
5. Instruct each student to write a description of this activity. Ask students what adaptations they could make that would make the work even easier. Have students draw and describe their adaptations.

Students might consider spraying the slide with a cooking spray, wrapping the books in cloth, or using garbage bags to reduce friction. Or they may suggest placing the books in some type of smooth container.

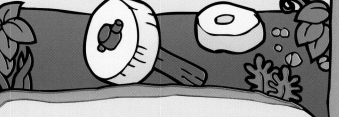

VIEW THE SCREW
(TEACHER DEMONSTRATION)

Materials needed: 2 pieces of 1/4-inch Plexiglas™, screw, screwdriver, drill

Directions: Predrill a small hole in the top of a piece of Plexiglas™. This hole is to help start the screw and should not go all the way through the Plexiglas™. Call a small group of students together to watch the demonstration. With the two pieces of Plexiglas™ held together, start the screw in the predrilled hole. Call on students in the group to use the screwdriver to screw the screw into the Plexiglas™. Students should observe the path of the screw through the Plexiglas™ and note how the screw works to cut through the glass. Continue to screw the two pieces together, but don't allow the screw to go completely through the bottom piece of Plexiglas™. Have students examine the tiny hole at the bottom where the screw is about to emerge. They should see how the screw, a simple machine based on the inclined plane, helps make work easier.

If the thread of a screw could be unwrapped and flattened, it would make an inclined plane. A screw is used to hold things together. The spiral motion of putting a screw into something actually requires less force and is less work for the builder. When a screw is put into an object, it moves material up and out of the hole it creates. A modern machine based on the design of a screw is a grain elevator.

MONKEY-BARS PULLEY
(TEACHER DEMONSTRATION)

Materials needed: monkey bars (or a tall stepladder), pulley, strong string or twine, large book, spring scale

Directions: Have a student stand near the top of the monkey-bars ladder. Tie the string around the book; then hand the opposite end of the string up to the student. Instruct the student to pull the book straight up to the bars, which may be difficult. Next have the student come down from the monkey bars. Place the book on the ground under the bars and toss the opposite end of the string over any bar. Make sure the student can reach the end of the string. Now have the student pull on the string until the book reaches the bars. This task introduces the concept of a pulley.

Have students hypothesize why the second task was easier to complete. Show students how they can measure the amount of force needed to lift an object by using a spring scale. Repeat the steps above with a spring scale attached to the end of the string. Record the measurement on the scale for each lift. Next hang a pulley from a monkey bar and pass the string over the pulley's wheel. Repeat both lifts again, using the spring scale to measure the amount of force needed. Record each measurement on the scale.

Discuss with students that the pulley gives no mechanical advantage of lift, but changes the direction of the force applied to the load. This is especially important when it's difficult to reach the space underneath a load.

WONDER WEDGE (SMALL-GROUP ACTIVITY)

Materials needed for each group: box of heavy books; triangular, wooden doorstop; hammer

Directions:

1. The object of this activity is for students to understand the difference between an inclined plane and a wedge. Remind students of the playground slide activity (page 135). Ask them to describe an inclined plane.
2. Show students the doorstop. Discuss how an inclined plane and a wedge are alike *(similar shapes).*
3. Divide students into small groups with the materials listed. Instruct each group to gently use the hammer and doorstop to lift an edge of the box of books off the ground. *The doorstop should be used as a wedge that students drive under the box with the hammer. The wedge will lift the box from the floor.*
4. Have students contrast the use and function of the inclined plane with the wedge.

An inclined plane allows something to be moved to a higher level with less energy than lifting. A wedge is shaped like an inclined plane, but actually moves into a space, separating an object. This can also cause a type of lift. Other common wedges include knives, axes, and wood splitters.

BICYCLE BREAKDOWN (TEACHER DEMONSTRATION/ CULMINATING ACTIVITY)

Materials needed: 1 old, unused bicycle; tools (hammer, adjustable wrench, screwdriver); safety glasses

Directions: Several weeks before this activity, send a note home with students asking for the donation of an old, unused bicycle. Make it clear that the bike won't be returned. Provide each student with a copy of page 137 and a 6" x 24" piece of white construction paper. Have students make accordion books as described on page 134.

Discuss with students that a bicycle is a machine made up of many simple machines. These simple machines work together to make a very efficient machine that helps us move distances much faster than on foot. Have students examine the bike for several days; then direct each student to draw each type of simple machine he observes in the bike in his accordion book. Next use tools to begin dismantling the bike, being sure to wear safety glasses. Discuss with students the different parts of the bike that are simple machines.

Students should have several parts drawn as examples of simple machines. For example, the wheel and axle category may include gears, sprocket wheels, and the tires. The lever category may include the hand brake and the pedals, and students should note the many screws that hold various parts of the bike together.

BARRY SLATE

BRICK SLIDE (SMALL-GROUP ACTIVITY)

Materials needed for each group: 1 brick, 3-foot-long piece of string, 10 round pencils

Introduction: Share several pictures of ancient structures with your students, such as the pyramids, Stonehenge, and the Greek Parthenon. Compare the types of machines we would use today to build these structures with the tools used by ancient builders. (Ask your librarian to locate resources that include pictures of ancient tools.) Have students brainstorm ways that ancient builders may have moved the huge stones used to build the pyramids. Then tell students they're going to experiment with one method.

Directions:

1. Divide students into small groups and provide each group with the materials listed.
2. Go outside to a hard-topped area. Instruct each group to first try to pull its brick across the ground by looping the string around it and pulling it. Also have each student try to push the brick along with just one finger.
3. Next have students duplicate the ancient method of using rollers. Instruct one student to lay the pencils side by side in front of the brick. Then, using the string still attached to the brick, instruct two or three students to gently pull the brick onto the pencils. (Other students in the group may need to hold some pencils in place.)
4. As the brick moves forward off a pencil, have a student pick up that pencil and place it in front of the rolling brick.

After all groups have completed the activity, discuss their experiences. Students will note that it was much easier to move the brick using the pencils and that ancient builders may have moved large stones using rollers.

LEVER

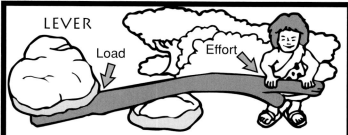

The lever is one of the earliest machines. A lever helps lift weights with less effort.
Examples:

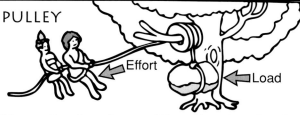

WHEEL AND AXLE

The wheel and axle can lift heavy weights for us with only a little effort on our part.
Examples:

PULLEY

The pulley is a form of the wheel and axle. A pulley changes the direction of the force.
Examples:

INCLINED PLANE

The inclined plane is so simple, it doesn't even look like a machine! An inclined plane makes it easier to slide a load upward than to lift it directly.
Example:

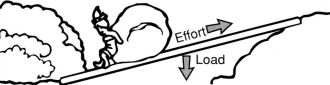

WEDGE

The wedge is related to the inclined plane. It can be used to lift a heavy load over a short distance or to split a log.
Examples:

SCREW

The screw is an inclined plane wrapped around a cylinder or a cone. Its main purpose is to raise a load over the *threads* (the spiral part of the screw) by applying a small force.
Examples:

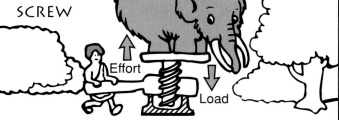

Note To The Teacher: Use with "A Machines Miniposter" on page 134 and "Bicycle Breakdown" on page 136.

Name(s) ____

____

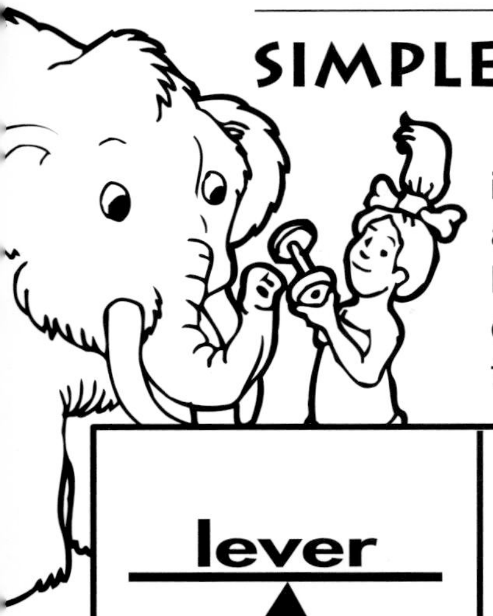

SIMPLE MACHINES SCAVENGER HUNT

Do you realize that you're being surrounded—by machines, that is! Your school and its grounds are marvelous places to find examples of every type of simple machine. Work with your group to locate at least two examples of each simple machine listed in the chart. Draw the machine and label its parts. Also write where you found each example.

lever		
wheel and axle		
pulley		
inclined plane		
wedge		
screw		

 Note To The Teacher: After students have become familiar with the six simple machines, divide the class into groups to complete this activity.

Name(s) _____

CATAPULT SHOOTER

What do you think would happen if you were sitting on one end of a seesaw and a huge rock was dropped on the other end? You would go flying up into the air! A long time ago, people used this idea to create a weapon called a *catapult.* Catapults were used to throw rocks and other objects over castle moats and walls.

Today we use catapults to make work easier. They help us lift loads because catapults are really levers. Complete the following activity to learn how this ancient machine works.

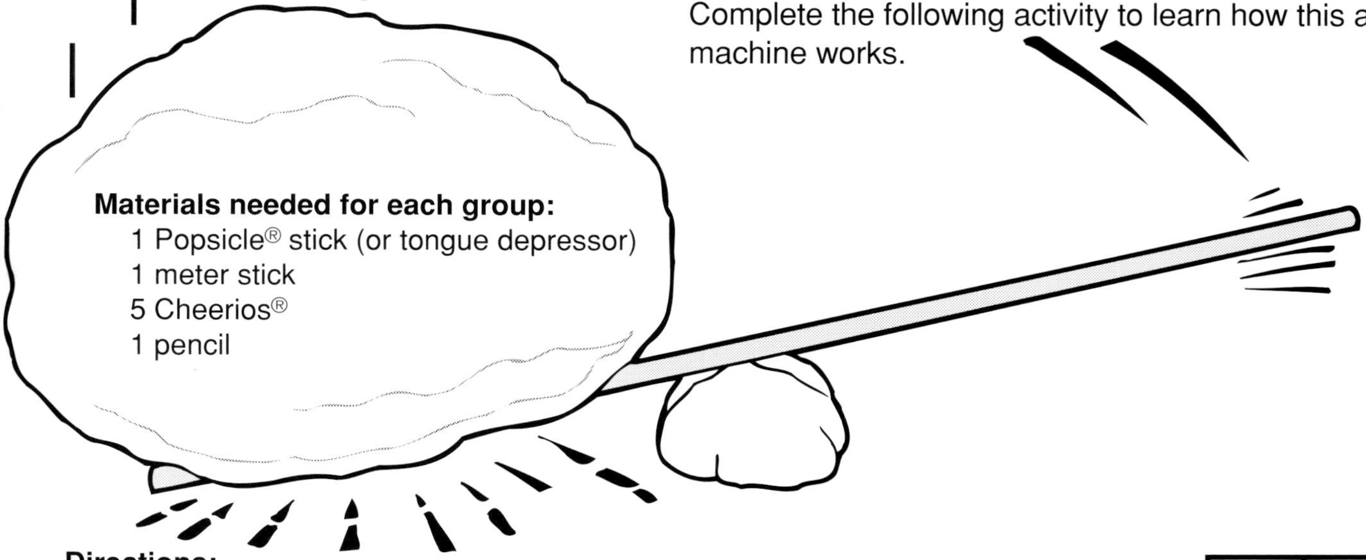

Materials needed for each group:
1 Popsicle® stick (or tongue depressor)
1 meter stick
5 Cheerios®
1 pencil

Directions:
1. Make a catapult on the floor by laying the Popsicle® stick across the pencil.
2. Place one piece of cereal on the end of the stick that is touching the floor.
3. Write "1" on the Popsicle® stick at the spot where it lies across the pencil (the *fulcrum*).
4. Flip the piece of cereal by hitting the end of the stick that is in the air.
5. Measure the distance the piece of cereal flew. Measure from the pencil.
6. Record the distance in the chart.
7. Change the location of the fulcrum—the spot where the Popsicle® stick crosses the pencil. Write "2" on the stick at the spot where it now crosses the pencil.
8. Repeat steps 2, 4, 5, and 6. Try to hit the end of the Popsicle® stick with the same force each time.
9. Complete steps 2–6 three more times, changing the location of the fulcrum each time (step 7).

How does the location of the fulcrum affect the distance the piece of cereal flies?

_____

_____

fulcrum number	distance
1	
2	
3	
4	
5	

Bonus Box: Extend the catapult activity by having an accuracy competition. Set a paper cup several feet from your group's catapult. Have each student in the group shoot a piece of cereal to see who can get it in the cup, or closest to the cup.

EXPLORING ENERGY

Creative, Hands-On Activities For Teaching Energy Concepts

An age-old adage says, "Seeing is believing." With this collection of creative activities and teacher demonstrations, seeing is understanding! Help your students better understand energy with the following hands-on ideas.

by Jim Martino

Background: Ever-Changing Energy

Energy is the ability to do work. For example, the burning of gasoline moves an auto. There are two kinds of energy: potential and kinetic. *Potential energy* is stored energy that a body has because of its position or structure. A lump of coal, which releases energy when it burns, has potential energy. Kinetic energy is energy in motion. The water at the top of a waterfall has potential energy. As it falls, its potential energy is changed to kinetic energy. One true constant of energy is change. Energy can change from one form to another, but it cannot be created or destroyed.

Energy Hide-And-Seek

Your classroom is filled with things that either use or store energy. Use these items in a game that helps students become more aware of the forms of energy that surround them. Label a set of small index cards according to these directions (examples of each form of energy likely found in a typical classroom are listed in parentheses):

Label 4 cards **electrical energy** (electric lights, clock, TV/VCR, computer).
Label 4 cards **light energy** (electric lights, TV/VCR, sun coming in windows, overhead projector).
Label 4 cards **heat energy** (heater, lights, TV/VCR, computer).
Label 7 cards **chemical energy** (paper, wood, humans, food, animals, animal food, desks).
Label 4–5 cards **potential energy** (any object that can fall).
Label 2–3 cards **kinetic energy** (any moving object).

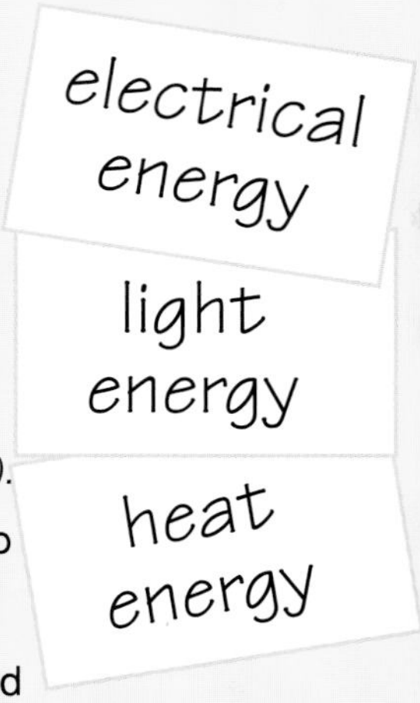

electrical energy

light energy

heat energy

Adapt the number of cards for each category to match energy sources in your own room. Mix up the cards and divide students into two teams. Have a player from team 1 draw the top card, read aloud its category, and identify a source or example of that energy found in the classroom. If the energy is stored in an object, the student must tell in what form it is stored and how it might be released. Once it has been named, the item cannot be used again for that category. Award a team one point for correctly identifying the energy source. Continue with teams taking turns until all cards have been played.

Energy-Use Survey

Most students don't realize the amount of energy they use in one day or think about the sources of that energy. Challenge students to take a closer look at energy use by completing 24-hour activity lists. Have each student divide a sheet of paper into three columns, labeled as shown. Beginning the next morning, instruct students to list all of their activities and the type of energy that is involved with each one. Remind them that any activity requires food, or *chemical*, energy, so it should be mentioned only once. Related activities, such as running and walking, should also be listed once. After students have noted their activities for 24 hours, discuss the energy-using activities and whether they are necessary. Be prepared for lively discussions about the necessity of hair dryers, television, and video games!

Activity	Energy Source	Necessary?
brushing teeth	natural gas to heat water (chemical) / pump to supply water (electrical)	yes
eating breakfast	chemical	

Rolling Along

The farther an object is from the center of Earth, the more *gravitational potential energy* (GPE) it has. The greater the *mass* of an object, the greater its GPE. With your students' help, demonstrate how gravitational potential energy is changed to kinetic energy. Make a ramp with a 1' x 4' board and several equal-sized books. You'll also need an empty two-liter pop bottle with cap, a measuring cup, masking tape, water, and rulers. Provide each student with a copy of the half-page reproducible on page 143.

- Pour a cup of water into the pop bottle and recap it. Mark a starting line on the ramp with tape. Have a student measure the height of the tape from the floor. Next have a volunteer hold the bottle on the ramp behind the tape, and then release it. Have a pair of students measure the distance the bottle rolls from the bottom of the ramp. Have students record this data on their reproducibles. Repeat the procedure two more times and have each student find the average distance the bottle traveled. Next mark a new starting line on the board, higher than the first one. Have volunteers repeat the steps: find the height of the tape, roll the bottle down the ramp three times, find the average distance rolled. Repeat the procedure one more time from an even higher starting line. Have students record all data on their reproducibles, then make their conclusions. *(Increasing the height of the starting line increases the GPE of the bottle, thus increasing its kinetic energy as it leaves the ramp. This should make the bottle travel farther.)*

- Pour a second cup of water into the bottle. Beginning at the first tape mark, have student volunteers roll the bottle down the ramp three times and measure the distance of each roll. Then have all students find the average of the three rolls. Repeat this procedure with three cups of water, then with four cups—beginning at the same starting line. Have students record all data on their reproducibles, and then make their conclusions. *(Adding water increases the mass of the bottle, which increases its GPE, thus increasing its kinetic energy. The bottle will travel farther each time more water is added.)*

Bottle Bowling

Sir Isaac Newton's first law of motion states, in part, that objects at rest tend to remain at rest unless acted upon by an outside force. The force applied must be great enough to overcome this tendency to remain at rest or the object will not move. Scientists refer to this tendency to remain at rest as *inertia*. Divide students into groups of four and provide each group with a copy of page 144. Have students in each group work together to collect the needed materials. Then, on a predetermined day, have each group complete the experiment. *(The ball has gravitational potential energy because it is above the floor. When released, the ball rolls down the ramp, converting its GPE into kinetic energy. When the ball hits the bottle, it transfers this kinetic energy to the bottle. If it transfers enough energy, it will overcome the bottle's inertia and cause it to move. The bottle will then have energy received from the ball, and it will roll.)*

Bottle Demolition Derby

Momentum is a property of all moving objects. Momentum depends on the *velocity* (speed) of an object in motion and its *mass* (weight). Divide students into small groups and provide each group with a copy of page 145. Have each group collect the materials it needs to complete the experiment. You may need to send some groups into a hallway so that everyone has plenty of room. In the activity, students will vary the mass and the velocity of colliding bottles, then compare the momentum of one bottle to the other. *(The bottle with greater momentum will continue moving in its original direction, while the bottle with less momentum will change directions in the collision.)*

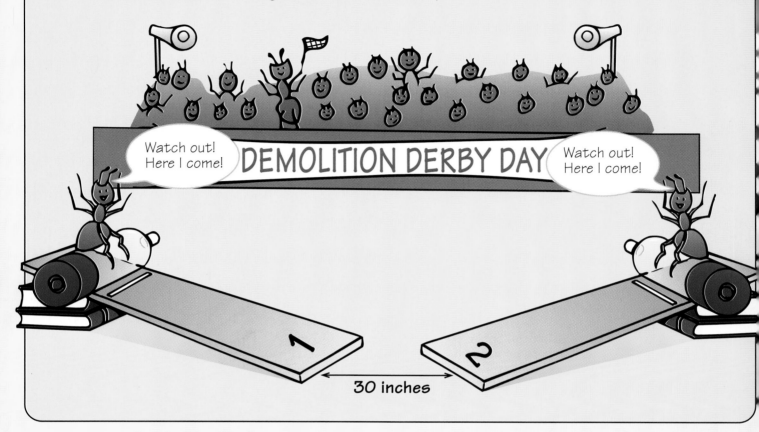

Sandpaper Surfing

When writing, the friction between a pencil's graphite and paper is great enough to wear away some of the graphite. The rougher the surface, the more the graphite wears away. Divide your students into pairs and provide each pair with a copy of the experiment on the bottom of page 143. Also provide each pair with several sheets of sandpaper of various grits: 80, 120, 200, and 400 will result in observable differences. Each student will also need a sheet of regular notebook paper, some scrap paper, a glossy magazine page, a ruler, and a pencil. Have each pair of students follow the directions on the reproducible. *(Different pencils, although they are the same number hardness, wear differently. Be sure that each student uses the same pencil for the entire activity. Students will also apply different amounts of pressure when making their marks; encourage them to try to exert the same force on each writing surface. The smoother the surface, the less friction between the pencil and paper. Thus less graphite wears away. The glossy paper may not wear away enough graphite to leave an observable mark.)*

What Happens When A Candle Burns?

Most students probably don't think that a candle loses mass as it burns. But a burning candle converts *chemical energy* stored in its paraffin into *heat* and *light energy*. Its carbon and hydrogen atoms change into carbon dioxide and water vapor. Show this change to your class with a simple demonstration. Mount a candle on a fireproof base by lighting it and dripping candle wax onto the base; then stick the candle in the liquid wax and allow it to harden. Make sure that none of the wax escapes. Next blow out the candle and place it and its base in one pan of a double-pan balance. Add weight to the other pan to balance the candle. Ask students to predict what they think will happen as the candle burns: Will it lose any of its mass? Will its mass remain the same? Then relight the candle and have students observe the light and heat produced. *(As the candle burns, it loses mass. The resulting imbalance will be visible to all your students.)*

Name ______________________________ Experiment: gravitational potential energy

Rolling Along

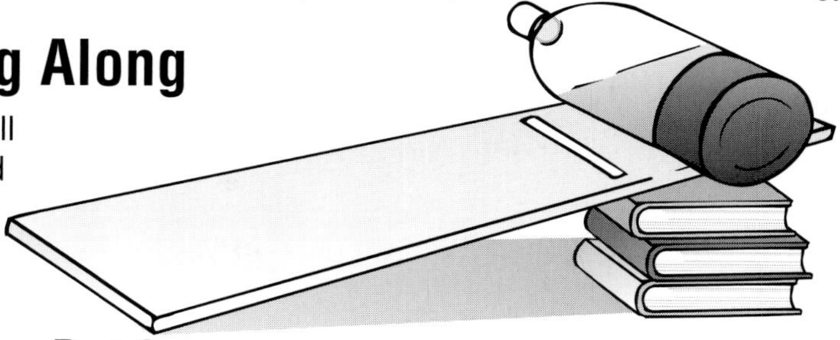

Does the height from which an object begins to roll affect how far it rolls? What about its weight? Record the data from the class experiments in the charts below. At the end of each demonstration, write a conclusion based on the data.

Part 1

height of starting line	test 1 distance	test 2 distance	test 3 distance	average distance

Conclusion: ______________________________

Part 2

mass of bottle	test 1 distance	test 2 distance	test 3 distance	average distance
2 c. water				
3 c. water				
4 c. water				

Conclusion: ______________________________

Names ______________________________ Experiment: friction

Sandpaper Surfing

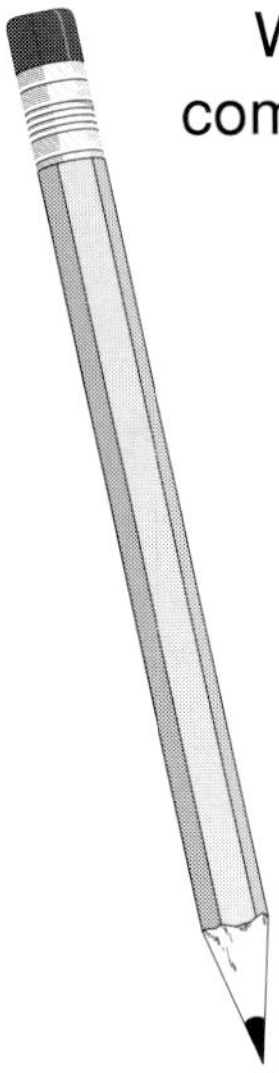

What type of surface wears down a pencil the fastest? Work with a partner to complete the experiment below.

Materials: pencil, ruler, various grits of sandpaper (80, 120, 200, 400), sheet of notebook paper, one glossy magazine page, another type of paper of your choice, scrap paper

Procedure:

1. Sharpen your pencil. Measure its length and record it in the chart in the 80 grit column.
2. Rub your pencil point across the 80 grit sandpaper 20 times or until the graphite is worn off, whichever comes first. (Place the sandpaper on scrap paper so you won't mark on your desk.)
3. Measure the pencil again and record its length in the chart. Then subtract to find the difference.
4. Repeat steps 1–3 with each sandpaper and with the other paper listed in the chart.

Observations: ______________________________

Conclusions: ______________________________

	80 grit	120 grit	200 grit	400 grit	other:	notebook paper	glossy paper
pencil's starting length							
pencil's ending length							
difference							

Note To The Teacher: Use "Rolling Along" with the activities on page 141. Use "Sandpaper Surfing" with the idea on page 142.

Names ______________________________

Bottle Bowling

Inertia is a property of all matter. It makes an object that is not moving remain still unless a force causes it to move. Inertia also makes a moving object continue to move at the same speed and in the same direction—unless an outside force changes it.

With the other students in your group, collect the materials listed below. Then complete the experiment that follows.

Materials needed:
a 1' x 4' board or piece of strong cardboard
a clean, empty two-liter pop bottle with the cap
a softball
masking tape
5–8 similar books
a ruler
water

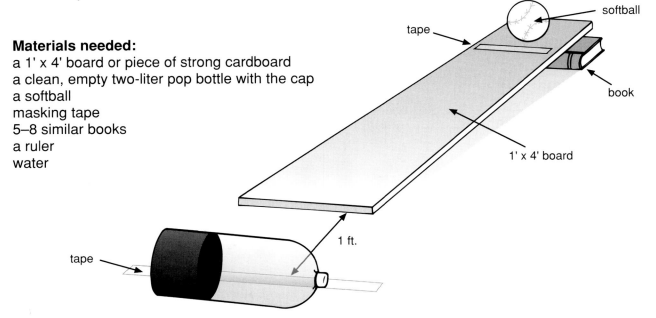

Procedure:
1. Make a ramp with the board and one book.
2. Measure one foot from the end of the ramp and mark a line on the floor with masking tape. The line and the end of the ramp should be parallel to each other.
3. Measure about six inches from the top of the ramp and mark a line with masking tape on the board.
4. Fill the pop bottle with water.
5. Place the bottle of water on the floor along the tape line as shown.
6. Hold the softball on the ramp directly behind the tape line.
7. Release the ball, allowing it to roll down the ramp and strike the pop bottle.
8. Did the pop bottle move? If so, how far did it move? Measure its distance from the tape line and write your response in the chart below.
9. Now add a second book to raise the height of the ramp and repeat steps 5–7. Did the pop bottle move? If so, how far did it move? Measure its distance from the tape line and write your response in the chart below.
10. Repeat steps 5–7 after making the ramp three books high, then four, five, six, seven, and eight books high. Measure; then write the results of each test in the chart.

height of ramp

	1 book	2 books	3 books	4 books	5 books	6 books	7 books	8 books
number of inches bottle moved								

Conclusion: ______________________________

____

____

____

 Note To The Teacher: Use with "Bottle Bowling" on page 141.

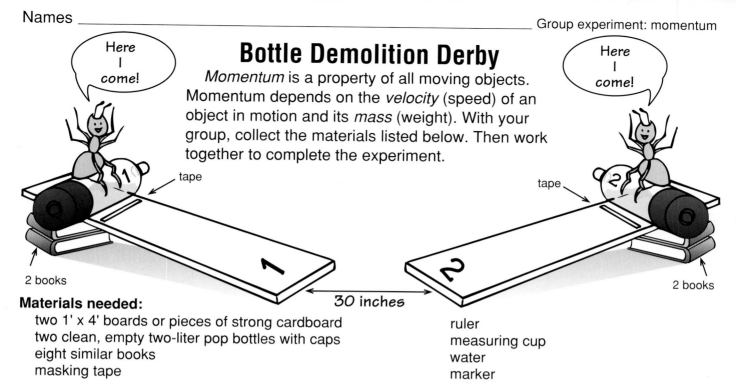

Bottle Demolition Derby

Momentum is a property of all moving objects.
Momentum depends on the *velocity* (speed) of an
object in motion and its *mass* (weight). With your
group, collect the materials listed below. Then work
together to complete the experiment.

Materials needed:

two 1' x 4' boards or pieces of strong cardboard
two clean, empty two-liter pop bottles with caps
eight similar books
masking tape

ruler
measuring cup
water
marker

Procedure:

1. Make two ramps that are exactly alike. Begin with each ramp resting on two books. Place the ramps so that their bottoms face each other and are about 30 inches apart (see the diagram).
2. Measure and mark with masking tape a line one foot from the top of each ramp. Use this starting line for all tests.
3. Label one pop bottle and ramp #1. Label the other bottle and ramp #2.
4. Fill each bottle with two cups of water. Recap each bottle.
5. Hold a bottle on each ramp behind the starting line.
6. On a signal, release both bottles.

Observations:

What happened? _____

_____

_____

Why do you think this happened? _____

_____

_____

Procedure (continued):

7. Complete each test below. First set up each test according to the directions. Then run the test. Write the results in the chart.

ramps	bottles with water	results
both—2 books high	#1—2 cups, #2—4 cups	
#1—2 books high #2—4 books high	#1—4 cups, #2—2 cups	
#1—2 books high #2—6 books high	#1—6 cups, #2—2 cups	
both—4 books high	#1—4 cups, #2—4 cups	

Note To The Teacher: Use with "Bottle Demolition Derby" on page 142.

Catch The Electricity Bug!

How do you electrify your students' interest in science? Charge them up, of course! The following how-tos, hands-on ideas, and minds-on activities—plus a class full of "eager Edisons"—will ensure that your electricity unit is wired for success.

by Bonnie Pettifor

Making Electricity Run Smoothly In Your Classroom

- If you don't have enough supplies for the entire class, demonstrate each activity; then undo the activity and put it in a center for partners to visit.
- Pool your supplies with those of colleagues to create one electricity kit to share.
- Choose quality supplies that will last. Lantern batteries will keep for two or three years if stored in a cool, dry place.
- Reduce the chance of burning out lightbulbs by matching the voltage of the bulb to that of the battery.
- Strip one-half inch of insulation off the ends of the wires needed for each experiment. Add alligator clips to the ends of the wires to make them easier to attach and to reduce wear.

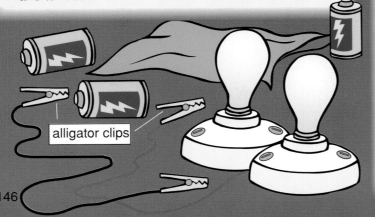

alligator clips

Static Electricity

Introducing Page 149: Rub an inflated balloon on a wool cloth. Ask students if they know why the balloon sticks to the wool. *(Static electricity—the buildup of positive or negative charges on an object—causes the balloon to stick.)* Demonstrate how static electricity works by giving each of eight students a card labeled "+." Give another eight students cards labeled "–." Form two lines, each with four + charges and four – charges. Instruct the lines to walk past each other. As they pass have two of the positive charges from one line switch places with two of the negative charges in the other line. Point out that one line now has more negative than positive charges, and the other line has more positive than negative charges. Explain that this happens when the wool and the balloon are rubbed together. *Electrons* move from the cloth to the balloon, making the balloon negatively charged and leaving the cloth positively charged. Since unlike charges are attracted, the negatively charged balloon is attracted to the positively charged wool, causing them to stick together.

Using Page 149: Divide your class into pairs. Give each pair one copy of page 149, one copy of the horse pattern on page 152, and the materials listed on page 149. Instruct the pair to complete the page as directed. Refer to the answer key on page 160 for the results of each experiment.

Series Versus Parallel Circuits

Introducing Page 151: Select six students. Tape one of six different signs—Battery, Wire, Lightbulb A, Wire, Lightbulb B, and Wire—to each student's shirt. Arrange the students as shown, holding hands, in Figure 1. Direct Lightbulb B to drop her hands. Ask students what would happen to both bulbs. Accept all responses, but do not reveal the answer. Next add another student wearing a Wire sign. Arrange the students as shown in Figure 2. (Have Lightbulb A hold hands with two of the Wire students and touch toes with the other two Wire students.) Again have Lightbulb B drop her hands. Ask students what will happen to the other bulb. Accept all responses, but do not reveal the answer.

Using Page 151: Divide your class into small groups. Give each group one copy of page 151 and the materials listed on that page. Refer to the answer key on page 160 for the results of each experiment. After completing the experiment, repeat the demonstration above, having students explain the difference between a series circuit and a parallel circuit.

Current Electricity

Introducing Page 150: Demonstrate how electrons move, creating a *current,* with this activity. Form your students into a circle. Have each student turn to the right and extend his arm forward until his palm is about one inch from the back of the person in front of him. Select one child to step forward so that his hand touches the back of the person in front of him. Have the person touched take a step forward and touch the back of the classmate in front of her, and so on. After each student has moved, explain that this movement represents *free electrons* (electrons that break away from atoms and wander within the material) transferring energy. The free electrons move forward and bump into other free electrons, creating a current.

Using Page 150: Divide your class into small groups. Give each group a copy of page 150 and the materials listed on that page. Refer to the answer key on page 160 for the results of the experiment.

Extending Page 150: Place one cup of water in a container. Dissolve two tablespoons of salt in a second container filled with one cup of warm water. Then place two tablespoons of salt on a paper plate. Ask students to predict whether each item—the water, the salt water, and the dry salt—is a *conductor* or an *insulator.* Test each as done in Step 5 on page 150. The bulb will only light up when the wires are in the salt water. *Therefore salt water is a conductor, while the dry salt and the plain water are insulators.*

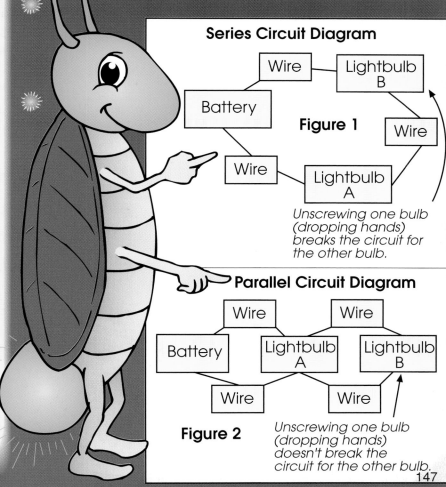

Series Circuit Diagram

Wire — Lightbulb B

Battery

Figure 1

Wire

Wire — Lightbulb A

Unscrewing one bulb (dropping hands) breaks the circuit for the other bulb.

Parallel Circuit Diagram

Wire   Wire

Battery   Lightbulb A   Lightbulb B

Wire   Wire

Figure 2

Unscrewing one bulb (dropping hands) doesn't break the circuit for the other bulb.

Electricity And Magnetism

Demonstrate the connection between electricity and magnetism with the following small-group or learning-center activity:

1. Bring a magnet close to a compass. Observe what happens. *(The compass needle will move. Like poles of a magnet repel and unlike poles attract, just as positive and negative electrons do.)*
2. Wrap a coil of wire around a large iron nail or bolt about 20 times; then remove the nail and connect the ends of the wire to a battery.
3. Place the coiled wire close to the compass. Observe what happens. *(The compass needle moves, indicating the presence of a magnetic field created by the electrical current flowing through the wire.)*
4. Insert the nail into the coil. The nail will become magnetized because of the electrical current. Use the magnetized nail (or *electromagnet*) to pick up small metal objects such as paper clips.
5. Disconnect the battery from the electromagnet and try to pick up the same paper clips with the nail. Observe what happens. *(When the battery is disconnected, the nail loses its magnetic force.)*

We All Need Each Other!

Connect your electricity studies to building cooperation in the classroom. Post a battery cutout on a bulletin board. Have each student complete one copy of the lightbulb pattern on page 152. Connect the cut-out lightbulbs to the bulletin-board battery by drawing a black line or by using real electrical wire. Fill the center of the resulting series circuit with photos of students working together. Remind students that if one lightbulb in a series circuit is loose or missing, all the bulbs go out. Likewise, if one student isn't doing his share, everyone is affected.

Get A Charge Out Of This!

Zap! Have you ever touched a door handle and felt a tiny electric shock? If so, you've felt static electricity. *Static electricity* is the buildup of positive or negative charges on an object. Complete each experiment below to get a real charge out of static electricity!

Experiment 1: Electroscope

Materials: flexible drinking straw; one small lump of clay; 1" x 8" strip of tissue paper; inflated balloon; piece of wool, nylon, fur, or flannel fabric; large metal paper clip; one piece of transparent tape; timer or watch with a second hand

Procedure:
1. Bend the straw and push the bottom end of it into the lump of clay. Stick the clay base to the edge of a desk.
2. Fold the tissue paper in half and place it over the straw as shown. Tape it to the straw.
3. Bring the balloon close to the tissue paper. Record your observations. _____
   _____
4. Rub the balloon along the fabric for 30 seconds.
5. Bring the balloon close to the tissue paper again. Record your observations. _____
   _____
6. Why do you think the paper acted as it did? _____
   _____
7. Touch the balloon to the paper clip to clear the balloon of the static electricity.
8. Why do you think the paper clip clears the balloon of its static electricity? _____
   _____

Experiment 2: Jumping Cereal

Materials: handful of puffed-rice cereal, sheet of notebook paper, two-foot length of plastic wrap

Procedure:
1. Ball up the plastic wrap. Place the cereal on a desk.
2. Rub the plastic-wrap ball on the notebook paper several times quickly.
3. Hold the plastic-wrap ball over the cereal. Record your observations. _____
   _____
   _____
4. Why do you think the cereal acted as it did?
   _____
   _____
   _____
   _____

Experiment 3: Static Horse Race

Materials for each student: one copy of the horse pattern; scissors; inflated balloon; piece of wool, nylon, fur, or flannel fabric

Procedure:
1. Cut out the horse pattern. Fold it on the dotted line so that it stands.
2. Charge your balloon by rubbing it on the fabric.
3. Hold your charged balloon in front of your horse to pull it along. Then have a race with your partner.
4. Why does your horse follow the charged balloon? _____
   _____
   _____
   _____

Bonus Box: For Experiment 3, does it matter which material you use to charge your balloon? Experiment with different materials. For each material used, record the amount of time the balloon held the charge on the back of this paper. Then explain your observations.

Name(s) ________________________________

Go With The Flow!

Some materials—called *conductors*—allow electricity to flow through them easily. Other materials do not make it so easy for electricity to get through. These are called *insulators*. Complete the experiment below to make a simple circuit. Then use the circuit to test objects to see if they are conductors or insulators.

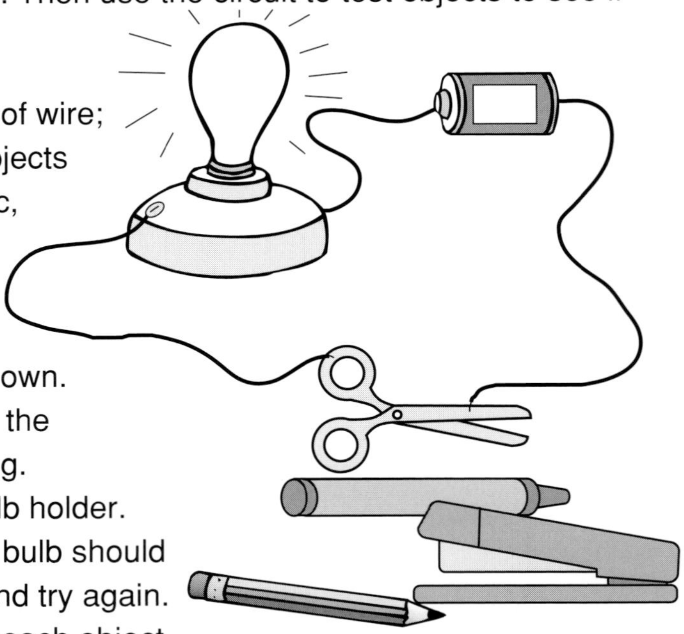

Materials: one C-size battery; three 5-inch lengths of wire; flashlight bulb in a holder; masking tape; several objects made from various materials including metal, plastic, and wood

Procedure:

1. Tape one wire to each end of the battery as shown.
2. Attach one of the battery's wires to one side of the bulb holder. Leave the other battery wire resting.
3. Attach the third wire to the other side of the bulb holder.
4. Touch the two free wire ends together and the bulb should light. If it does not, check all the connections and try again.
5. Touch both free wire ends at the same time to each object. If the bulb lights, the item is a conductor. If the bulb does not light, the item is an insulator. Record your data in the chart below.

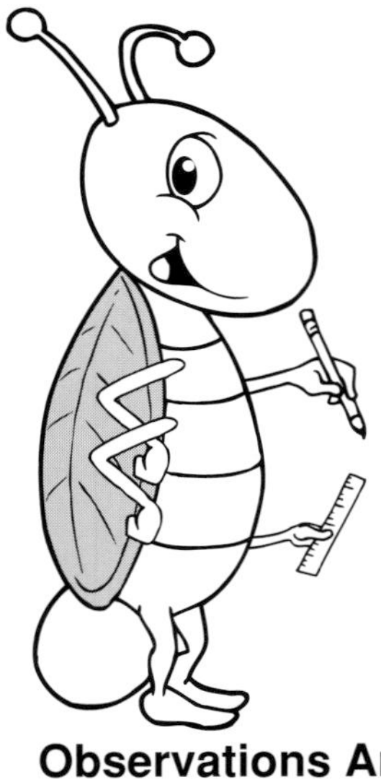

Object	Type of material of object	Conductor or insulator

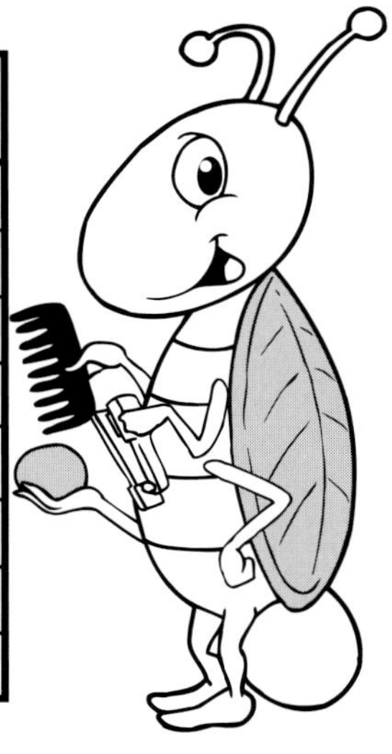

Observations And Conclusions:

1. From what materials are the conductors made? ________________________
2. From what materials are the insulators made? ________________________
3. Look at the wires connecting your circuit. What part is the conductor? The insulator? ________

____

4. What purpose do you think insulators might serve? ________________________

____

Bonus Box: On the back of this page, list three places where you have seen insulators being used.

 Note To The Teacher: Use with "Current Electricity" on page 147.

Comparing Circuits

Electrical currents follow paths called *circuits*. A *series circuit* connects everything in a single path. A *parallel circuit* has more than one path for current. Complete the experiments below to make both a series and a parallel circuit.

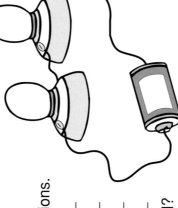

Experiment 1: Making A Series Circuit

Materials: two flashlight bulbs with holders
three 5-inch lengths of wire
C-size battery

Procedure:

1. Attach the wires to the battery and lightbulbs as shown in the illustration. If the bulbs do not light, check the connections and try again.

2. While the bulbs are lit, unscrew one bulb. Record your observations. _____ _____

3. Why do you think this happened? _____ _____

Experiment 2: Making A Parallel Circuit

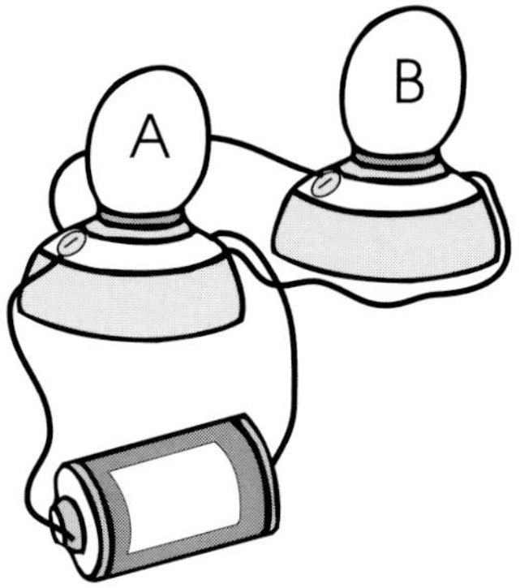

Materials: supplies listed for Experiment 1
one more length of wire

Procedure:

1. Attach the wires to the battery and light-bulbs as shown in the illustration. If the bulbs do not light, check the connections and try again.

2. While the bulbs are lit, unscrew bulb B. Record your observations. _____

3. Why do you think this happened? _____

4. Screw bulb B back in and unscrew bulb A. Record your observations. _____

5. Why do you think this happened? _____

6. Which type of circuit do you think is more reliable? Why? _____

Bonus Box: Why wouldn't you want to wire a house with series circuits? Write your answer on the back of this page.

Note To The Teacher: Use with "Series Versus Parallel Circuits" on page 147.

Patterns

Use with "Experiment 3: Static Horse Race" on page 149.

fold

©The Education Center, Inc.

Use with "We All Need Each Other!" on page 148.

I can help my classmates learn more by

Name:

©The Education Center, Inc.

SOLAR POWER!

Is it gas? Is it coal? Is it nuclear? No! It's solar power! And it's coming to a home near you to heat and purify water, warm the air, and provide for every electrical need. Examine this amazing energy source with your students by conducting the following experiments.*

by Bill O'Connor

For many of these activities, you will need small, inexpensive thermometers, which can be purchased from science supply companies. Thermometers with metal backs work best.

Heat Energy From The Sun

How Solar Energy Heats The Earth

Everyone knows that the sun gives us energy. The following experiment shows how the sun's energy provides warmth.

Materials: sunny day, data record sheet for each group (page 157), six or eight thermometers (Cover the bulb of each thermometer with a square of folded aluminum foil to prevent the sun from heating the thermometers directly.)

Directions: Divide your class into six or eight teams. Go outside and identify three to four different ground surfaces such as grass, blacktop, white concrete, and bare soil. Locate a sunny and a shaded spot for each surface. Assign one team to each of the six or eight spots; then give each team a covered thermometer and a data sheet. Instruct each team to place its thermometer on the ground; then have the team record the temperature after three minutes and again after five minutes. Return to the classroom and have each team report its results. Compile the data onto a large chart. What conclusions can the students draw from the data?

A Simple Solar Energy Collector

Collect solar energy with the following experiment.

Materials: sunny day, two plastic soda bottles, black tempera paint, two thermometers, paintbrush, water

Directions: Paint the outside of one bottle with black paint. Fill both bottles with water and place them in the sun for two hours. Measure the water temperature in each bottle. Which bottle got warmer? Why? Have students explain their answers based on what they learned from the previous experiment, and the ones that follow on page 154.

As a variation, use a green bottle and a clear bottle. Have students predict which one will get warmer.

What Color Best Captures Solar Energy?

Compare the heat-absorbing capacity of different colors.

Materials: sunny day; data record sheet for each group (page 156); eight identical clear glass or plastic containers; eight thermometers with bulbs covered; construction paper in white, black, and five colors; aluminum foil; clear plastic wrap; rubber bands; scissors

Directions: Line the bottom and halfway around the side of each container with a different color of paper or the foil (see the illustration). Place one thermometer inside each container. Cover the top of each container with two layers of plastic wrap. Secure the wrap with a rubber band.

Provide each of eight teams with one copy of page 156. Have each team predict which container will reach the highest temperature, second highest, and so on. After groups have recorded their predictions, assign one container to each team. Go outside and place all of the containers on a similar surface in direct sunlight. Position each container so that its unlined side faces the sun. Have each team record its container's internal temperature every two minutes. Instruct students to stop recording once they have three consecutive measurements that show no change in temperature.

Return to the classroom. Write on the board the highest temperature recorded for each container. Rank the colors and foil and their temperatures 1–8. Have each team fill in its result column with this new information. Then ask each group to subtract to find the difference between its prediction and the observed result for each color. Have each team add the numbers in its difference column. The team with the smallest total has the closest predictions. Which team's predictions were most accurate? Which colors behaved according to the predictions? Which did not? Why are colors like orange called *warm colors,* and colors like blue called *cool colors?* Which colors would you use in a solar heat collector?

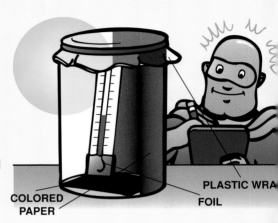

COLORED PAPER

PLASTIC WRA

FOIL

The Greenhouse Effect

The earth's atmosphere allows sunlight to pass through. The sunlight warms the earth's surface. However, the infrared (or heat) waves given off by the earth are trapped in the atmosphere. Without the greenhouse effect, the earth would be a frozen world!

Gases such as carbon dioxide and methane are produced through both natural and man-made activities. These gases, along with man-made chlorofluorocarbons (CFCs), absorb infrared rays. Today many scientists believe that the earth's climate may be warming because of increased amounts of these gases. Try this simple simulation to demonstrate the greenhouse effect.

Ask students if they have ever gotten into a car that has been parked in the sun with the windows closed. How could the temperature in the car become warmer than the temperature outside? Measure the temperatures inside and outside several closed-up cars that have been in the sun in your school parking lot. Does the color of the car or its upholstery make any difference in the temperature? What variables would need to be controlled in order to make this a "fair" experiment?

Conduct the "It's Getting Hot In Here!" experiment on the bottom of page 157. Then ask students these follow-up questions: Did the temperature rise at the same rate in each bottle? Which bottle reached the higher temperature? Why does the temperature in each bottle level off after awhile? What conclusions can you draw about the earth's atmosphere?

In this simulation, the clear plastic of the bottle acts like a car's windows. Sunlight enters through a car's windows, strikes the material inside, becomes absorbed, and changes into heat. The plastic wrap, like the closed car windows, traps the heat.

A Chemical Change

The sun's energy can cause chemical changes. For example, plants use the sun's energy to make food. Try this activity to study changes caused by sunlight.

Materials: sunny day, several colors of construction paper, scissors, foil, tape, ruler

Directions: Cut 4 1/2" x 6" rectangles from construction paper. Tape a smaller piece of foil in the center of each paper rectangle. Place the papers outdoors in bright sunlight for four to six hours. Weight the papers with small rocks to prevent them from blowing away. Remove the foil from each piece and observe the difference between the covered and uncovered areas. Which colors changed the most? The least?

Making Pictures With Solar Energy

Materials: sunny day; a collection of easily recognizable objects such as leaves, scissors, paper clips, etc.; blueprint paper or Ozalid® (black line) paper; water or covered pot or bucket, gravel or marbles, and household ammonia (Ozalid may be purchased from drafting supply stores. Get the slowest speed available.)

Directions: Give each student one small object. Go outdoors on a sunny, windless day. Remove the blueprint paper from its envelope and immediately have students arrange their objects on top of it in direct sunlight. After a minute or two, return the paper to its envelope. (You may have to experiment a bit with the time.) Indoors, wash the paper in water until an image appears. Can students recognize their objects in the "sun picture"?

If using Ozalid paper, develop it in a covered pot or bucket into which you have placed a few centimeters of gravel or marbles and a small amount of household ammonia. Keep the container covered while the paper develops. You will see the images appear on the paper.

Purifying Water With Solar Power

Solar Drinking Water Machine

Use solar energy to purify water. Students will be fascinated by this simple solar "still."

Materials: sunny day, large shallow bowl, small bowl, plastic wrap, tape, small weight or rock, salt, water

WEIGHT

Directions: Pour water into the large bowl to a depth of 2 cm. Add some salt to represent impurities. Place the smaller container into the center of the bowl. Cover the large bowl with plastic wrap and secure it with tape. Place a small weight or rock on the plastic wrap directly over the center of the smaller bowl. Place the "still" in direct sunlight for four to six hours.

Remove the weight and plastic wrap. Examine the small bowl. Does it contain water? If so, taste it. Is it salty? How did water get into the smaller bowl?

Solar energy causes the water from the large bowl to evaporate. The water then condenses on the plastic wrap and drips into the small bowl. Because the impurities do not evaporate, the water in the small bowl is not salty. This process, called solar desalinization, is used in coastal desert areas to obtain drinking water from sea water.

PLASTIC WRAP

WATER

155

What Color Best Captures Solar Energy?

Test different colors to see which one best holds heat. Fill in five additional test colors in the chart below. Predict how each color will respond to solar heat. In the prediction column, write a "1" by the color that your team predicts will hold the most solar energy. Number the other colors in the order you think they will heat up, with "8" representing the color that you think will absorb the least solar energy.

Place the collector that has been assigned to your team in a sunny spot with the uncovered side facing the sun. Record the starting temperature in the first box of the time/temperature chart. Continue to record the temperature every two minutes. Do not move the container or block the sun from shining on it. Once you get the same temperature three times in a row, stop.

TIME (minutes)	TEMPERATURE
starting	
2	
4	
6	
8	
10	
12	
14	
16	
18	

COLOR	PREDICTION	RESULT	DIFFERENCE
White			
Black			
Foil			
Total Difference			

Bonus Box: Using a cardboard box, clear plastic, tape, and other materials, design and build a solar collector that will reach the highest possible temperature. Use a thermometer to measure the temperature. Experiment to improve your solar heater. Report your results to the class.

©The Education Center, Inc. · *The Best Of* THE MAILBOX® *Science · Intermediate* · TEC1475